THE
VATICAN

THE
VATICAN

FATHER MICHAEL COLLINS

LONDON, NEW YORK, MELBOURNE,
MUNICH, AND DELHI

This book is dedicated to Florence B. D'Urso, who
for many years has been a wonderful supporter of
the Holy See and the Vatican Museums and, most
importantly, a constant and loving friend.

FOR THIS EDITION
Senior editor Kathryn Hennessy
Senior art editor Gadi Farfour
US editor Margaret Parrish
Managing editor Esther Ripley
Managing art editor Karen Self
Art director Phil Ormerod
Associate publisher Liz Wheeler
Reference publisher Jonathan Metcalf
Pre-production controller Rebecca Fallowfield
Jacket designer Mark Cavanagh
Jacket editor Manisha Majithia

PREVIOUS EDITION
Managing editor Debra Wolter
Managing art editor Karen Self
Editors Tom Broder, Ferdie McDonald,
Marianne Petrou, Paula Regan,
Steve Setford, Anna Streiffert
US editor Shannon Beatty
Art editors Anna Hall, Gadi Farfour,
Dean Morris, Adam Walker
Production editor Luca Frassinetti
Production controller Norma Weir
Art director Bryn Walls
Publisher Jonathan Metcalf
Picture researcher Louise Thomas
Photography Christopher Pillitz
Additional photography Gary Ombler
Endpaper Illustration Cathy Brear

First American Edition, 2008
This revised edition, 2014
Published in the United States by
DK Publishing, 4th floor, 345 Hudson Street
New York, New York 10014

14 15 16 17 18 10 9 8 7 6 5 4 3 2 1

001–259409–Mar/2014

Published in Great Britain by Dorling Kindersley Limited.

A catalog record for this book is available from the
Library of Congress.
ISBN: 978-1-4654-1920-0

DK books are available at special discounts when purchased in
bulk for sales promotions, premiums, fund-raising,
or educational use. For details, contact:
DK Publishing Special Markets, 345 Hudson Street, New York,
New York 10014 or SpecialSales@dk.com.

Printed and bound in Hong Kong

Discover more at
www.dk.com

CONTENTS

FOREWORD

 In the Spring of 2013, for the first time in the 2,000-year history of the papacy, two popes resided at the Vatican. The unprecedented events that led to the resignation of Pope Benedict XVI and the election of Pope Francis brought the world of the Vatican into sharp focus and a global interest in its activities, interest which has continued during the new pope's first year.

Over the centuries, the area and influence of this small patch of land has changed in extraordinary ways. Today, more than one billion Catholics look to the Vatican, the seat of the papacy, as their spiritual home. It is the place where, according to tradition, the apostle Peter, a trusted friend of Jesus, was executed by the emperor Nero. His successors, the popes, have wielded enormous influence. While the early Bishops of Rome were persecuted for their faith,

successive popes became important political figures, anointing emperors and deposing them at will. Although their political power waxed and waned, the spiritual influence of the papacy has been enormous, affecting everything from theology to art, science to astronomy, politics to morality.

Visitors are fascinated by St. Peter's Basilica, the majestic church built on the site of St. Peter's tomb. For some, the experience of visiting this magnificent building is overwhelming. The Vatican Museums house one of the greatest art collections in the world. Many wonder why the Vatican does not simply sell these works of art and give the money to the poor; after all, the Catholic Church is one of the largest humanitarian agencies in the world. But these masterpieces, commissioned in the past when popes were patrons of the arts, inspire and educate people in the Christian faith. Today, responding to our changing world, the popes more often use social media to spread the Christian message.

Shortly after his election, Pope Francis said that he wanted a Church that would truly act for the poor and be poor itself. His remarks and subsequent actions indicate a change in direction. In an institution such as the Vatican there is much to preserve and much to reform. Pope Francis has already shown himself to be someone who intends to tackle head-on the difficult issues the Catholic Church has faced.

The Vatican is one of the most visited places on Earth. Each year, millions of people cross the boundaries of the smallest city-state in the world. Some come as pilgrims, others as curious tourists.

With this book, I have taken you behind the scenes of this fascinating city-state, and in this latest edition offer insight, too, into the extraordinarily compelling personality of our new pope. You will meet a variety of the other people who live and work in the Vatican, too, and admire the incomparable artistic treasures housed in the museums. Although tucked into a corner of Rome, you will discover that the Vatican has almost a village atmosphere. If you have visited the Vatican, perhaps this book will be a pleasant souvenir. If you have not had that opportunity, I sincerely hope this "insider's guide" will give you a real taste of this unique place, which has played such an important part in world history.

Michael Collins

September 2013

CALENDAR

THE VATICAN YEAR

Throughout the year, the Church observes a series of seasons and festivals, many of which celebrate the life, death, and resurrection of Jesus. In his role as bishop of the diocese of Rome, the pope presides over all these ceremonies within the Vatican, which are attended by Romans and visitors from all over the world. The season begins in December with Advent, as the Church recalls Christ's Incarnation and his promise to return at the end of the world; at Christmas, the birth of Jesus is commemorated. The numbers of tourists and pilgrims swell during the season of Lent, which begins 40 days before the great feast of Easter in the spring. During the summer, the stifling heat drives many people from the city. On his election, Pope Francis broke the tradition of retiring to the country residence at Castelgandolfo outside Rome, choosing to live and work as usual at the Vatican.

✝ **THE CHRISTMAS SEASON AT THE VATICAN IS A TIME TO REJOICE IN THE BIRTH AND MIRACULOUS** EVENTS IN THE LIFE OF THE INFANT JESUS. THE TRADITIONAL MIDNIGHT MASS AT ST. PETER'S BASILICA AND THE POPE'S CHRISTMAS BLESSING FORM THE CLIMAX TO THE CHRISTMAS CELEBRATIONS, BUT THE WINTER PERIOD IS FILLED WITH OTHER FESTIVITIES, FROM THE CELEBRATION OF THE IMMACULATE CONCEPTION IN EARLY DECEMBER, THROUGH TO THE FESTIVITIES MARKING THE REVELATION OF JESUS TO MANKIND, HIS BAPTISM, AND—AT THE CLOSE OF THE CHRISTMAS SEASON—THE PRESENTATION OF JESUS AT THE TEMPLE.

THE CHRISTMAS SEASON

CELEBRATION OF THE BIRTH OF JESUS CHRIST

CHRISTMAS HOMILY ➤
Pope Benedict delivers his Christmas homily
in front of the High Altar at the center of St. Peter's
Basilica during the Midnight Mass on Christmas Eve.

MIDNIGHT MASS AT THE VATICAN ⋀
Crowds gather in the square outside St. Peter's to join worshipers inside the basilica
in the celebration of Midnight Mass on the evening of December 24, 2000. The
words of Pope John Paul II's homily are relayed to the multitude outside through
large television screens dotted around the piazza. The tall Christmas tree, donated
to the Vatican by a different country each year, shelters a life-sized nativity scene.

Immediately coming up from the water, he saw the heavens parting, and the spirit descending on him like a dove. MARK 1:10

FEAST OF THE EPIPHANY >
Pilgrims dressed as the Magi—the three wise men who followed the star to Bethlehem to worship at the crib of the infant Jesus—approach St. Peter's Square for the Feast of the Epiphany on January 6.

FEAST OF THE BAPTISM OF THE LORD ʌ
Pope Benedict XVI baptizes a baby during Mass in the Sistine Chapel on the first Sunday after Epiphany, a Vatican tradition established by his predecessor, John Paul II. The feast commemorates the baptism of Jesus by St. John the Baptist in the Jordan River.

They brought him up to Jerusalem, to present him
to the Lord, as it is written in the law of the Lord.

LUKE 2:22–23

BLESSING THE CANDLES ＞
Benedict XVI presides over the ceremonial blessing of candles during the Mass held in St. Peter's Basilica to commemorate the Feast of the Presentation of the Lord.

FEAST OF THE PRESENTATION OF THE LORD ∧
Nuns and other members of the congregation hold candles representing Christ "light of the world" during Mass in St. Peter's Basilica. The candle-lit Mass is celebrated on February 2 to mark the presentation of the infant Jesus in the Temple at Jerusalem, 40 days after his birth. The Feast of the Presentation of the Lord marks the end of Christmas and is traditionally a time for members of religious orders to renew their religious vows.

✝ HOLY WEEK IS THE MOST SACRED TIME IN THE VATICAN'S LITURGICAL CALENDAR. BEGINNING ON PALM SUNDAY, CHRISTIANS RECALL THE LAST DAYS IN THE LIFE OF THE LORD JESUS, FROM HIS TRIUMPHAL ENTRANCE INTO JERUSALEM, TO HIS CRUCIFIXION AND RESURRECTION. ALTHOUGH THE HOLY WEEK CELEBRATIONS FORM THE PRINCIPAL FOCUS OF THE EASTER PERIOD AT THE VATICAN, THE SEASON CONTINUES UNTIL THE FEAST OF PENTECOST, 50 DAYS AFTER THE RESURRECTION OF JESUS AT EASTER, MASS IS CELEBRATED AT ST. PETER'S TO MARK THE DESCENT OF THE HOLY SPIRIT ON THE APOSTLES.

THE EASTER SEASON
CELEBRATION OF CHRIST'S RESURRECTION

HOLY THURSDAY CHRISM MASS >
On the morning of Holy Thursday, the pope celebrates
the Mass of the Chrism in St. Peter's Basilica and
blesses the vessels containing the holy oils used in the
administration of the sacraments throughout the year.

PALM SUNDAY PROCESSION ∧
Priests bearing olive branches blessed by the pope lead
the procession preceding the Mass of the Lord's Passion
on the Sunday before Easter. The procession recalls the
welcome that Jesus received on his entry into Jerusalem
from crowds waving palm leaves and olive branches.

We adore your Cross, O Lord,
and we praise and glorify your resurrection.
Through the wood of the Cross came joy
to the whole world.

CRUCEM TUAM, ANTIPHON OF THE LITURGY, GOOD FRIDAY

GOOD FRIDAY LITURGY AT ST. PETER'S ➤
Pope Benedict XVI lies prostrate as he venerates the
Cross during the Celebration of the Lord's Passion
on Good Friday. The penitential act commemorates
the moment when Christ died on the cross.

VIA CRUCIS PROCESSION ⌃
Thousands of pilgrims gather in the shadow of
Rome's ancient Colosseum as the pope leads the
traditional *Via Crucis* (Way of the Cross) procession
on the evening of Good Friday. The procession
commemorates Christ's own journey to Calvary.

EASTER VIGIL MASS >
Pope Francis holds the Book of the Gospels during the Easter Vigil in St. Peter's Basilica. Catholics renew their baptismal vows as they celebrate the resurrection of Jesus.

EASTER BLESSING ∧
On the morning of Easter Sunday, thousands of pilgrims and Romans crowd into St. Peter's Square and the streets around the Vatican to hear the pope deliver his traditional Easter address and blessing *Urbi et Orbi* (to the city and the world) from the balcony of St. Peter's Basilica.

I swear to faithfully, honestly, and honorably serve the supreme pontiff and his legitimate successors, and to dedicate myself to them with all my strength, ready to sacrifice, should it become necessary, even my own life for them.

OATH OF THE SWISS GUARD

SWEARING OF THE OATH >
With three fingers raised in honor of the Holy Trinity, a new recruit to the Pontifical Swiss Guard grasps the standard and pledges his life and loyalty to the pope.

SWISS GUARD SWEARING-IN CEREMONY ʌ
Wearing full dress armor with halberds at the ready, members of the Pontifical Swiss Guard march through the Vatican on their way to the Paul VI Hall for the annual swearing-in ceremony for new recruits. One of the most colorful events in the Vatican calendar, the Swiss Guard ceremony is held every year on May 6 in honor of the 147 Swiss halberdiers who died on that day in 1527 defending Pope Clement VII.

Even the weakest and most vulnerable, the sick, the old, the unborn and the poor are masterpieces of God's creation.

POPE FRANCIS, JULY 17, 2013

PENTECOST VIGIL IN ST. PETER'S BASILICA >
Pope Francis greets a Scout leader at a Prayer Vigil to mark the Feast of Pentecost. This feast commemorates the descent of the Holy Spirit on the apostles 50 days after the resurrection of Jesus on Easter.

PENTECOST MASS IN ST. PETER'S SQUARE ^
Pope Francis tours St. Peter's Square in an open-top jeep in order to salute the thousands who attend a Pentecost Mass. For many, this visit to the Vatican is a once-in-a-lifetime experience, and the pope makes the pilgrims welcome.

DURING THE HOT SUMMER MONTHS, THE CONSTANT BUZZ OF ACTIVITY AROUND THE VATICAN GRADUALLY SUBSIDES AND THE POPE LEAVES ROME FOR HIS COUNTRY RESIDENCE AT CASTEL GANDOLFO IN THE ALBAN HILLS, 15 MILES SOUTHEAST OF ROME. THE FEAST OF THE APOSTLES PETER AND PAUL IN LATE JUNE GENERALLY MARKS THE LAST OFFICIAL FUNCTION OF THE VATICAN PRIOR TO THE SUMMER RECESS, ALTHOUGH THE POPE RETURNS TO ROME EACH WEDNESDAY TO GIVE A GENERAL AUDIENCE TO THE PILGRIMS WHO CONTINUE TO FLOCK TO THE VATICAN THROUGHOUT THIS PERIOD.

SUMMER AND FALL

THE VATICAN YEAR AFTER THE FEAST OF PENTECOST

MONTH OF MAY CLOSING CEREMONY >
Pope Benedict addresses pilgrims and the faithful gathered
at the Lourdes Grotto in the Vatican gardens to celebrate
the close of the month honoring the Virgin Mary.

MONTH OF MAY CELEBRATIONS ʌ
Acolytes carrying torches lead worshipers on a candle-lit procession through the Vatican
gardens to the Lourdes Grotto, a shrine reproducing the grotto at Lourdes in southern
France where the Virgin Mary appeared eighteen times to the young Bernadette
Soubirous in 1858. The procession celebrates the close of the Marian month of May, the
month traditionally dedicated to the veneration of the Blessed Virgin Mary.

Whoever wants to become great among
you shall be your servant; whoever wants to
become first among you, shall be servant of all.

MARK 10:43–44

RITE OF ORDINATION >
Deacons prostrate themselves in front of the altar
during the rite of ordination. As they lie prostrate, the
assembled faithful pray the Litany of Saints for them.

ORDINATION OF THE DEACONS IN ST. PETER'S BASILICA ʌ
Young deacons who are about to be ordained as priests by Pope Benedict XVI stand
ready to make their promise of obedience and celibacy during the rite of ordination.
Each year, hundreds of young men from all over the world prepare for the priesthood
in Rome and many are ordained as priests by the pope. The ceremonies are held at
St. Peter's Basilica at various times throughout the year, often during the summer months.

CORPUS DOMINI PROCESSION >
A solemn procession of worshipers headed by
the pope carries an ornate, jeweled monstrance
containing the Sacred Host through the streets of Rome.

CORPUS DOMINI BENEDICTION ʌ
During a ceremony in St. Peter's Basilica, Pope Francis lifts the monstrance containing
the consecrated Host—the unleavened bread that becomes the body (*corpus*)
of Christ during the celebration of the Eucharist—and gives the Eucharistic
Benediction. For the first time in history, on June 2, 2013, the ceremony was
replicated simultaneously in all the Catholic churches throughout the world.

You are Peter, and on this rock
I will build my Church

MATTHEW 16:18

IMPOSITION OF THE PALLIUM ›
Pope Francis bestows the pallium on a newly
appointed archbishop. The woolen band is symbolic
of the archbishop's role as the shepherd of his flock.

FEAST OF ST. PETER AND ST. PAUL ʌ
Archbishops gather after a Mass celebrated in St. Peter's Basilica on June 29 to
commemorate the martyrdoms of the apostles Peter and Paul. On this day, the
archbishops appointed the previous year receive the pallium, the symbol of their office,
from the pope. On the eve of the feast day, the pope also celebrates Mass in honor of
the apostles at St. Paul-Outside-the-Walls, the basilica dedicated to St. Paul in Rome.

PAPAL BLESSING >
Pope Benedict XVI blesses the faithful and
onlookers gathered in St. Peter's Square as he arrives
to celebrate a Mass of canonization in October 2006.

CANONIZATION MASS IN ST. PETER'S SQUARE ∧
Pilgrims and worshipers pack into St. Peter's Square during a rite of canonization, the
climax of the long process by which the Vatican recognizes an individual as a saint.
Canonization ceremonies form an irregular but spectacular addition to the Vatican
calendar and popular candidates for sainthood can attract huge crowds—over half a million
pilgrims gathered in 2001 for the canonization of the Italian mystic Padre Pio.

NOON BLESSING ➤
Benedict XVI appears at the window of his apartments in the Apostolic Palace overlooking St. Peter's Square to give his blessing at noon on the Feast of All Saints.

ALL SAINTS DAY ʌ
Pope Benedict blesses a group of nuns as he leaves St. Peter's Basilica after Mass on the Feast of All Saints. This annual feast day is celebrated on November 1 to honor all the saints in heaven, known and unknown. The following day, as a counterpart to the celebration of the saints in heaven, the Feast of All Souls commemorates the departed faithful who have not yet been purified and reached heaven.

HISTORY

 ## FAITH AND POWER

For almost two millennia, the papacy has influenced the lives of countless billions of people. St. Peter was the first to be entrusted with the care of the Christian community; his successors, the bishops of Rome—who took on the title of "pope" from the 4th century onward—have accepted this responsibility with varying degrees of success. Popes have not always limited their power to the spiritual realm; for more than a thousand years, the papacy played an important role in the power struggles of Western Europe, crowning emperors and regulating disputes among rulers. However, the temporal influence of the papacy waned dramatically in the 18th and 19th centuries. The role of the pope has undergone reevaluation in recent decades; his moral authority has been shown to have a unique and powerful influence on a significant proportion of the world's population.

FOLLOWING THE CRUCIFIXION OF JESUS CHRIST, IT WAS THE APOSTLE PETER—AS THE RECIPIENT OF THE SYMBOLIC KEYS TO THE KINGDOM OF HEAVEN FROM JESUS—WHO ASSUMED LEADERSHIP OF THE INFANT CHRISTIAN CHURCH. ST. PETER, LIKE MANY OF THE POPES WHO SUCCEEDED HIM, WAS MARTYRED FOR HIS BELIEFS BY THE ROMANS. DESPITE BITTER PERSECUTION, THE ROMAN CHURCH FLOURISHED UNDER THE LEADERSHIP OF THE POPES AND BY THE END OF THE 4TH CENTURY AD, CHRISTIANITY HAD EMERGED AS THE RELIGION OF THE ROMAN EMPIRE, AND BEYOND.

c.32–c.67	c.67–c.76	c.88–c.97	c.155–c.166

PETER	LINUS	CLEMENT I	ANICETUS

EVEN BEFORE THE DEATH of Jesus on the cross in c. 30 AD, the Galilean fisherman known as **Peter** had emerged as one of Jesus's foremost disciples. According to the Gospels, it was Jesus himself who named his disciple Peter, meaning "rock", telling him "upon this rock I will build my church." Peter often took the role of spokesman for the other apostles and it is this leadership role within the early Church, and Peter's position as the first Bishop of Rome, that lies at the heart of the papacy's leadership of the Roman Catholic Church.

Following the crucifixion of Jesus, the historical record for Peter's life is sparse. According to tradition, he left Jerusalem, possibly for Antioch in Turkey, before he finally settled in Rome. Although we do not know for certain how he died, the earliest traditions record that Peter met his death in the Circus of Nero, near the Vatican Hill, and was buried in a nearby cemetery. It is on this site that the great basilica dedicated to St. Peter at the Vatican now stands.

THE PERSECUTION OF NERO

In antiquity, the Vatican Hill lay outside the city walls in an area infested with snakes and covered by vineyards producing a notoriously sour wine. Emperor Nero's circus, where his guests were invited to witness games, cut through the valley which ran between the Janiculum and Vatican hills, where the fields were sometimes flooded by the River Tiber. On the night of July 18 in 64 AD, a fire broke out, destroying a large tract of Rome close to the emperor's city residence. The Roman historian, Tacitus, recounts how Nero blamed the Christians for the fire. Several Christians were brought to his circus, where they were tied to wooden poles and painted with tar—the first organized and state-sponsored martyrdoms of Christians. Tacitus records how "insult was added to the injury of torture, such as wrapping men in the skins of animals so that the dogs might rip them to pieces while others were nailed to crosses or condemned to be burned alive." It was probably at this time that St. Peter himself was martyred—according to some traditions, he was crucified upside down at his own request, lest his crucifixion be equated with that of his Lord Jesus.

THE APOSTOLIC SUCCESSION

The Christians who had escaped death after the great fire of Rome needed a new leader so, accordingly, the clergy and the Christian people of Rome elected a successor to St. Peter as leader of the fledgling Christian Church. To begin with there may have been a group of administrators, but by the end of the second century, Bishop Irenaeus of Lyons cites a list of Bishops of Rome in chronological order. In this way, the papacy can claim an unbroken line of succession stretching from the apostle Peter, through his immediate successor as Bishop of Rome, **Linus**, to the present day—the "Apostolic" or "Petrine succession."

< THE FEAST OF ST PETER
Each year, during celebrations at the Vatican to mark his feast day on June 29, the bronze statue of St. Peter in the nave of the basilica is adorned in sumptuous papal vestments.

THE ROMAN ERA

FROM IMPERIAL PERSECUTION TO A STATE RELIGION, 32–606

> I will give to you the keys of the Kingdom of Heaven, and whatever you will bind on Earth will be bound in Heaven; and whatever you will loose on Earth will be loosed in Heaven.

JESUS TO ST PETER, MATTHEW 16:19

189–199	217–222	230–235	236–250
VICTOR I	CALLISTUS I	PONTIANUS	FABIAN

After the destruction of Jerusalem in the Jewish War of 66–73, a rebellion in Judea against Roman rule, Rome emerged as the empire's most important Christian center; the Bishops of Rome (titled popes from c.384, *see p.43*), as successors of St. Peter, enjoyed great prestige and influence throughout the whole Christian community. Toward the end of the first century, for example, **Clement I** intervened to settle a dispute in Corinth—from such beginnings, the papacy gradually acquired authority over the wider Church.

THE EARLY CHURCH

As the Church developed over the centuries after the martyrdom of St. Peter, two other offices began to emerge: presbyter and deacon. By 250, there was a structured hierarchy in Rome to administer the local Christian community. The bishop was the overall leader of the local Christian family whose principal role was to gather Christians in prayer at the Eucharist. In this he was assisted by presbyters, who also presided at the Eucharist and oversaw the administration of the sacraments, while deacons took care of widows, orphans, and the poor.

In the early years of the Church, uniformity of discipline and practice was uneven. Around 155, a dispute arose between Bishop **Anicetus** of Rome and the Bishop of Smyrna regarding the dating of Easter. A little later, in an attempt to settle the dispute and to bolster the authority of the papacy, **Victor I** convened a synod in Rome and called for Church meetings to be held throughout the empire. Despite his strong stance, the controversy would continue to simmer.

Questions of Christian morality could prove equally divisive. **Callistus I**, elected Bishop of Rome in 217, adopted a conciliatory attitude to moral lapses, re-admitting adulterers and murderers to the Christian community. Such reconciliation was rejected by the presbyter, Hippolytus, whose followers also elected him Bishop of Rome: the first rival, or "antipope." The schism continued until 235, when Emperor Maximinus Thrax exiled both Hippolytus and the legitimate pope, **Pontianus**, to Sardinia. Reconciled on the island, they both died as a result of forced labor in the salt mines.

THE DECIAN PERSECUTION

A number of the early Bishops of Rome, together with many of their fellow Christians, died as martyrs for their faith. From around 250, the Roman emperor, Decius, required all citizens to perform pagan sacrifice to the state gods, thereby proving loyalty to the emperor, and to obtain a document known as a *libellus* as confirmation of this act. Those who refused, such as the Jews and Christians, faced intense persecution. Some gave in to the pressure, renounced their faith and left the community; others paid for their resistance to the emperor's edict with their lives. In January 250, the Bishop of Rome, **Fabian**, was martyred by the imperial guard. With much of the Roman clergy in prison, it would be another 14 months before a new election could be held and the vacant seat could be filled.

> **CHRISTIAN PERSECUTION**
> Many early Christians were martyred at the hands of the Roman authorities. Some, like the figure in this mosaic, torn to pieces by wild animals at the circus.

257–258	283–296	296–304	308–309
SIXTUS II	**CAIUS**	**MARCELLINUS**	**MARCELLUS I**

The death of Emperor Decius in 251 did not end the persecution of the Christians. A few years later, a new period of repression broke out under Emperor Valerian. **Sixtus II**, one of the first victims, was beheaded and many other Christians were exiled or put to death. After Valerian's death in 260, an uneasy truce between Church and empire prevailed—although **Caius** allegedly was martyred in 296—until the last and most ferocious of the Roman persecutions was initiated by Diocletian in 303. In that year, Bishop **Marcellinus** was forced to abdicate and four years were to pass before a successor, **Marcellus I**, was elected. His pontificate was brief; incurring the emperor's displeasure, Marcellus was imprisoned and sent to work in the imperial stables.

CONSTANTINE THE GREAT

The era of imperial persecution finally came to an end with the accession of Emperor Constantine. The historian Eusebius relates how Constantine had a vision of the Cross of Christ and saw the words "in this sign you will conquer" on the eve of the Battle of the Milvian Bridge in 312. Fighting under a Christian banner against his co-ruler, Maxentius, Constantine went on to take control of the entire Western Roman Empire. The following year, he ended the centuries of persecution against the Christians with a proclamation, the Edict of Milan, allowing freedom of worship throughout the empire.

Constantine embraced Christianity, endowing the Christian community with lands and churches. He donated to **Miltiades** a palace at the Lateran, close to the Roman walls, which was to remain the pontifical residence until the start of the 14th century. The emperor razed the adjoining buildings, previously barracks belonging to the bodyguard of the defeated Maxentius, to build the world's first Christian basilica, St. John Lateran. Among various other projects, Constantine constructed a large basilica over the tomb of St. Peter close by the ruins of the Circus of Nero on the Vatican Hill. This monument dominated the Vatican until the 16th century, when the modern basilica of St. Peter's was built. A 6th-century biography of the popes, the *Liber Pontificalis,* also details the warm relationship between the emperor and Miltiades's successor, **Sylvester I,** as well as the extravagant gifts given to the Christian community in Rome.

While the Church in the West enjoyed Constantine's patronage and protection, the situation was not so favorable in the Eastern Roman Empire. In 313, as a part of the Edict of Milan, Constantine had come to an arrangement with Licinius, emperor in the East, to allow religious toleration in his territories.

< THE CONVERSION OF CONSTANTINE
According to Constantine's biographer, Eusebius, Constantine had a vision of a cross of light emblazoned against the sun and saw the words "in this sign you will conquer." The Christian emblem he adopted is the Chi-Rho symbol, a combination of the Greek letters *X* and *P.*

> It is our will that all the peoples we rule shall practice the religion that Peter the Apostle transmitted to the Romans.

EDICT OF THE EMPEROR THEODOSIUS, 380

311–314	314–335	366–384	384–399
MILTIADES	SYLVESTER I	DAMASUS I	SIRICIUS

When Licinius renewed his persecution of Christian sects in 320, Constantine's armies advanced eastward underneath the sign of the cross and seized control of the Eastern Roman Empire in 324.

THE ARIAN CONTROVERSY

With the threat of imperial repression receding, the greatest danger to the growing Church arose from internal dissent. In 318, Arius, a presbyter of Alexandria, caused consternation within the Christian community by declaring that Jesus was created by God, thereby denying the true divinity of Christ. With Arius rapidly gathering followers, Constantine convened all the bishops of the empire to meet at Nicaea, in modern-day Turkey. An agreement was reached and enshrined in the Nicene Creed, which declared that Jesus was "of one substance with the Father." The Arians, however, refused to abide by the decrees of the Council of Nicaea. The doctrinal argument raged on for more than a century, dividing both Church and empire.

TOWARD A STATE RELIGION

In 380, **Damasus I**, the first Bishop of Rome to refer to his seat as the Apostolic See, took advantage of his good relations with Emperor Theodosius to have Christianity declared the official religion of the empire. A decade later, the pagan temples were finally closed for cultic sacrifice. The Roman emperors also abandoned the title *Pontifex Maximus*, supreme pontiff, which had traditionally denoted them high-priests of the state religion. This title was instead assumed by Damasus's successor as Bishop of Rome, **Siricius**. Asserting the primacy of the popes over other bishops, Siricius decreed that no bishop should be ordained without a mandate from "the Apostolic See" of Rome. By the close of the 4th century, Christianity was firmly established both as the religion of state and the religion of the majority of people in the empire. From now on, with the title of pope, the Bishops of Rome were widely recognized as the supreme authority within the Christian Church.

⋀ DEATH OF ST. SEBASTIAN
St. Sebastian was martyred during the Diocletian persecution and his remains placed in a basilica built by Pope Damasus I on the site of the modern church of San Sebastiano fuori le mura in Rome.

401–417	432–440	440–461	468–483
INNOCENT I	SIXTUS III	LEO I	SIMPLICIUS

The 5th century was a period of transition throughout the Roman Empire. As the power of the emperors declined, an influx of barbarian tribes swept through Western Europe. In 410, disaster struck: the city of Rome itself was attacked. **Innocent I** tried in vain to enlist the aid of Emperor Honorius, who resided in Ravenna, but for several days the city was plundered by an army under the Visigothic king, Alaric—the first time that the city had fallen in 800 years.

The Visigoths did not remain in Italy and imperial authority in Rome was, for the time being, restored. During the pontificate of **Sixtus III**, the city even enjoyed a building boom, with the construction of Santa Maria Maggiore, one of the four great patriarchal basilicas of Rome. Nonetheless, the sack of Rome was a deeply traumatic event, an indication that the Church could no longer rely upon imperial protection. As the empire began to disintegrate, the papacy increasingly sought to take its own lead in temporal affairs.

LEO THE GREAT

Elected in 440 while he was on a diplomatic mission to Gaul on behalf of Emperor Valentian III, **Leo I** proved an effective and influential pontiff, leading the Church for two decades. Leo's diplomatic skills proved invaluable when he met with Attila, leader of the Huns—a confederation of barbarian tribes that had laid waste to northern Italy—and persuaded him not to march on Rome. In 455, when Rome was ransacked by the east-Germanic Vandals, Leo obtained a promise from their leader, Genseric, that the inhabitants should be spared.

< GOLD COIN OF JUSTINIAN I
The Byzantine emperor Justinian I is shown as a mounted warrior preceded by a winged Victory on this coin commemorating his conquests in Italy, including Rome, and North Africa.

Leo also did much to assert the authority of the popes as successors to St. Peter. At the Council of Chalcedon in 451, Leo challenged the monophysite heresy: the belief that Jesus had only one nature, rather than two, human and divine. According to one account, the council fathers leaped to their feet in recognition of Leo's authority, exclaiming that "Peter has spoken through the mouth of Leo."

GOTHIC KINGS AND BYZANTINE EMPERORS

In 476, the last emperor to rule from Rome, Romulus Augustus, was deposed by the barbarian king, Odoacer, leader of the Heruli. This date is often held to mark the end of the Roman Empire in the West. Although Odoacer was a Christian, he was an Arian—a form of Christianity regarded as heretical by the Roman Church (see p.43). Despite this, Pope **Simplicius** agreed that Odoacer, like the Roman emperors, would confirm the appointment of the popes.

The Eastern, or Byzantine, Empire continued to prosper for many centuries after the fall of the West. Determined to recover the western portion of the empire from the barbarians, the Byzantine emperor, Justinian I, invaded Sicily in 535 and prepared to invade Italy. The Ostrogothic king of Italy begged Pope **Agapetus I** to travel to Byzantium to dissuade the emperor from invading. Agapetus failed in his mission, becoming embroiled in a conflict with the

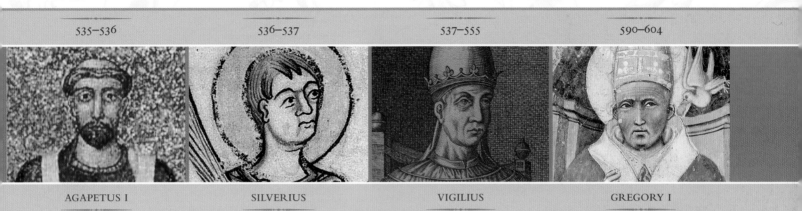

535–536	536–537	537–555	590–604
AGAPETUS I	SILVERIUS	VIGILIUS	GREGORY I

Patriarch of Constantinople over the patriarch's support of the monophysite heresy. The following year, Justinian's armies entered Rome. Over the next two decades, Rome changed hands regularly, with the Ostrogoths finally defeated only in 552. With Justinian controlling Italy, the papacy soon became embroiled in Byzantine Church politics, and in particular with Justinian's attempts to appease the adherents of monophysitism, a doctrine that still held much support in the East. In 537, Pope **Silverius** was deposed in favor of **Vigilius**, the ambitious papal ambassador in Constantinople. Vigilius had secured imperial backing in return for a promise to promote the monophysite position but, unable to deliver on his promises, he was arrested and brought to Constantinople. Vigilius died in Sicily a few years later while attempting to return to Rome.

GREGORY THE GREAT

Byzantine control over Italy was short-lived. Within a few years of Justinian's death in 565, Rome faced a new barbarian threat from the Lombards, a Germanic tribe that had settled in northern Italy, making regular raids into papal territory. Yet, in these least promising circumstances, in a city beset by plague and floods, a pope was elected who would do more than any other to help the Church come to terms with the decline of the Roman Empire. A monk at the time

of his election in 590, **Gregory I** had gained administrative experience as Prefect of Rome and papal legate to Constantinople. He soon put this to good use, reorganizing the civil administration of Rome, giving economic and social rebirth to the city. He also consolidated the lands owned by the Church, creating a territory that would later form the basis of the Papal States. As pope, Gergory continued to live a simple life of service to the Church, styling himself *servus servorum Dei*—servant of the servants of God. Contemporary accounts describe him sailing through the flooded city of Rome, bringing food and rescuing stranded people.

A man of culture, Gregory reorganized the liturgy (Church ritual), founding choirs at the Lateran and St. Peter's to sing the liturgies performed in the basilicas. But perhaps his most important contribution was to recognize that the future of Christianity lay not with the fading Roman Empire, but with the new kingdoms of Western Europe. By sending missionaries such as St. Augustine to evangelize the English and establishing monasteries in barbarian lands, Gregory helped to lay the foundations of Christianity in the medieval era.

< LEGEND OF THE CASTEL SANT'ANGELO
In this scene from the life of Pope Gregory the Great, an angel appears above the Castel Sant'Angelo in Rome, sheathing his sword to indicate the end of the city's plague.

AS THE PEOPLES OF EUROPE UNDERWENT A STEADY CONVERSION TO CHRISTIANITY, THE PAPACY BEGAN TO TURN AWAY FROM THE EASTERN EMPERORS AND SEEK ALLIANCE WITH THE NEW CHRISTIAN EMPIRE ESTABLISHED BY THE FRANKISH KING, CHARLEMAGNE. IN THE 9TH CENTURY, THE FORTUNES OF THE PAPACY DECLINED DRAMATICALLY AS THE PAPAL THRONE BECAME A PRIZE FOR FEUDING ROMAN FAMILIES. YET BY THE END OF THE EARLY MEDIEVAL PERIOD, A SERIES OF STRONG AND REFORM-MINDED POPES HAD REVITALIZED THE CHURCH AND RESET THE PAPACY'S MORAL AND POLITICAL COMPASS.

607	649–655	654–657	657–672	731–741
BONIFACE III	MARTIN I	EUGENE I	VITALIAN	GREGORY III

 DURING THE early medieval period, the Italian peninsula was riven by political instability. The emperors of Byzantium controlled only a small area around the cities of Rome and Ravenna, with a thin corridor linking the two cities. The land around these territories was held by the Lombards—pagans or Arian Christians *(see p.43)* who owed no allegiance to the popes in Rome.

Ten popes lived and died between the death of Gregory the Great in 604 and the election of Martin I half a century later. Each had to request confirmation from the emperor in Constantinople before their coronation, a procedure that could take up to a year. **Boniface III**, who enjoyed excellent relations with the Byzantine emperor, was forced to wait almost a year for his confirmation as a result of wrangling in Rome. Finally confirmed in 607, Boniface died nine months later, although he was at least able to persuade the emperor to formally recognize the Roman Church as the head of all Churches.

IMPERIAL TENSIONS

In 649, **Martin I** was crowned pope just two days after his election and without the imperial mandate. The Byzantine emperor, Constans II, already irritated by Martin's independence, was outraged when he called a synod (meeting of bishops) at the Lateran that criticized the theological opinions of the court. In 653, the pope was arrested in the Lateran basilica, having narrowly avoided an assassination attempt ordered by the emperor; the frail pontiff was bundled into a cage and shipped to Constantinople, where, after months of solitary confinement and suffering from dysentery, he was put on trial. Accused of heresy, Martin was deposed, flogged, and exiled to the Crimea, where he died shortly afterward.

When news of Martin's death was relayed to Rome, the clergy and people set about electing a new pope. An elderly presbyter was elected, taking the name **Eugene I**. His efforts to placate the emperor and the Romans failed but his successor, **Vitalian**, succeeded in re-establishing good relations between Rome and Constantinople. In 726, however, the Byzantine emperor, Leo III, caused a crisis by ordering the destruction of icons. Pope **Gregory II** rejected Leo's demands, noting that it was not the business of princes to interfere in questions of theology. With theological differences mounting, and the emperors in Constantinople distracted by the growing Islamic threat to the east, the papacy began to turn to allies closer to home.

THE DONATION OF PEPIN

As imperial power waned in the Italian peninsula, the papacy found it increasingly difficult to defend Rome from an invasion by their Germanic neighbors, the Lombards. In 739, Pope **Gregory III** unsuccessfully appealed to Charles Martel, King of the Franks (a Germanic people settled in the area of present-day France). After the Lombards had taken the imperial city of Ravenna, **Stephen II** traveled to Paris in 754 in a new attempt to seek help. During the negotiations with Pepin, the Frankish ruler, it seems probable that the pope presented him with a document purporting to be an edict issued by the Emperor Constantine in the 4th

> **LOMBARD CROSS**
As the various peoples of Europe became more settled and powerful, their religious art grew more sophisticated. This jeweled cross from northern Italy is a stunning example of Lombard craftmanship.

THE EARLY MIDDLE AGES

CONSOLIDATION, CORRUPTION, AND REFORM, 607–1159

> He [Charlemagne] honored more than any of the other venerable and holy places, the Church of St. Peter in Rome.
>
> EINHARD, *LIFE OF CHARLEMAGNE*, c.820

752–757	772–795	795–816	817–824	828–844
STEPHEN II	HADRIAN I	LEO III	PASCHAL I	GREGORY IV

century. As a reward for the emperor's baptism by Pope Sylvester I and for curing him of leprosy, this document claimed, Constantine bestowed on the papacy dominion over all the provinces in the Western Roman Empire. The Donation of Constantine, as the document became known, was used throughout the medieval period to bolster papal claims to territorial power in Europe. It was not until 1440 that an Italian scholar finally proved that the document was a forgery.

As a result of Stephen's appeals, Pepin crossed the Alps and descended into Italy, routing the Lombards during two campaigns in 754 and 756. The Frankish ruler donated the former imperial territories occupied by the Lombards to the papacy. Over the following centuries, these lands came to form the basis of the Papal States—the territories over which the papacy exercised civil, as well as spiritual, power.

THE NEW ROMAN EMPIRE

The alliance between the Frankish rulers and the papacy proved ever more important as the Frankish Empire continued to expand. Pepin's son, Charles, reigned for almost half a century from 768, his reputation for justice, his aggressive military campaigns, and his piety earning him the epithet Charles the Great, or Charlemagne. In 773, when Pope **Hadrian I** appealed to the Franks once again for protection from the Lombards, Charlemagne entered Italy and took for himself the title "King of the Lombards."

Charlemagne was deeply affected by his Roman connections and ordered Roman practices, especially in liturgy, to be observed throughout his territories.

Like Constantine, Charlemagne appreciated the unifying force of religion in his empire. He carried out reforms in the Frankish Church, imposing higher levels of literacy on the clergy and issuing new laws to counter errors and abuses.

In 800, a violent dispute broke out between Pope **Leo III** and the Roman aristocracy. Leo was accused of adultery and other misdemeanors and was set upon while riding through the streets. Seeking refuge in the nearby monastery of San Silvestro, the pope then escaped Rome, appealing to Charlemagne for aid. After a delay of several months, Charlemagne made the journey to Rome, where he was lodged at a palace specially built for him at the Vatican. On Christmas Day 800, Leo crowned Charlemagne "Emperor of the Romans" in St. Peter's Basilica. Thus began the long association between the papacy and the emperors of what would later become known as the Holy Roman Empire. Initially constructive, the relationship would become increasingly fraught with tension.

> CHARLEMAGNE SHRINE
Emperor Charlemagne is shown flanked by Leo III and Bishop Turpin on this exquisite reliquary in Aachen Cathedral.

847–855	872–882	891–896	903
LEO IV	JOHN VIII	FORMOSUS	LEO V

In August 846, a fleet of ships carrying Islamic warriors from North Africa sailed through the mouth of the River Tiber and inland toward Rome—Saracens intent on pillaging Rome. Disembarking at the old grain docks in the Greek Quarter, the raiders swarmed west towards the Vatican, where they looted the tomb of St. Peter while others pillaged the tomb of St. Paul on Via Ostiensis. After three days, the Saracens withdrew, having stripped the churches bare.

Still recoiling after the attack, the newly elected Pope **Leo IV** ordered the construction of a high wall around the Vatican, fortified with a series of strong towers—two of which still stand in the Vatican gardens today. During the construction of the Leonine walls, word arrived of a new Saracen fleet gathering off Sardinia. The pope swiftly organized a papal fleet to join the ships of the Italian maritime cities. Aided by a storm that scattered their opponents' ships, the Christian fleet routed the Saracens off Ostia in 849. The prisoners captured at Ostia were put to work building the new walls.

NICHOLAS THE GREAT
Few popes emerge with great credit during the late 9th and 10th centuries but one notable exception was the energetic and

> **THE BATTLE OF OSTIA**
Painted by Raphael to decorate the walls of the Apostolic Palace, this fresco shows the Saracen prisoners captured at the Battle of Ostia being presented to Pope Leo IV.

autocratic pontiff, **Nicholas I**, elected in 858. Nicholas asserted the papacy's independence from the emperors in Constantinople by refusing to support their appointment of Photius as Patriarch (Archbishop of Constantinople), and took a strict line against bishops he considered lax. He censured the Archbishop of Ravenna for unjust behavior, threatening to depose and excommunicate him unless he submitted to pontifical authority. He also clashed with the powerful Frankish Archbishop Hincmar of Rheims over the question of papal prerogative, eventually forcing him to capitulate to the authority of the papacy.

Nicholas was equally willing to intervene in matters of state. When King Lothair of Lorraine divorced his wife, Nicholas interceded in favor of the queen. Although Lothair's brother attacked Rome and imprisoned Nicholas in St. Peter's, the beleaguered pope remained firm.

VIOLENCE AND ASSASSINATIONS
The later 9th century was marked by a dramatic decline in the fortunes of the papacy. The papal throne became little more than a prize to be fought over by feuding Roman families such as the dukes of Spoleto, the Tusculani, and their bitter rivals, the Crescentii. In 882, the unthinkable occurred: **John VIII** was poisoned and then battered to death by members of his own entourage—the first pope to be assassinated. However, the real nadir of the papacy came in 897, when

904–911	914–928	931–935	1012–1024
SERGIUS III	JOHN X	JOHN XI	BENEDICT VIII

Stephen VI carried out an act as violent as it was shocking. After some eight months in the tomb, the body of his predecessor, Pope **Formosus**, was disinterred and placed in the Synod Hall of the Lateran, arrayed in pontifical vestments. Charges were read out against the deceased and as the bizarre trial ended, Stephen ordered the corpse to be stripped of its vestments and thrown in the Tiber. Pope Stephen was himself later strangled by a Roman mob.

Two camps had been created, those faithful to Formosus and those who followed Stephen. Five popes and one rival, or "antipope," succeeded each other in a period of eight years. After just one month in office, Pope **Leo V** was overthrown and imprisoned. One of his own clerics, Christopher, had himself elected antipope. In 904, with the support of the powerful duke of Spoleto, a new contender, **Sergius III**, was elected. Marching on Rome, Sergius imprisoned Christopher along with Leo. Some months later, both men were strangled in the papal dungeon.

MAROZIA AND THE TUSCULANI
Frequent incursions by Islamic armies continued to threaten central Italy. When the archbishop of Ravenna was elected as **John X** in 914, he gathered an army of Italian princes and led them into battle against the Saracens, routing his opponents near the River Garigliano in 915. Later that year, John crowned his Carolingian ally, Berenger, as Holy Roman Emperor, sealing his diplomatic success. For more than a decade, John controlled Rome, but in 928, he was deposed by an aristocratic faction headed by the notorious Roman noblewoman, Marozia. A member of the Tusculani family, Marozia was a former wife of the Duke of Spoleto and allegedly the mistress of Pope Sergius III. John was imprisoned in the Castel Sant'Angelo, where he died some months later.

With Marozia in control of Rome, John's immediate successors were little more than puppets in the hands of the Tusculani. In 931, Marozia secured the election of her own son to the papal throne as **John XI**. According to the *Liber Pontificalis*, a medieval biography of the popes, John was the illegitimate child of Pope Sergius III. There followed a long period in which first the Tusculani, then the Crescentii family gained ascendency inside Rome.

Not all of the popes in this period were lacking faith or principles: **Benedict VIII**, elected in 1012, introduced reforms, holding a council at Pavia to legislate against simony (the sale of Church offices) and clerical marriage, and encouraging the monastic reform movement. But it would not be until the papacy freed itself from the grip of the Roman aristocracy that the popes would regain the moral and spiritual leadership of the Church.

< FIRE IN THE BORGO
Raphael's fresco shows the fire that broke out near the Vatican in 847. According to legend, Leo IV miraculously extinguished the blaze through the power of his prayer.

> The Roman pontiff alone can with right be called universal … he alone can depose or reinstate bishops.
>
> DOCUMENT IN THE REGISTER OF GREGORY VII, 1075

1049–1054	1061–1073	1073–1085	1088–1099
LEO IX	ALEXANDER II	GREGORY VII	URBAN II

In 1046, the young ruler of the Holy Roman Empire, the German king, Henry III, crossed the Alps into Italy, determined to remedy the turbulent situation in Rome, where three claimants from aristocratic Roman families were vying with one another for control of the papacy. Deposing all three, Henry imposed a German bishop, the short-lived **Clement II**. After the death of another German appointee in 1048, the emperor offered the papacy to his own cousin. Reluctantly accepting the emperor's nomination, the new pope took the name **Leo IX**.

REFORM AND SCHISM

Leo moved decisively against the Roman families whose fighting had done so much to discredit the papacy. He attempted to reform the Church, enforcing clerical celibacy, limiting the sale of Church positions, and traveled widely as he sought to extend papal authority. Perhaps most significantly, Leo gathered around himself a group of reformers such as Peter Damian and Cardinal Humbert. One member of the circle, a young monk named Hildebrand, would later write his own chapter in the history of the reformed papacy as Pope Gregory VII.

Leo did much to improve the reputation of the papacy in the West, but his efforts were marred by a dispute with Constantinople. Trouble flared when Leo attempted to impose the Latin (Western) rite in southern Italy, an area that looked toward the Eastern Church rather than Rome. Infuriated by this interference, the Patriarch of Constantinople retaliated by ordering Christians who followed the Latin rite to leave Constantinople. In

ʌ BYZANTINE CROSS
The Byzantine Empire produced exquisite ornaments such as this cross depicting Mary, mother of Jesus.

1054, Leo attempted to heal the rift by dispatching an embassy under Cardinal Humbert. Unfortunately, Humbert proceeded directly to the church of Santa Sophia, where he slammed a bull of Excommunication on the high altar—a step that Leo had intended only as a last resort. With this deliberately provocative action, the already strained relations between Rome and Constantinople were ruptured definitively.

THE INVESTITURE CONTROVERSY

Leo's successor, **Nicholas II**, took steps to limit the influence of the Roman nobility by decreeing that only the seven cardinal bishops could select a candidate. Nicholas's aspirations, however, were ignored at the death of **Alexander II**, when the Roman crowds clamored for the election of Hildebrand, now archdeacon and one of the most influential men in the Church. Elected in 1073 as **Gregory VII**, the new pope would prove to be one of the key figures of the medieval period, determined to promote the authority of the papacy in both the spiritual and temporal spheres.

Above all, Gregory sought to tackle lay investiture—the system in which secular rulers were able to influence the appointment of bishops and other Church officials. Gregory was determined that control over investiture should lie with the Church alone—and ultimately with the papacy. Events came to a head in 1076, when Gregory opposed the appointment of the Archbishop of Milan by the Holy Roman Emperor, Henry IV. The emperor persuaded the German bishops to declare the pope deposed; Gregory responded by excommunicating

1099–1118	1119–1124	1130–1143	1145–1153	1154–1159
PASCHAL II	CALLISTUS II	INNOCENT II	EUGENE III	HADRIAN IV

Henry and freeing his subjects from their oaths of loyalty to their monarch. Outmaneuvered, Henry traveled to Canossa in northern Italy to be reconciled with the pope but soon reneged on his promises and in 1080 was excommunicated once again. The controversy continued long after Gregory's death in 1085, dividing the Church and causing half a century of civil war inside Germany.

THE CRUSADE TO THE HOLY LAND

Against this backdrop of conflict and controversy occurred one of the most extraordinary episodes in the history of the papacy. In 1095, during a council at Clermont in France, Pope **Urban II** led the bishops into a field outside the town walls and, from a wooden platform, launched an impassioned appeal urging his listeners to mount a military expedition to the Holy Land to liberate Jerusalem from the Muslims, who had captured it from the Byzantines in 638. Any soldier who died fighting for their Lord, Urban stated, would earn remission from all sins. The crowd erupted with cries of "God wills it!". Over the next two years alone, thousands of crusaders from every section of society took the cross and joined the armed pilgrimage to the Holy Land.

Despite Urban's exalted rhetoric, the march of the crusaders to Jerusalem was rarely either noble or glorious. The path eastwards was marked by episodes of anti-semitism, where crusaders attacked Jewish enclaves. The first army to cross into Asia—the ragged "People's Crusade"—was massacred soon after entering hostile lands, and many thousands of soldiers died in the harsh conditions on the journey to Jerusalem. Nonetheless, the ultimate success of this first crusade was remarkable; arriving before the walls of Jerusalem in 1099, the Christian army laid siege to the city and a week later the Holy City fell into their power.

THE CONCORDAT OF WORMS

Urban II died in July 1099, before the news of the capture of Jerusalem had time to reach him in Rome, and the pontificate of his successor, **Paschal II**, was dominated by the struggle with the Holy Roman emperors in Germany over control of the Church. In 1122, Pope **Callistus II** reached a compromise with Emperor Henry V—the Concordat of Worms—which drew a clear distinction between the temporal and spiritual responsibilities of bishops, granting the emperor a say in the former but not in the latter. This compromise allowed subsequent popes, such as **Innocent II** and **Eugene III**, to focus on Church reform. In 1146, Eugene was able to persuade the Holy Roman Emperor Conrad to take part in a new, though ill-fated, crusade. Inevitably, relations soured; when the English pope, **Hadrian IV**, died in 1159, he was in the process of excommunicating Emperor Frederick Barbarossa—the beginning of a renewed period of conflict between the papacy and the Holy Roman Empire over the vexed question of papal supremacy.

➤ CRUSADER KNIGHT
Inspired by Urban II's theory of legitimate religious warfare, thousands of Christian knights fought and died in the Holy Land.

✝ **PAPAL POLITICS IN THE LATE MEDIEVAL PERIOD CONTINUED TO BE DOMINATED BY FRICTION** BETWEEN THE PAPACY AND EUROPE'S POWERFUL SECULAR RULERS, WITH GERMAN EMPERORS AND FRENCH KINGS BOTH VYING FOR INFLUENCE IN ITALY AND CONTROL OVER THE CHURCH. BUT IT WAS INFIGHTING BETWEEN RIVAL FACTIONS IN ROME THAT FINALLY FORCED THE PAPACY TO ABANDON ITALY FOR AVIGNON IN FRANCE. AFTER A 70-YEAR EXILE, THE POPES RETURNED TO ROME IN 1376, BUT A BITTER SCHISM SOON THREATENED TO UNDERMINE THE VERY BASIS OF PAPAL AUTHORITY.

1159–1181	1181–1185	1185–1187	1187	1187–1191	1191–1198
ALEXANDER III	LUCIUS III	URBAN III	GREGORY VIII	CLEMENT III	CELESTINE III

THE LATE 12TH CENTURY witnessed the apogee of papal claims to spiritual and temporal power—but even at their height, such claims were rarely uncontested. Following the election of **Alexander III** in 1159, a small band of disaffected cardinals elected a rival candidate, who took the name Victor IV. The Holy Roman Emperor Frederick Barbarossa, ever keen to extend his influence inside Italy, convened a council at Pavia to decide between the rivals. When Barbarossa sided with Victor, the infuriated Alexander immediately excommunicated the emperor, throwing the papacy and empire into a period of renewed conflict.

The split initiated by Victor's election lasted for almost 18 years, with two more rival popes, known as antipopes, elected. Gradually, however, Alexander won support from the rulers of Europe, many of whom opposed Barbarossa's expansionist policies. In 1176, a group of northern Italian towns, supported by Alexander, defeated the emperor's armies at Legnano, forcing him to enter into negotiations with the pope, and the following year, in return for lifting his excommunication, Barbarossa acknowledged Alexander's pontificate.

ANTIPOPES AND HERETICS

The election of these rival popes must have been at the forefront of Alexander's mind in 1179 when he convened the Third Lateran Council, a General Council of bishops held at the Lateran Palace in Rome. Among the decrees of the council was a canon requiring a majority of two-thirds of the cardinals' votes for a valid papal election, a provision that remains in effect today. Significantly, the council also published canons condemning a number of heretical movements, most notably the Cathars, a breakaway Christian sect based in

southern France. This desire to define the limits of orthodox Christian behavior would become increasingly evident in papal policy of the period, and led Alexander's successor, **Lucius III**, to establish an episcopal inquisition—forerunner of the Papal Inquisition—against the Cathars in 1184.

THE PAPACY RESURGENT

At the Concordat of Worms in 1122 *(see p.51)*, the papacy had reached an uneasy compromise with the Holy Roman emperors over secular interference in Church appointments. However, popes and princes continued to dispute ecclesiastical appointments throughout the medieval period, and, during a series of short pontificates from Lucius to **Celestine III**, the papacy tried unsuccessfully to assert its authority over secular powers who wished to control the lucrative revenues brought in from Church-owned land.

With the unanimous election of the 37-year-old **Innocent III** in 1198, the papacy finally found a determined leader capable of defending the Church's interests. A noted canon lawyer, the young pontiff combined a formidable intellect with great diplomatic skill, and sought to strengthen the power of the papacy by various means; he obliged the Roman senate and

> RELIQUARY BUST OF FREDERICK I
The formidable Holy Roman Emperor Frederick Barbarossa (r.1152–90) clashed repeatedly with popes as he sought to impose his political will on the papacy.

THE LATE MIDDLE AGES
IMPERIAL POLITICS, EXILE, AND PAPAL SCHISM, 1159–1415

> Three doves were flying around the room where the cardinals had taken their seats and when Innocent was elected ... the whitest of doves flew to him and settled next to his right hand.
>
> "THE DEEDS OF POPE INNOCENT III", c.1208

1198–1216	1216–1227	1227–1241	1241	1243–1254	1254–1261
INNOCENT III	HONORIUS III	GREGORY IX	CELESTINE IV	INNOCENT IV	ALEXANDER IV

aristocracy to take an oath of loyalty and intervened regularly in the affairs of European courts. In 1209, Innocent excommunicated King John of England for his refusal to acknowledge Stephen Langton as Archbishop of Canterbury, while he declared Aragon, Poland, Portugal, and Ireland as fiefdoms to be held at the pope's pleasure. He also adroitly handled the papacy's sensitive relationship with the rulers of the Holy Roman Empire. Following the death of Frederick Barbarossa's son, Henry VI, Innocent allied himself first with Otto of Brunswick, whom he crowned Holy Roman Emperor Otto IV in 1209, then with Otto's rivals, King Philip II of France and Barbarossa's grandson, Frederick II.

After his election, Innocent III launched the Fourth Crusade to liberate Jerusalem, which had been retaken by the Muslims in 1187. In 1204, the galleys carrying the crusaders docked at Constantinople, capital of the Christian Byzantine Empire with around 150,000 inhabitants. Disastrously, the crusaders sacked the city, setting a destructive fire and ending any hopes of a resolution of the rift between the Roman Catholic and Eastern Orthodox Churches.

PIETY AND PERSECUTION

As the papacy came to define the Church orthodoxy with increasing precision in the 13th century, there was a corresponding intolerance of unorthodox behavior. In 1208, Pope Innocent III demanded that King Philip II of France undertake a military campaign, the Albigensian Crusade, against Cathar heretics in his realm. With papal approval, thousands of Cathars were massacred by the civil authorities. According to one Cistercian historian, the papal legate ordered the indiscriminate slaughter of the townsfolk of Béziers with the words "Kill them all; the Lord knows his own." It was during a mission among the Cathars

that the Spanish preacher, Dominic de Guzmán, was inspired to found the Friars Preachers, or Dominicans, an order of mendicant friars dedicated to combating heresy through preaching. Another charismatic figure, Francis of Assisi, founded the Friars Minor, seeking to emulate the poverty and simplicity of the early Church. Pope Innocent approved the Franciscans in 1209, while his successor, **Honorius III**, formally established the Dominican order in 1216. The scholarly and fiercely orthodox Dominicans proved staunch allies of the papacy, and in 1233, **Gregory IX** established a permanent tribunal staffed by Dominicans and dedicated to eradicating heresy—the Inquisition.

Meanwhile, the delicate relationship with Frederick II, crowned Holy Roman Emperor by Honorius in 1220, continued to cause friction. In 1245, **Innocent IV** declared Frederick deposed and sent aid to his adversaries in Germany. The impasse was resolved only by Frederick's death in 1250.

∨ SUPPRESSION OF THE HERETICS

King Philip II watches as a group of heretics is burned outside Paris in 1210. Pope Innocent III encouraged the French king to pursue the suppression of the Cathars in southern France.

> There are two swords, the one wielded …
> by priests, the other by kings and soldiers,
> but by the will and permission of the priests.
>
> POPE BONIFACE VIII, 1302

1261–1264	1265–1268	1271–1276	1276	1276
URBAN IV	CLEMENT IV	GREGORY X	INNOCENT V	HADRIAN V

With the death of the Holy Roman Emperor Frederick II in 1250, the German Hohenstaufen dynasty of emperors began to disintegrate. Freed from overbearing imperial interference, the papacy quickly sought to restore its authority in the Papal States and promote its influence within the former imperial territories of Sicily and southern Italy. In 1262, in an attempt to prevent Sicily falling into the hands of Frederick's son, Manfred, the French-born Pope **Urban IV** offered the kingdom to the French prince, Charles of Anjou. Urban died just two years later while fleeing from Manfred's allies, but he was succeeded by another French pope, **Clement IV**, who maintained his policy. In 1266, Charles of Anjou recognized Clement as his feudal overlord and in return was crowned King of Sicily by the Roman cardinals. However, King Charles quickly acquired more influence in Italy than the popes had intended; Clement soon discovered that he had simply exchanged the domineering Hohenstaufen emperors for an increasingly imperious Angevin king.

THE PAPAL INTERREGNUM

The death of Clement IV in 1268 sparked a succession crisis of unprecedented proportions. For almost three years, the cardinals were locked into deliberations in the Italian town of Viterbo, where Clement had died. Two cardinals expired, while a third resigned his right to vote and returned home. Eventually, the mayor of Viterbo decided to take matters into his own hands. The cardinals were confined to the papal residence and their food was gradually reduced. When this failed to achieve an election, part of the roof was removed. Finally, in September 1271, they elected Pope **Gregory X**. The new pope was neither a cardinal nor a member of the conclave (the assembly of cardinals gathered to elect a pope)—he was not even in Italy at the time of his election, but on crusade in Palestine where he was serving as chaplain to the future King Edward I of England.

THE PONTIFICATE OF GREGORY X

Once elected, Gregory was keen to prevent the recurrence of the election crisis, and in 1274 he laid down new rules for papal elections, summarized in a papal bull (a special decree named after the *bulla,* or seal, used to authenticate it). Ten days after a pope's death, Gregory stated, the cardinals were to be locked into a room in the palace where the pope had died, their meals passed to them through a small opening. If after three days an election failed to take place, food would be reduced. A further inducement was the suspension of cardinals' salaries during the conclave.

Having experienced first hand the plight of the Christian states in the Holy Land, Gregory was determined to organize a new crusade. To this end, he tried to reconcile the divided monarchies of Europe and negotiated with the Byzantine emperor in an attempt to heal the great schism between the Eastern and Western Churches (see p.50). A temporary reunion of the Churches was achieved at the Second Council of Lyons in 1274, but proved short-lived. The council also debated the new crusade and secured a six-year tithe, or

< CORONATION OF CHARLES OF ANJOU
In January 1266, Charles of Anjou was crowned King of Sicily at the Vatican. Invited to Italy by the papacy to counterbalance imperial power, Charles soon became a dominant figure in papal and Italian politics.

1276–1277	1277–1280	1281–1285	1294	1294–1303
JOHN XXI	NICHOLAS III	MARTIN IV	CELESTINE V	BONIFACE VIII

tax, to finance the expedition, but with Gregory's death early in 1276 this also came to nothing. Barely 15 years later—and almost two centuries after Urban had first preached the crusades—the last area controlled by the crusaders in the Holy Land fell to the Muslims.

SCHOLARS, HERMITS, AND STATESMEN

Neither **Innocent V** nor his successor, **Hadrian V**, long outlived Gregory; both popes died just a few months after their elections. The uneventful pontificate of the scholarly and pacific pontiff, **John XXI**, was almost as brief, coming to an end after just ten months when the roof of his study collapsed on him. The new pontiff, **Nicholas III**—the first pope to reside regularly in the Vatican Palace—was more deeply involved in European politics than his predecessor. Nicholas checked the influence of Charles of Anjou in Italy and negotiated with the imperial claimant, Rudolf I of Germany, persuading him to cede the region of Romagna, north of Rome, to the Papal States.

A new French-born pope, **Martin IV**, reversed Nicholas's policy toward Charles of Anjou, welcoming him to Rome. Martin also abandoned attempts to reconcile the Roman Church with Constantinople and authorized Charles to attack the Byzantine Empire. Nonetheless, the boundaries of the Papal States would stand, more or less as they had been defined by Nicholas III, for the next 600 years.

Λ THOMAS AQUINAS
The teachings of the 13th-century Dominican theologian Thomas Aquinas provided an intellectual foundation for the medieval Church—and still form the basis of Catholic doctrine today.

Both Martin and his successor, **Honorius IV**, greatly admired the Franciscan and Dominican friars *(see p.53)* and promoted them throughout the Church. The first Franciscan pope, **Nicholas IV**, was elected in 1288. However, the cardinals had less success when they elected an elderly hermit, **Celestine V**, in 1294. Reluctantly traveling to Rome, the pious but unworldly Celestine soon realized that he had neither the desire nor the aptitude for papal politics. Less than five months after his election, Celestine abdicated. He was succeeded by **Boniface VIII**, who immediately had his predecessor imprisoned. Celestine died in captivity less than two years later.

Like many popes before him, Boniface was determined to defend the papacy from secular interference. In 1302, in order to assert the spiritual superiority of the Church, Boniface published the bull *Unam Sanctam* ("One Holy"), which asserted that it is "absolutely necessary for salvation that every human creature be subject to the Roman pontiff." Such elevated claims did not go uncontested. In 1303, having clashed with King Philip IV of France over the payment of clerical taxes, the elderly pontiff withdrew to his family palace at Anagni, southeast of Rome. Pursued and detained for several days by Philip's chief minister, the pope died a few weeks later. Despite Boniface's exalted claims to supremacy, his successors would find themselves unable—and often unwilling—to escape the domination of the French king.

1303–1304	1305–1314	1316–1334	1334–1342	1342–1352
BENEDICT XI	CLEMENT V	JOHN XXII	BENEDICT XII	CLEMENT VI

Following the brief pontificate of **Benedict XI**, the cardinals gathered in conclave in the hill town of Perugia. They were divided into two camps, those who sought revenge for King Philip IV of France's treatment of Pope Boniface VIII *(see p.55)* and those who sought a compromise with the French monarch. After 11 months, the French cardinals prevailed and the Archbishop of Bordeaux was elected as pope, taking the name **Clement V**. Suspicious of his welcome in Rome, a city still riven by violent factions, the new pope chose to remain under the protection of the French king and was crowned in the French city of Lyon in 1305. Clement spent the next five years at various places around France before finally moving his papal court to Avignon in southern France; as a result of his actions, no pope would set foot in Rome for six decades.

SUPPRESSION OF THE TEMPLARS
Clement soon proved willing to submit to the French king's demands, meekly acquiescing to his master's request to suppress the Knights Templar, a quasi-monastic military order established during the crusades. By the time of their suppression, the Templars had grown hugely wealthy and King Philip undoubtedly coveted their riches and extensive territories. With Clement's permission, Philip moved against the Knights on the night of October 13, 1307, arresting prominent members of the order and using torture to extract confessions of blasphemy. In 1312, at the insistence of King Philip, Pope Clement issued a series of bulls dissolving the order, and their lands in France fell to the crown. Two years later, the Grand Master of the Templars, Jacques de Molay, was burned at the stake.

THE AVIGNON PAPACY
Clement was the first in a series of French popes chosen from among the increasing number of French cardinals, followed by **John XXII**. With the election of **Benedict XII** in 1334 and the construction of a huge palace in Avignon worthy of the pontifical court, it became clear that the popes intended to stay there indefinitely, away from the factions and turbulence of Rome.

Any hopes that the papacy would return to Italy in the short term were dashed when the Black Death swept through Europe in 1348, during the papacy of the pompous **Clement VI**, decimating the population. When Pope **Urban V** attempted to transfer the papacy back to Rome in 1367, he found the city sadly dilapidated after decades of neglect. As the papal procession wound its way through the shabby streets, the court passed the basilica of St. John Lateran, whose roof had collapsed in 1360 due to neglect, while the Forum of the Caesars was a grazing ground for cattle, and shacks lined the Tiber. The pope made his residence at the Vatican, the Lateran palace being uninhabitable, but the French cardinals, with their strange cuisine and foreign language, were resented by a Roman populace grown used to freedom from papal government. Three years later, Urban was persuaded by his cardinals to return to the security and relative tranquillity of Avignon. The papacy, however,

< PALAIS DES PAPES
The magnificent Gothic palace built in Avignon by Pope Benedict XII and his successors remains as a monument to the papacy's long soujorn in France.

Now I am living in France, in the Babylon of the West … here reign the successors of the poor fishermen of Galilee; they have strangely forgotten their origin.

PETRARCH, LETTER TO A FRIEND, 1350

1352–1362	1362–1370	1370–1378	1389–1404	1406–1415
INNOCENT VI	URBAN V	GREGORY XI	BONIFACE IX	GREGORY XII

could not remain indefinitely in Avignon, a town prey to the political vicissitudes of various neighboring states, and the seven-decade exile finally came to an end in 1377, when the last elected French pontiff, **Gregory XI**, visited Rome and established his court at the Lateran. Five months later, clashes between the native Romans and the French court obliged Gregory to move south to the city of Agnani, where he died the following year.

THE WESTERN SCHISM

The conclave that met in Rome to elect a new pope did so in an atmosphere of great excitement. With the city's populace clamoring for a Roman pope, the mainly French cardinals finally settled on an Italian candidate, the Archbishop of Bari. While the archbishop was traveling to Rome, however, the cardinals grew concerned that their choice would not satisfy the populace and, intimidated by the Roman mob, the prelates hastily robed an elderly Italian cardinal and presented him to the people as the new pope. Satisfied with this candidate, the mob withdrew, leaving the cardinals to reconfirm the Archbishop of Bari as Pope **Urban VI** when he finally arrived in Rome.

If the cardinals had hoped that Urban would prove a compliant appointee, they were soon disappointed. A well-respected administrator before his election as pope, Urban proved haughty and autocratic, quickly alienating his supporters. Withdrawing one by one from Rome to Agnani, the cardinals held a new

⋏ TREE OF SCHISMS
This 15th-century allegory of the schism as the Tree of Fortune shows the supporters of Urban VI on one side of the tree and those of the antipope, Clement VII, on the other.

conclave, and, claiming that Urban's election had been invalid, they elected an antipope, Clement VII. Urban excommunicated Clement, who reciprocated the gesture from Avignon. Having lost most of his cardinals to Clement, Urban shrewdly created 29 more, choosing them from countries most likely to support his beleaguered position. An international diplomatic crisis soon developed, with the Holy Roman emperor recognizing the Roman claimant, the French king supporting his rival, and most of the other states and kingdoms of Europe taking one side or the other. Hopes of reconciliation were briefly raised when Urban died in 1389, but the Roman cardinals elected Pope **Boniface IX** in his stead. With Clement's death four years later, a new antipope, Benedict XIII, was elected in Avignon.

In 1408, Pope **Gregory XII** convened a Church Council at Pisa in order to resolve the question. The council declared both popes deposed and elected a new candidate, Alexander V. With neither Gregory nor Benedict willing to abdicate, three rival popes now each claimed legitimacy. The situation was not resolved until 1415, when the Council of Constance deposed both Benedict and Alexander's successor, John XXIII, and secured the abdication of Gregory XII. Three months later, Gregory died, and an end to the schism was finally in sight. The line of Roman popes is now recognized as the legitimate papal line—but the affair had badly damaged the prestige and authority of the Holy See.

THE RENAISSANCE PERIOD WITNESSED A REMARKABLE FLOWERING OF ART AND CULTURE IN ITALY. THROUGH THEIR ENTHUSIASTIC PATRONAGE OF THE GREAT ARTISTS AND ARCHITECTS OF THE AGE, THE POPES TRANSFORMED ROME AND THE VATICAN INTO A CENTER OF RENAISSANCE CULTURE TO RIVAL FLORENCE. BUT THE 16TH AND 17TH CENTURIES WERE ALSO MARKED BY POLITICAL AND IDEOLOGICAL TUMULT, WITH THE UPHEAVALS OF THE PROTESTANT REFORMATION LEADING ON TO THE RELIGIOUS AND ARTISTIC REJUVENATION OF THE CATHOLIC COUNTER-REFORMATION.

1417–1431	1431–1447	1447–1455	1455–1458

MARTIN V	EUGENE IV	NICHOLAS V	CALLISTUS III

 THE ELECTION OF THE wealthy patrician Odo Colonna as **Martin V** in 1417 finally ended the Western schism *(see pp.56–57)*, bringing to a close three decades of bitter fighting within the heart of Christendom. It was the start of a new era in other ways too. A long sojourn in Florence before entering Rome in 1420 introduced Martin to the ideals of the Renaissance, new concepts that influenced his approach to the reconstruction of Rome. Following an intense campaign to bring order to the Papal States, Martin began a program of restoration of ancient buildings, most notably the basilicas of St. Peter's and St. John Lateran, and moved the papal residence from the Lateran to the Vatican.

STRUGGLE FOR SUPREMACY

Unlike his predecessors, Martin never had to contend with a rival pope in Avignon but he was instead faced with the increasingly assertive conciliar movement whose supporters held that the final authority in Church matters lay with Church Councils rather than the pope. By 1430, Martin could no longer ignore the clamor for reform. Just three weeks before his death from an apoplectic fit, Martin reluctantly convened a council at Basel in Switzerland.

Suspicious of the council's intention to assert their rights over those of the pope, Martin's successor, **Eugene IV**, attempted to dissolve the Council of Basel in 1431. However, the members refused to disperse and renewed resolutions declaring the council superior to the pope. Exasperated by this temerity, Eugenius excommunicated the prelates at Basel. The cardinals responded by declaring the pope deposed and elected the ambitious Duke of Savoy as antipope, Felix V. However, Felix received little support from the kings and princes of Europe. Papal victory over the council was confirmed in 1449 when Eugenius's successor, **Nicholas V**, secured the resignation of the antipope, restoring the papacy to the dominant position it held before the papal schism.

THE EARLY RENAISSANCE

The early 15th century witnessed the beginning of a great flowering of art and culture in Italy as scholars, artists and thinkers sought to emulate the achievements of the Classical past. The cultured and scholarly pontiff, Nicholas V, was very much a part of this new world.

< FRA ANGELICO ALTARPIECE
The Tuscan painter Fra Angelico was one of many Early Renaissance artists who enjoyed the patronage of popes such as Eugene IV and Nicholas V.

THE RENAISSANCE

ART, CULTURE, AND RELIGIOUS REFORMATION, 1417–1621

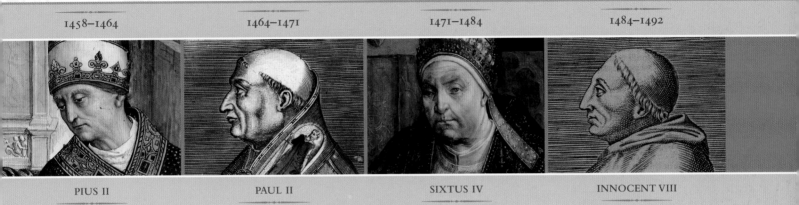

1458–1464	1464–1471	1471–1484	1484–1492
PIUS II	PAUL II	SIXTUS IV	INNOCENT VIII

As a youth, he had worked as a tutor in Florence—birthplace of the Renaissance—and had made the acquaintance of leading humanist scholars of the day. As pope, Nicholas introduced the Renaissance to the Vatican, employing notable artists such as Fra Angelico, Leon Battista Alberti, and Bernardo Rossellino. Never happier than when among his precious books, Pope Nicholas constructed a new library at the Vatican, enriching it with five thousand Greek and Latin texts. The pope also initiated an ambitious program of urban reform, restoring the Roman aqueducts, renovating the Vatican Palace, and raising money for the rebuilding of St. Peter's Basilica.

THE FALL OF CONSTANTINOPLE

Both Eugene and Nicholas had held high hopes for the reunification of the Greek (Eastern) and Roman (Western) Churches. In 1439, at Eugene's council in Florence, the Eastern delegates had agreed to a union and had even recognized the pope as the highest authority in Christendom. The agreement faltered, but the growing threat to Byzantium from the Ottoman Turks led the emperor to appeal again to Nicholas in 1452, raising new hopes of an end to the schism.

Discussions were quickly overtaken by events. In 1453, the city of Constantinople, the great capital of the Byzantine Empire, fell to the Ottomans. To Nicholas, and his Spanish-born successor, **Callistus III,** the conquest of Christian lands by the Ottoman armies was nothing less than a catastrophe but they both strove fruitlessly to mobilize the rulers of Europe in a new crusade against the Turks. In 1464, Pope **Pius II**—poet, author, and adventurer in his youth, and a true son of the Renaissance—assumed the cross himself, intending to place himself at the head of a new crusade, but after traveling to the port of

Ancona on the Adriatic, Pius died of fever while waiting for the fleet to muster. Pope **Paul II,** less quixotically but no more effectively, negotiated in vain for a crusade with the Holy Roman Emperor Frederick III.

THE SISTINE CHAPEL

The contribution of the popes to the arts in the mid-15th century is incalculable. Pope **Sixtus IV** added one of the most famous edifices in the Vatican in 1473, when he commissioned Giovannino de Dolci to construct the Sistine Chapel. Sixtus was also patron to several artists who painted the frescoes on the walls of the Sistine Chapel (although Michelangelo's famous ceiling was added later). The pope also refounded and enlarged the Vatican library, and gathered an important collection of artworks and sculptures. Outside the Vatican, he restored or rebuilt almost 30 churches, and constructed the first new bridge over the Tiber since antiquity. His successor, **Innocent VIII,** was also a patron of the arts. Under the Renaissance papacy, a grand new city was rising once again from the ashes of the past.

> SIXTUS IV'S LIBRARY
This fresco by Renaissance artist Melozzo da Forlí in the Vatican Museums, shows Pope Sixtus IV and the director of the Vatican library, Bartolomeo Platina.

1492–1503	1503	1503–1513
ALEXANDER VI	**PIUS III**	**JULIUS II**

The year 1492 saw momentous changes in Europe and the wider world. In March that year, having recently defeated the last Moorish King of Granada, the Catholic monarchs, Ferdinand and Isabella, expelled the Jews from Spain, and a few months later, in October 1492, the Genoese navigator Christopher Columbus reached the Americas, opening up the New World to Christian influence. Meanwhile, in Rome, less than two weeks after Columbus first set sail, the worldly Spanish cardinal, Rodrigo Borgia, ascended to the papal throne, taking the name **Alexander VI**.

THE BORGIA PAPACY

A nephew of Callistus III, Rodrigo Borgia had used his uncle's influence to rise quickly through the ranks of the curia. At the conclave following the death of Innocent VIII—the first papal conclave to be held in the Sistine Chapel—his obvious ambition led to accusations of bribery. Whatever the truth of these allegations, Alexander's pontificate was to prove notably secular in character. As the doting father of several illegitimate children, Alexander used the papacy as an instrument to enrich his offspring and further his family's interests.

< TOMB OF POPE JULIUS II
Michelangelo's marble statue of Moses, now in the church of San Pietro in Vincoli in Rome, was commissioned as a part of the tomb of Julius II.

Early in his reign, in 1493, Alexander drew a line of demarcation in the Atlantic, dividing newly-discovered lands in America and Africa between Spain and Portugal. It was a grand gesture. In Europe, however, the security of the Papal States depended on a delicate web of family interests. In 1497, when Alexander's favorite son, Juan, was murdered, the distraught pope shut himself in Castel Sant'Angelo and swore to reform his life, though his resolve soon weakened. Another son, Cesare, was made a cardinal but resigned to pursue a military career, becoming the model for Machiavelli's study in political pragmatism, *The Prince*. At the Vatican, Alexander continued as a patron of the arts and commissioned the influential painter, Pinturicchio, to decorate his private apartments.

THE WARRIOR POPE

Alexander died in 1503, probably from malaria, though many contemporaries suspected poison. Following the brief ten-day pontificate of **Pius III**, a new pope, **Julius II**, was elected, who proved to be an energetic defender of the Papal States as well as a noted patron of the arts. Personally leading his military campaigns in full battle dress, he soon earned the nickname Julius the Terrible. It was Pope Julius who first established a permanent corps of the Pontifical Swiss Guard at the Vatican, granting them the title "Defenders of the Church's Freedom," an honor of which they would soon prove themselves worthy.

In 1506, Julius laid the foundation stone for a great new basilica at St. Peter's. Initially entrusted to the architect, Donato Bramante, the project would take another 120 years to complete and would involve many of the most notable artists and architects of the Renaissance and the Baroque. The pope also commissioned a young Umbrian artist, Raphael, to decorate the

1513–1521	1522–1523	1523–1534
LEO X	HADRIAN VI	CLEMENT VII

walls of his private apartments at the Vatican, and persuaded Michelangelo to paint his masterpiece, the magnificent fresco that adorns the ceiling of the Sistine Chapel.

PROTESTANT SCHISM

Elected in 1513 at the relatively young age of 37, Pope **Leo X** was a son of Lorenzo the Magnificent, the Medici ruler of Florence. A benign ruler, happier hunting game on his estates than conducting the affairs of Church government, Leo squandered vast sums on the arts; one anonymous contemporary complained he spent "the treasure of Julius II, his own, and that of his successor." This extravagance transformed Rome into a center of High Renaissance art and culture—but at a great cost to the Church. To help cover his expenditure and pay for the construction of St. Peter's Basilica, Leo authorized the sale of indulgences—promises of remission from time spent in purgatory for sins already committed. It was the exchange of indulgences for money that inspired Martin Luther to post his 95 theses (statements) on the church door at Wittenberg in 1517, sparking the great schism known as the Protestant Reformation.

A university-educated priest and friar, Luther was a reluctant revolutionary. Inevitably, however, his open challenge to Leo and his stubborn defense of his arguments in the face of papal censure soon provoked his excommunication. What had begun as a religious debate rapidly developed into a political revolt as princes and rulers saw in the new movement a way to seize control of the

⋏ MARTIN LUTHER
New printing technology helped to spread Luther's ideas in books and pamphlets and undermined the authority of the popes.

Church from the papacy and strengthen their own authority inside their realms. When Leo died suddenly in December 1521, the Reformation was already in full flow.

THE SACK OF ROME

Leo's immediate successor to the See of Peter, **Hadrian VI**, was a learned scholar who died too soon to put into place an effective programme of reform. He was followed in 1523 by **Clement VII**, a cousin of Leo X. Clement's pontificate was overshadowed by the Holy Roman Emperor Charles V's military campaigns in Italy, which prevented the pope from responding vigorously to the Lutheran threat. In May 1527, Charles V's unpaid and mutinous troops marched on Rome, ransacking the city and pillaging the Vatican. The pope fled for safety along the raised tunnel connecting the Vatican to the nearby Castel Sant'Angelo. Most of the Swiss Guards who defended his escape paid for their loyalty with their lives—a sacrifice commemorated today in the annual swearing-in ceremony for Swiss Guards at the Vatican. A month later, Clement agreed to pay a huge ransom to Charles, before he was released to the Papal Palace at Viterbo (*see pp. 162–65*).

It was in order to avoid provoking Charles again that Clement refused to annul the marriage between Henry VIII of England and Catherine of Aragon, a relative of the emperor. Unable to gain the pope's permission to remarry, Henry founded the Church of England, establishing himself as "supreme head" of the English Church in place of the pope in Rome.

To reform morals and restore ecclesiastical discipline, to bring about peace and harmony among the Christian people, an ecumenical and general council has ... been summoned ... to meet in the city of Trent.

PAPAL BULL OF POPE PIUS IV PROMULGATING THE COUNCIL OF TRENT, 1564

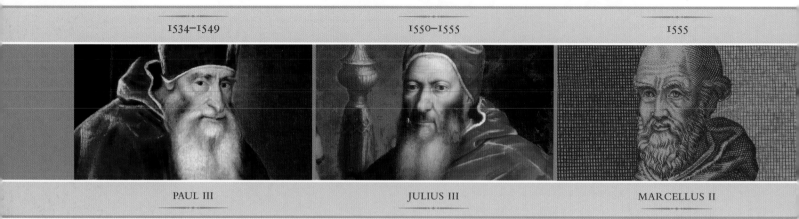

1534–1549	1550–1555	1555
PAUL III	JULIUS III	MARCELLUS II

Elected in 1534 at the age of 66, Pope **Paul III** seemed an unlikely architect of ecclesiastical reform. A member of the aristocratic Farnese family, the new pope had fathered four illegitimate children prior to his elevation to the papacy and after his election his love of the arts and entertainment remained undiminished; in 1534, to the delight of the Roman populace, he restored the city's Carnival. Yet Paul also set in motion the first effective Catholic response to the criticisms of the Protestant reformers.

THE COUNCIL OF TRENT

In March 1537, a group of cardinals met with Paul III in the Hall of the Parrot at the Apostolic Palace. During the secret meeting, the cardinals presented the pontiff with a damning report that accepted that many of the reformers' criticisms were valid. Most pertinently, they blamed the Roman Curia (the government of the Catholic Church) for many abuses and for the failure to address them. The pope forbade the cardinals to publish their report—although a copy was leaked—but set about arranging a council to address the issues it had raised.

Delayed by political intrigue, the council finally opened in the northern Italian town of Trent, meeting in three sessions between 1545 and 1563. In 1552, shortly after Pope **Julius III** convened the second session of the council, the Protestant ruler of Saxony attacked the Holy Roman Emperor Charles V, near Trent. Alarmed at this outbreak of hostilities, the bishops suspended the proceedings of the council, putting an end to any hopes of reconciliation with the Protestant reformers.

A PAPAL INDEX
Pius IV compiled a new *Index of Forbidden Books* in 1564 to help Catholic censors decide which works to authorize.

The council did not meet again for almost a decade. **Marcellus II**, a committed reformer and previously a president of the Council of Trent, was elected pope in 1555 but died less than a month later. His successor, the 78-year-old Neapolitan **Paul IV**, was an austere man who had little time for the council. Paul preferred to institute his own reforms within the Roman Curia. As a former Inquisitor he had acquired a reputation for harshness in the face of heresy, and in 1559 he compiled the first *Index of Forbidden Books*—an attempt to restrict the publication of works deemed corrupting to the Catholic faith. It was left to **Pius IV** to reconvene the Council of Trent in 1559, and through his delegates on the council, Pius skillfully steered the remaining sessions to a triumphant conclusion in 1563. The following year, Pius undertook to implement all the decrees of the council, introducing the Catechism of the Council of Trent (or Roman Catechism) and reforming the Council of Cardinals. Pius also compiled a new *Index* to moderate Paul IV's more restrictive version, in line with the decrees of the Council of Trent.

THE COUNTER-REFORMATION

Although the Council of Trent failed to reunite the various strands of the Christian Church, the period immediately following the council was characterized by a confident, ebullient leadership from the papacy, most notably during the pontificate of **Pius V**. Critics bemoaned the fact that Pius, a former Dominican friar, "turned Rome into a convent." Prostitutes were banned and criminals faced harsh sentences, including

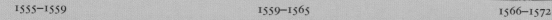

PAUL IV

PIUS IV

PIUS V

the death penalty. Insisting that bishops reside in their own diocese rather than in Rome, the pope reformed the morals of all the clergy, and seminaries were set up to train candidates for priesthood. Critical of concessions to reformers, in 1570, Pius published an encyclical (circular letter) declaring Elizabeth I of England a heretic and releasing her Catholic subjects from obedience.

The period also saw a flowering of new religious orders, with the Jesuits, Ursulines, Oratorians, and Theatines energetically combating heresies while reaffirming Catholic doctrine. The most effective of these new orders was the Society of Jesus, or Jesuits, founded by Ignatius Loyola and confirmed by Paul III in 1540. The aims of the Jesuits were threefold: to provide a rigorous academic training for the ministry; to establish missions in non-Christian regions; and to counter the spread of Protestantism. In all three areas the society proved highly successful, earning the members a reputation as the "elite troops" of the papacy.

Following suggestions made at the Council of Trent, the late 16th-century papacy also employed art as a means to express the renewed confidence of the Church. Michelangelo's majestic dome, rising over St. Peter's tomb, was a symbolic expression of the papacy's vigor. Art served both as a tool of education in the Catholic faith and as a rebuttal of the claims of the Reformers.

BEYOND THE BORDERS OF CHRISTENDOM

In the second half of the 16th century, Christian Europe faced a growing threat from outside its borders. After the fall of Constantinople in 1453 (see p.59), the armies of the Ottoman Turks had advanced almost unchecked into Europe, their progress halted only at the gates of Vienna. In the Mediterranean, the Ottoman fleets dominated the waters, enabling the Turks to invade Cyprus in 1570,

threatening Venice, Naples, and Rome. In 1571, Pope Pius V, through delicate and painstaking negotiations, succeeded in uniting the quarrelsome Catholic powers of Europe into a Holy League against the Turks. In October, the galleys of the Holy League engaged the Turkish fleet off Lepanto in Greece. The decisive Christian victory dealt a major blow to Ottoman naval power.

Meanwhile, the secular rulers of Europe were equally concerned with a struggle for supremacy in the New World, a source of extraordinary wealth. While the papacy strained to rebuild its authority inside Europe, Catholic and, later, Protestant missionaries sought to extend Christianity in the vast new territories that were rapidly being discovered in the Americas. To the East, the Jesuit missionaries in particular proved highly effective, establishing successful missions in India and Japan and, later, in China.

> LEPANTO MONSTRANCE
This ornate monstrance (vessel used to hold the consecrated Host during Eucharist celebrations) commemorates the victory of the Holy League over the Turks at Lepanto in 1571.

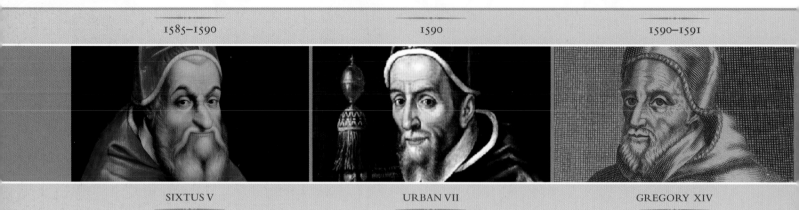

1585–1590	1590	1590–1591
SIXTUS V	URBAN VII	GREGORY XIV

In 1572, following a conclave lasting less than 24 hours, the Italian cardinal, Ugo Buoncompagni, was elected as Pope **Gregory XIII**. The new pontiff, an expert in canon law who had participated in the proceedings of the Council of Trent *(see p.62)*, enthusiastically sought to implement the decrees of the council and improve clerical discipline and education. To this end, Gregory founded a number of colleges in Rome, most notably the Gregorian University, which he entrusted to the care of the Jesuits.

In a Europe still riven by bitter religious conflict, Gregory had little sympathy for those Christians who rejected Catholic teaching, even holding a thanksgiving ceremony when news of the St. Bartholomew's Day massacre of French Protestants reached Rome. Politically, Gregory supported the Catholic monarch, Philip II, of Spain in his failed attempt to invade England and Ireland, and backed the Spanish against Protestant rebels in the Netherlands. Outside Europe, Gregory sponsored Catholic missions to India, China, and Japan.

THE GREGORIAN CALENDAR

It is, however, with the reformed calendar that still bears his name, that Pope Gregory is most closely associated. The lunar calendar devised under Julius Caesar and still in use at the time of Gregory's reforms, divided the year into 365 days, with a leap day added every four years. This resulted in an average year length that was slightly too long for the solar cycle. Every 131 years, the Julian and the solar calendar diverged by one day, and by the 16th century, more than ten days had been gained. In order to correct the discrepancy, Pope Gregory appointed the Jesuit astronomer, Christopher Clavius, to make a new set of computations, and in 1582, published the reforms in an encyclical, *Inter Gravissimas* (Among the Serious). With effect from the following October, ten days were omitted, meaning October 4 was followed by October 15. To prevent the discrepancy recurring, three leap days were omitted every 400 years.

The loss of these days from the calendar was bitterly resented by the populace, who feared that the reforms would be used by landlords to cheat them out of ten days rent. Nonetheless, the Gregorian calendar was soon implemented in most Catholic countries, although many Protestant nations refused to accept the reforms until the middle of the 18th century.

REBUILDING ROME

Gregory was succeeded in 1585 by Pope **Sixtus V**, who conceived an ambitious program for the aggrandizement of Rome. Decrepit areas of the medieval city were demolished and Rome was rebuilt on a grid plan with large piazzas laid out in front of the major Roman basilicas; at the center of each piazza rose an ancient Egyptian obelisk, a tribute to Rome's imperial past. Domenico Fontana, the architect who supervised the erection of the ancient obelisks, was also commissioned to provide a

> **THE VATICAN OBELISK**
It took almost a year to erect the great Egyptian obelisk in front of St. Peter's Basilica, a feat noted to have required the muscle power of 900 men and 75 horses.

1591	1592–1605	1605	1605–1621
INNOCENT IX	CLEMENT VIII	LEO XI	PAUL V

balcony of benedictions at the Lateran and a new palace attached to the cathedral. The ancient aqueducts were repaired and a new library laid out in the Vatican Palace. Although Sixtus's five-year pontificate was not sufficient to implement all of his grandiose schemes, many of them were concluded by his successors.

Sixtus successfully reformed the Roman Curia (the government of the Catholic Church), which remains in substantially the same form to the present day. Insisting that bishops reside in their sees, he also ordered that they visit Rome every five years to give an account of their stewardship. In the Papal States, which had recently become overrun by brigands, Sixtus reasserted papal authority by introducing harsh penalties and executing thousands of bandits.

REVIVAL OF PAPAL POWER

Three brief pontificates passed within two years, until the election of Pope **Clement VIII** in 1592. A member of the aristocratic Aldobrandini family, Clement was personally pious, making visits to hospitals and tending the sick himself. He became a familiar sight, washing the feet of pilgrims who arrived in the Eternal City. Clement also proved to be an astute statesman, encouraging the conversion of the French king, Henry IV, to Catholicism, and reducing the dominance of the Spanish monarchs over the papacy. His successor, the Medici pope, **Leo XI**, died after only 27 days in office.

The renewed confidence of the papacy at the outset of the 17th century was evident in the election of the ebullient Camillo Borghese as Pope **Paul V** in 1605. A noted canon lawyer, Paul insisted on the Church's privileges, including exemption from taxes and civil laws in certain jurisdictions. When the city of Venice passed laws concerning property rights and restricting the

Church's rights to build places of worship, Paul placed the city under interdict, forbidding the citizens from participating in certain sacraments. A year later, the Venetian authorities capitulated. Paul also founded a bank, the Banco Santo Spirito, to administer the revenues of the Holy See.

THE JAPANESE EMBASSY

In November 1615, Paul V received a delegation from the Shogun of Japan. The delegation asked the pontiff to send missionaries to Japan and to intervene on Japan's behalf to establish trade relations with Mexico. The pope gladly received the invitation to dispatch more missionaries, but on the question of Mexico he referred the delegation to the King of Spain, who declined to sign a trade agreement. This decision (together with contemporaneus events involving Christians in Japan) irritated the shogun, who in 1639 banned all foreign ships from entering Japan without his approval. Christianity was effectively stifled in Japan for two centuries.

> SAMURAI AT THE VATICAN
The samurai Hasekura Tsunenaga led the first official Japanese delegation to visit the Vatican in 1615. It would also be the last Japanese embassy to travel to Europe for over 200 years.

EUROPEAN VIEWS ABOUT THE ORIGINS OF THE UNIVERSE UNDERWENT A FUNDAMENTAL CHANGE DURING THE 17TH AND 18TH CENTURIES AS "NATURAL PHILOSOPHERS" SUCH AS FRANCIS BACON, DESCARTES, AND GALILEO LAID THE FOUNDATIONS OF MODERN SCIENCE AND USHERED IN THE AGE OF THE ENLIGHTENMENT. THE NEW INTELLECTUAL CLIMATE—AND THE POLITICAL AND IDEOLOGICAL UPHEAVAL THAT FOLLOWED—PRESENTED THE CHURCH WITH NEW OPPORTUNITIES AS WELL AS NEW CHALLENGES, AND THE PAPACY CONTINUED TO PLAY A KEY ROLE IN EUROPEAN POLITICS, AND CULTURE.

1621–1623	1623–1644	1644–1655	1655–1667
GREGORY XV	URBAN VIII	INNOCENT X	ALEXANDER VII

AFTER THE SHORT BUT EFFICIENT papacy of **Gregory XV** which included a new constitution, Cardinal Maffeo Barberini was elected as Pope **Urban VIII** in 1623. A diplomat by training, he was no stranger to the intellectual currents of the age and had been a friend and admirer of the astronomer Galileo Galilei for more than a decade. In the first year of his pontificate, Urban received Galileo six times and endowed him with a papal pension. Difficulties arose when Galileo published the hypothesis (made originally by Copernicus a century earlier but now confirmed by Galileo's telescope) that the earth revolved around the sun, a view that appeared to contradict the sacred scriptures, which indicated that the sun rose and set above the earth. Initially, Urban was intrigued by Galileo's thesis and indicated his private approval but urged the astronomer not to teach in public lest he attract the attention of the Inquisition.

In 1632, Urban gave his permission for Galileo to publish the arguments for and against his thesis in a book, asking only that the astronomer include the pope's own views on the matter. Galileo did so, but alienated his powerful patron by presenting these views in a way that Urban felt made them seem foolish. The papal Inquisition forced Galileo to sign a humiliating recantation of his theories and ordered that he be confined to his home in Florence where, forbidden from publishing, and blind from years spent gazing at the stars, Galileo passed his last years. Not until Benedict XIV authorized the publication of his works in 1741 were Galileo's views finally rehabilitated.

∧ BARBERINI BEES
Urban VIII was a keen patron of artists and architects and his family crest can be seen on buildings all over Rome.

BUILDING THE BAROQUE

Although the 17th-century papacy sometimes struggled to come to terms with the scientific advances of the age, popes remained at the forefront of artistic developments. The Council of Trent *(see pp.62–63)* had identified art as a means to communicate the power and vitality of the Church and by the time of Urban's election in 1623, papal patronage had transformed Rome into the center of the Baroque—a style of art and architecture characterized by extravagant ornamentation and dramatic effect. Urban commissioned several works of art from Gian Lorenzo Bernini, one of the most prestigious sculptors and architects of his day, including the magnificent bronze canopy, the *baldacchino*, over the tomb of St. Peter. The pope plundered the bronze for the great canopy from the ceiling of the Pantheon's portico, leading contemporaries to quip that *quod non fecerunt barbari, fecerunt Barberini*—what the barbarians failed to do, the Barberinis did. In November 1626, 120 years after work had first commenced, it was Urban who finally dedicated the magnificent new basilica at St. Peter's, the largest and most spectacular church in Christendom.

THE THIRTY YEARS WAR

For three decades, throughout Urban's pontificate and well into that of his successor, **Innocent X**, Europe was embroiled in bitter religious conflict. The hostilities had broken out in 1618, ostensibly over a dispute between Catholic and Protestant rulers. The conflict gradually spread through the continent, setting

THE ENLIGHTENMENT

THE PAPACY IN THE AGE OF REASON, 1621–1799

1667–1669	1670–1676	1676–1689	1689–1691
CLEMENT IX	**CLEMENT X**	**INNOCENT XI**	**ALEXANDER VIII**

neighboring countries against each other and mixing religious tensions with political and dynastic strife. The Thirty Years War finally ended with the Treaty of Westphalia in 1648, effectively reiterating the 1555 Treaty of Augsburg that had allowed rulers to determine the religion to be followed in their territories. The papacy was sidelined from any direct negotiations, and Innocent protested against this humiliation in the bull, *Zelus Domus Meae* (Zeal for my House), lamenting that too many concessions had been made to the Protestants. The war-weary negotiators, however, refused to respond to Innocent's complaints—a poignant reminder of how the prestige of the papacy had declined.

ART AND POLITICS

Following the death of Innocent X in 1655, the new pope, **Alexander VII**, continued the papal patronage of Bernini, by now widely regarded as the foremost artist of the era. In 1657, the pope commissioned a large setting for a chair at that time believed to have been used by St. Peter while he instructed the Christians—a symbolic expression of the teaching authority of the pope as inspired by the Holy Spirit. Bernini also completed the restoration of the great Scala Regia, the steps leading from the Vatican Palace to the entrance of St Peter's Basilica, and he oversaw the construction of a vast colonnaded piazza in front of the basilica to accommodate the large crowds who flocked to the Vatican to view the pope during his public appearances. Bernini's elegant colonnades still hold visitors to St. Peter's, in the words of the architect, within the "maternal arms of Mother Church." With the completion of the new basilica and the construction of Bernini's commanding new piazza, the Vatican began to take on its modern appearance.

On Christmas Day 1655, the Lutheran, highly educated Queen Christina of Sweden, who had abdicated and moved to Rome, was received into the Catholic Church, an event marked by weeks of balls, fireworks, and splendid Baroque spectacles that drew crowds to the Vatican where she briefly lodged. The conversion of such a celebrated royal figure was seen as a highly political event and went a considerable way to restoring the prestige of the Roman Church. After her death in 1689, her extensive collection of books and manuscripts was bought by the then pope, **Alexander VIII**, and added to the Vatican Library.

The short pontificate of **Clement IX** was overshadowed by the growing threat of an Ottoman Turkish invasion of Europe. Clement sought in vain to encourage other Christian states in Europe to mount a crusade, and **Clement X**, elected the following year, attempted to counter the Turkish threat by providing financial support for the military endeavors of the Polish ruler, Jan Sobieski. It was not until the election of **Innocent XI** in 1676 that Europe found a truly effective response; with the Turks laying seige to the city of Vienna, the pope persuaded Jan Sobieski to form an alliance with the Holy Roman Emperor Leopold I. The combined Polish and Imperial armies routed the Turks outside the gates of Vienna in 1683. By the end of the century, the Holy League initiated by Innocent XI would completely regain control of Hungary, ending the Ottoman threat.

> **> TRIUMPH OF THE PAPACY**
> Bernini's expansive new piazza in front of St. Peter's is used as the setting for an allegory of the "Triumph of the Papacy" in this 17th-century painting by Pannini.

1691–1700	1700–1721	1721–1724	1724–1730
INNOCENT XII	CLEMENT XI	INNOCENT XIII	BENEDICT XIII

The early 18th century was dominated by the War of the Spanish Succession, a bloody conflict between the Austrian Habsburg and the French Bourbon dynasties who both had claims to the Spanish throne, which expanded into a pan-European dispute over balance of power and territory. Pope **Innocent XII** had advised the childless Spanish Habsburg king, Charles II, to nominate the French Philippe de Bourbon as his successor. The Habsburgs and their allies had to prevent the threat of a union of the French domains with the vast Spanish territories in Europe and overseas. Pope **Clement XI**'s appeals for peace to the warring parties went unheeded, even when the hostilities moved onto Italian soil. When Clement then sided with the French, the Austrian Habsburgs invaded the Papal States and he was forced to support the Habsburg claim. Diplomatic relations between Spain and the Holy See were severed for six years.

The Peace of Utrecht in 1713, which confirmed the Bourbon Philip V as King of Spain (but forced him to renounce any claims to the French throne), went some way to resolving the conflict, although the papacy was excluded from the negotiations. Unfortunately, the hostile relations revived during the conclave following Clement's death in 1721 as French

and pro-Habsburg parties haggled over the candidates. Eventually, the Italian Michelangelo Conti emerged as a compromise candidate, taking the name **Innocent XIII**. The new pope's efforts to improve relations between the Holy See and the European powers were moderately successful, but his successor, **Benedict XIII**, had little interest in international politics. A Dominican friar and a noted scholar, Benedict instead devoted himself to prayer and to improving the clergy in Rome. He was followed by the elderly Florentine patrician, **Clement XII**, whose efforts to improve relations met with little success.

ROME IN THE AGE OF THE GRAND TOUR

If Rome no longer exerted its former political influence in Europe, it continued to attract admiring visitors. Italy was a popular destination on the "Grand Tour," undertaken by many young aristocrats from Britain and other countries to expose them to the wonders of European history and culture. Rome exerted a special fascination, with its imperial ruins and the churches, palaces, and piazzas of Baroque and Renaissance heritage. Popes such as Clement XII continued to embellish the city: a palatial new façade was added to the basilica of San Giovanni in Laterano in 1735 and the majestic Trevi fountain, built at the rear of Clement's family palace, was completed in 1762.

> THE TREVI FOUNTAIN
Rome's grandest fountain was commissioned by Clement XII in 1730, one of the numerous buildings and monuments that drew visitors to Rome in the 18th century.

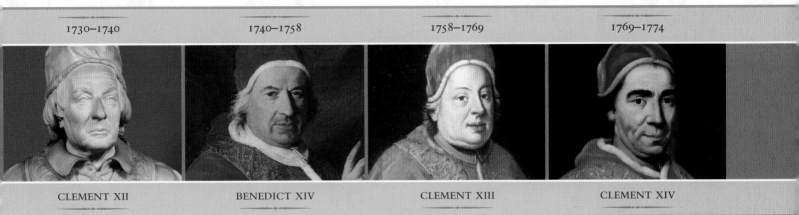

1730–1740	1740–1758	1758–1769	1769–1774
CLEMENT XII	BENEDICT XIV	CLEMENT XIII	CLEMENT XIV

Other foreign visitors to Rome added to papal prestige. In 1719, Clement XI offered the Palazzo Muti to James Stuart, the exiled Catholic claimant to the English and Scottish thrones. The Stuarts established their court in exile in Rome, and in 1747, James Stuart's son, Henry, was appointed as a cardinal by **Benedict XIV**. A marble monument to the Royal Stuarts in St. Peter's Basilica by the celebrated sculptor Antonio Canova commemorates their sojourn.

In 1758, the year of Pope **Clement XIII**'s election, the prime minister of Portugal expelled the religious order of the Jesuits from his territories. Very soon, France, Spain, Naples, Parma, and Sicily all followed suit. The Jesuits were resented for their independence of vision, and in particular their interference with the lucrative slave trade, so important to Portugal and Spain's economy. Pope Clement was put under pressure to dissolve the order, but in 1769, the day before his judgment on the matter was due, he died of a stroke. Under intense pressure from Spain and France, his successor, **Clement XIV**, finally dissolved the Jesuits in 1773. Clement's willingness to suppress a religious order so loyal to the papacy was evidence of how low papal authority had sunk among the rulers of Europe. The Jesuit order was not restored until 1814.

THE FRENCH REVOLUTION

The early part of the pontificate of Clement's successor, **Pius VI**, was relatively serene. An able administrator and attentive patron of the arts, Pius took steps to place the Papal States on a sound economic footing. In 1789, however, the old order of Europe was shattered by the outbreak of the French Revolution.

Under the *Ancien Regime*, the Catholic Church had been the largest landowner in France; the revolutionary government quickly moved to confiscate Church lands and outlaw religious orders. In 1790, the French Government passed the Civil Constitution of the Clergy, turning the Catholic Church in France into a mere arm of the secular state. The process of de-Christianization reached its climax during the Reign of Terror in 1792–94, when Catholicism was violently repressed in favor of the atheist "Cult of Reason" and then by Robespierre's Deist "Cult of the Supreme Being."

The fall of Robespierre in 1794 led to the return of some forms of Catholic worship in France, but the pope's efforts to improve relations with the revolutionary government suffered a severe setback in 1796, when French troops under the command of General Napoleon Bonaparte occupied part of the Papal States. Two years later, French troops entered Rome and established a new Roman Republic in Italy under French supervision. Artworks were plundered from the Vatican and for three days a fire smoldered in the courtyard of the Apostolic Palace as French soldiers burned sacred vestments. Monasteries, colleges, and seminaries were closed down and their properties confiscated.

The elderly pontiff was arrested on Napoleon's orders and sent to France. Worn out by the harsh treatment and the difficulty of the journey, Pius died at Valence in southern France in 1799.

> REVOLUTIONARY SATIRE
Marianne, the personification of Republican France, dismisses Pius VI's bulls condemning the Civil Constitution of the Clergy in this 18th-century French satirical cartoon.

✝ THE 19TH CENTURY WAS A PERIOD OF MOMENTOUS CHANGE, NOT ONLY FOR THE PAPACY, BUT FOR THE ENTIRE ITALIAN PENINSULA. THE DEFEAT OF NAPOLEON AND THE RESTORATION OF PAPAL POWER HAD APPEARED TO SIGNAL A RETURN TO THE OLD ORDER IN ITALY. BUT WITH THE RISE OF ITALIAN NATIONALISM AND THE FORMATION OF THE KINGDOM OF ITALY, THE TEMPORAL TERRITORIES OF THE PAPACY SHRANK TO THE VATICAN AND ITS IMMEDIATE ENVIRONS. THE HISTORY OF THE PAPACY IN THE 19TH CENTURY IS OF ITS STRUGGLE TO COME TO TERMS WITH THIS NEW POLITICAL REALITY.

1775–1799	1823–1829	1829–1830
PIUS VI	LEO XII	PIUS VIII

 THE CONCLAVE THAT MET in Venice following the arrest and death of Pius VI *(see p.69)* chose a Benedictine cardinal, Luigi Barnaba Chiaramonti. Elected as **Pius VII** in March 1800, the pope had to be crowned using a papier-mâché tiara, the original having been seized during his predecessor's arrest. When the new pope entered Rome, he received a hero's welcome. Houses along his route were decked with flower garlands, rich embroideries were hung from the windows of the palaces, and rose petals were strewn along his path. A group of young men unhitched the pope's carriage as it entered the city and carried it all the way to the Quirinal Palace.

Papal relations with Napoleon remained stormy. In 1801, Pope Pius negotiated a concordat with the French Government, which reaffirmed the position of the Catholic Church as the established Church of France; Napoleon overturned the agreement by adding the Organic Articles, which subjugated the Church to the French authorities. Despite this, a reluctant Pius travelled to Paris for Napoleon's coronation in 1804.

Pius continued to defend papal prerogatives in the face of French intransigence, but in 1809, was arrested by Napoleon's troops at the Quirinal

Palace and exiled first to Grenoble, then to Savona and Fontainbleau. Exhausted by his harsh treatment, Pius signed a new concordat favorable to Napoleon in 1813, though he retracted it two months later. Only after six years of captivity, as the tide began to turn against Napoleon in Europe, was Pius freed.

When the French emperor was finally defeated in 1815, the victorious powers who met at the Congress of Vienna to redraw the borders of Europe largely restored the Papal States to their former extent. It seemed like a victory for the papacy and the old order of Europe. Already, however, new concepts of national identity were emerging that would fundamentally transform the role of the papacy in Europe.

ITALIAN NATIONALISM

Pius was succeeded in 1823 by Pope **Leo XII** who, following the trauma of the Napoleonic wars, negotiated a number of concordats with foreign states in the hope of ensuring a tranquil future for the Holy See. But revolution was in the air all across Europe and, in 1830, during the brief pontificate of

< CONCORDAT WITH NAPOLEON
An allegorical painting of the 1801 concordat that restored Catholic worship in France depicts Pope Pius VII with figures representing Napoleonic France.

THE 19TH CENTURY
THE VATICAN AND THE UNIFIED ITALIAN NATION, 1800–1903

1831–1846	1846–1878	1878–1903
GREGORY XVI	PIUS IX	LEO XIII

Pius VIII, a series of nationalist insurrections broke out across the Papal States. The rebels were crushed the following year by the Austrian army at the request of the new pontiff, **Gregory XVI**. A deeply conservative pope, Gregory was suspicious of any moves toward democracy, refusing requests to establish a council of laymen to administer parts of the Papal States. Nonetheless, nationalist sentiment proved difficult to contain and Gregory's reign was dominated by political unrest.

THE UNIFICATION OF ITALY

During the pontificate of the long-serving pope, **Pius IX**, the movement for the unification of Italy, the *Risorgimento*, progressed rapidly. At first it seemed as though Pius was in favor of political reform and would be its champion. However, when revolutionaries assassinated the pope's prime minister in 1848 and declared a Roman Republic, Pius was forced to flee to nearby Gaeta in disguise. Austria sent troops into Rome to restore the pope, who adopted a much more conservative line.

Meanwhile, the *Risorgimento* continued to gather speed. In 1859, the northern Italian kingdom of Piedmont-Sardinia expelled the Austrians from Italy, leaving the way open for its armies to take control of most of northern and central Italy. The following year, the Italian soldier and patriot, Giuseppe Garibaldi, landed in southern Italy with an army of volunteer "Red Shirts" and quickly conquered Sicily and Naples. In 1861, Garibaldi proclaimed the new Kingdom of Italy and announced his intention to make Rome its

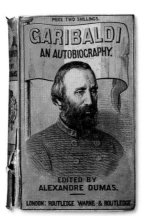

A NATIONALIST HERO
The charismatic Italian patriot, Garibaldi, led many of the campaigns to unify Italy, most famously the conquest of the Kingdom of the Two Sicilies in 1860.

capital with the slogan *Roma o Morte* (Rome or Death). The vow would not be fulfilled until 1870, when the Italian army finally laid siege to the papal city. After a long bombardment, the city walls were breached at Porta Pia. Rome became the new capital of a unified Italy.

PRISONERS IN THE VATICAN

Having taken control of Rome and the other papal territories, the new Italian government offered to allow the pope to continue using the Leonine city—that part of Rome contained within Pope Leo IV's ancient walls *(see p.48)*. Not wishing to legitimize the annexation of the Papal States, Pius angrily rejected the offer, declaring himself a "prisoner in the Vatican" and forbidding Catholics from participating in the usurping Kingdom of Italy. For the next 59 years, Pius and his successors were to remain confined to the Vatican.

Pius IX's long pontificate ended in disillusionment. During his funeral procession, an anticlerical mob attempted to throw his body into the Tiber. His successor on the papal throne, **Leo XIII**, is remembered above all for his enlightened teaching on social justice and political thought. Leo's long reign restored in some measure the fortunes of the papacy. International contacts improved and a number of foreign dignitaries—including Wilhelm II of Germany and the English king, Edward VII—visited the pope in his self-imposed confinement at the Vatican. In this way, Leo guided the papacy toward improved relationships with a rapidly changing world.

THE PAPACY BEGAN THE 20TH CENTURY STRIPPED OF POLITICAL POWER INSIDE ITALY AND WITH THE POPES CONFINED AS SELF-PROCLAIMED PRISONERS INSIDE THE VATICAN. FORTUNATELY, THIS LOSS OF TEMPORAL POWER FREED THE PAPACY TO FOCUS ON THE MORAL AND SPIRITUAL MISSION OF THE CHURCH. THROUGHOUT TWO WORLD WARS, AND THROUGH ALL OF THE SOCIAL AND POLITICAL VICISSITUDES OF THE 20TH AND 21ST CENTURIES, THE PAPACY HAS CONTINUED TO PROVIDE LEADERSHIP AND GUIDANCE TO THE UNIVERSAL CHURCH OF BELIEVERS ACROSS THE GLOBE.

1903–1914	1913	1914–1922	1922

PIUS X	WITH PAPAL COURT	BENEDICT XV	WORKING AT DESK

 ELECTED IN 1903, the saintly cardinal, Giuseppe Melchiorre Sarto, immediately signaled his sympathy for the conservative theology of his predecessor, Pius IX, by adopting the papal name **Pius X**. The first pope to be elected in the 20th century, Pius was nonetheless deeply suspicious of developments in modern theology. In 1907, he denounced the Modernist movement within the Church that sought to assimilate Catholic theology with scientific developments and advances in biblical studies. A highly principled and simple man, Pius also abandoned the large rooms of the Apostolic Palace used by former popes in favor of a small apartment at the top of the palazzo. After his death, many miracles were attributed to his intercession (the act of praying to God on behalf of others), and he was canonized by Pius XII in 1954.

THE PAPACY DURING WORLD WAR I

The death of Pius X in 1914 coincided with the outbreak of World War I. The cardinals who gathered in conclave to elect a new pope were aware that the difficult times called for an experienced diplomat and so elected the Cardinal Archbishop of Bologna as **Benedict XV**. The Great War and its aftermath were to dominate Benedict's pontificate.

Throughout World War I, which he memorably described as "the great suicide of Europe," Pope Benedict endeavored to send aid to those whose lives were affected by the atrocities. The pope made many attempts to negotiate

A LATERAN TREATY
The 1929 treaty between Mussolini and the Holy See created the Vatican City State, ending 59 years of papal confinement inside the Vatican.

peace, and in 1917, proposed a seven-point peace plan for the belligerent parties to consider. Germany was agreeable to the terms, but the plan was eventually rejected by the Allies. Benedict was careful to maintain the neutrality of the papacy during the war, a position that caused the victorious powers to exclude papal diplomats from the peace negotiations at Versailles. Despite this, Benedict issued an encyclical, *Pacem, Dei Munus Pulcherrimum* (Peace, a Most Beautiful Gift from God), calling for international reconciliation, and he backed the formation of the League of Nations. Benedict also urged forward the unification of the separated Churches of the East, and was an enthusiastic patron of the missions of the Church around the world. His death from pneumonia in 1922 was a shock to the Catholic world, and he was universally mourned for his sincerity and pacifist aspirations. Pope Benedict XVI, adopting his predecessor's papal name in 2005 (see p.78), described the pope as a "courageous prophet of peace, who guided the Church through turbulent times of war."

THE SOVEREIGN VATICAN CITY STATE

In February 1922, the scholarly Milanese cardinal, Achille Ratti, was elected pope, taking the name **Pius XI**. One of the new pope's first acts was to revive the traditional blessing, *urbi et orbi* (to the city and the world), from the balcony of St. Peter's Basilica—something that his predecessors had refused to do since the loss of Rome in 1871 (see p.71). The act was symbolic of the pope's

THE MODERN ERA

THE PAPACY AND THE MODERN VATICAN STATE, 1903–PRESENT

| PIUS XI | READING IN STUDY | PIUS XII | SPEAKING ON VATICAN RADIO |

intention to engage with the world, rather than withdrawing as a prisoner in the Vatican, and Pius soon went even further. In 1929, a treaty was signed at the Lateran Palace between the papacy and the Italian prime minister, Benito Mussolini. In return for the papacy's recognition of the Kingdom of Italy, the Lateran Treaty established the independent State of the Vatican City and granted Catholicism special status in Italy. Later that year, Pius became the first pope in 59 years to leave the confines of the Vatican. Ever since the treaty, the Vatican City has remained a sovereign territory of the Holy See, providing the papacy with the security and the autonomy to take an independent role in world affairs.

BUILD-UP TO WORLD WAR II

As Europe struggled to recover from World War I, the twin specters of Fascism and Communism loomed ever larger in world affairs. In 1933, Pius concluded a concordat with Germany in an attempt to protect German Catholics, although the agreement was almost immediately ignored by the Nazis. Four years later, he issued an encyclical, *Mit Brennender Sorge* (With Burning Sorrow), condemning the plight of Christians in Nazi Germany. When Hitler visited Rome in 1938, the pope withdrew to his country residence at Castel Gandolfo to express his disapproval. Pius also feared the spread of atheistic Communism and abhorred the Stalinist regime, forcefully condemning the political philosophy in his encyclical, *Divini Redemptoris* (Of the Divine Redeemer), in 1937.

Pius died in February 1939, just one day before he was due to deliver a blistering attack on Fascism and anti-Semitism. The cardinals who gathered to elect his successor again realized the need for a pope with diplomatic experience in the event of the outbreak of war. The choice fell on Pius XI's close collaborator, Cardinal Eugenio Pacelli, who took the name **Pius XII** in deference to the deceased pontiff. In 1933, while serving as Secretary of State to Pius XI, Pacelli had been the prime mover behind the concordat with Nazi Germany and as pope he remained committed to a diplomatic solution to the Fascist threat. In his first Christmas address, Pius proposed a five-point peace plan, which was ultimately rejected. Nonetheless, Pius was anxious to preserve the neutrality of the Holy See; the threat of the invasion of the Vatican by Nazi troops was a clear danger, and Pius realized that any careless words could enrage the Nazis and endanger lives throughout Europe.

Although Pius has been criticized posthumously for not being more outspoken in his criticism of the Nazis, the papacy led initiatives that saved over 850,000 Jewish lives, making it arguably more successful than those of all other governments and agencies. Hundreds of Jews in particular were housed at the Vatican, Castel Gandolfo, and in convents and friaries throughout Italy. During the war and the post-war period, the Vatican also ran a successful service to help people trace relatives and friends displaced by the war.

> **> ROYAL VISIT TO THE VATICAN**
> King Victor Emmanuel pays a ceremonial visit to Pius XI at the Vatican in 1929, a token of the new accord achieved between the Holy See and the Kingdom of Italy.

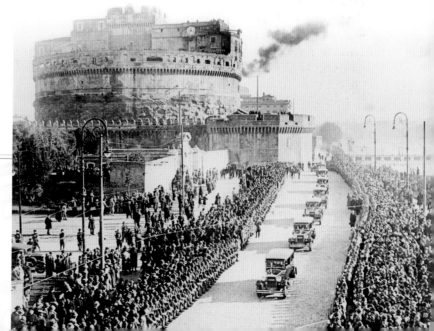

> I want to throw open the windows of the Church
> so that we can see out and the people can see in.
>
> JOHN XXIII EXPLAINS HIS REASONS FOR CALLING THE SECOND VATICAN COUNCIL, 1959

1958–1963	1960	1962
JOHN XXIII	ROME OLYMPICS OPENING CEREMONY	ADDRESS AT THE SANCTUARY OF LORETO

The election of the 76-year-old Angelo Roncalli as **John XXIII** in 1958 had an extraordinary effect on the Church and on the world. Few would have considered that such an elderly candidate would be more than a "caretaker pope," preparing the way for a younger, more energetic pontiff. Yet by calling the Second Vatican Council—a watershed in the history of the Catholic Church—in 1959, John helped the Vatican to renew its relationship with the modern world.

GOOD POPE JOHN

John XXIII spent most of his long life in the diplomatic corps of the Holy See before becoming Cardinal Patriarch of Venice in 1953 at the age of 72. Noted for his cheerfulness, optimism, piety, and sense of humor—in Italy he is affectionately remembered as *Il Papa Buono* (the Good Pope)—John never lost the common touch. On the first Christmas after his election, John visited sick children at the Bambino Gesù hospital in Rome, making sure that each child received a gift. A surprise visit to a Roman prison the next day was marked by simplicity and informality, with the pope explaining to the prisoners, "you could not come to me, so I came to you."

John was above all a man of dialog. By adopting a conciliatory approach toward Christians of other denominations, for example, he greatly boosted the ecumenical movement. But the defining event of John XXIII's pontificate was undoubtedly the opening of the Second Vatican Council in 1962, a conference of all the bishops of the Church. The council sought to bring the Church, in John's words, "up to date." Although the pope died before he could see its completion, the Second Vatican Council was to reorient the Church's teaching on a wide range of issues. Most notably, the council permitted that the liturgy should normally be celebrated in vernacular languages rather than Latin; pronounced in favor of religious liberty for non-Catholics; and called on the Catholic Church to work with other Churches and with secular society toward "the establishment of a world that is more human."

John welcomed many major official figures to the Vatican, including US First Lady Jacqueline Kennedy and Queen Elizabeth II of Great Britain. He also received the daughter of the Soviet premier Nikita Khrushchev, helping to thaw relations between the Soviet Union and the Catholic Church. His death in 1963 after a long struggle with cancer was met by an outpouring of grief among Catholics and non-Catholics alike. John was declared Blessed by Pope John Paul II during a beatification ceremony held in St. Peter's Square in 2000.

AFTER THE SECOND VATICAN COUNCIL

Elected while the Second Vatican Council was still in session, Pope **Paul VI** often appeared reserved in comparison to his more jovial predecessor but the new pope nonetheless steered the Second Vatican Council toward a successful conclusion in 1965. To continue the dialog initiated by the council, Paul

< SECOND VATICAN COUNCIL
Bishops and prelates from all over the world gather in St. Peter's Basilica in 1962 for a session of the Second Vatican Council. Over 2,500 prelates attended the opening session.

PAUL VI GREETING PATRIARCH ATHENAGORAS JOHN PAUL I

established the Synod of Bishops, a forum for the world's bishops to meet regularly in Rome to discuss issues of concern with Roman officials and each other. The pope also carried out a thorough reform of the Curia (the apparatus of papal government) and greatly simplified Vatican protocol.

The manner in which the Catholic Church changed in the years after the Second Vatican Council often proved controversial. Paul's authority was challenged by traditionalists such as the French archbishop Marcel Lefebvre, who refused to accept all its declarations, especially in the area of religious freedom and the liturgy. On the other hand, when Paul demonstrated more conservative views regarding the value of life and the sacrament of marriage in the encyclical *Humanae Vitae* (Of Human Life) in 1968, this too was met by dissent. The large number of priests and believers who abandoned their vows during his pontificate was a great source of suffering for the pope.

ᴧ PRESIDENT KENNEDY
US President John F. Kennedy visits the Vatican in July 1963: one of many foreign dignitaries received by Pope Paul VI.

In 1964, the pope met with the Orthodox Patriarch Athenagoras in Jerusalem, a warm encounter that led to both men rescinding the mutual excommunications of the Great Schism of 1054 *(see p.50)*. Paul also reached out to other Christian denominations, meeting the Anglican Archbishop of Canterbury in 1966 and describing the Anglican Church as "our beloved sister Church." In 1965, at the United Nations in New York, Paul made an impassioned plea for the end of war, then continuing the theme in the 1967 encyclical, *Populorum Progressio* (Progression of the Peoples), a powerful critique of many national philosophies that urged social economic stability and justice as a precondition for peace.

At the Vatican, Paul's architectural legacy lies in the building of the Audience Hall designed by Pier Luigi Nervi for the Holy Year of 1975. Paul is also remembered as a patron of modern art, and in 1973, he inaugurated the Gallery of Modern Religious Art at the Vatican Museums.

THE PILGRIM POPE

Like his predecessor, Paul VI sought to bring the papacy into closer contact with the world, and he became the first pope in modern history to travel extensively outside the Vatican. Paul's pastoral visits took him to the Holy Land, India, and America, and he became the first pope to visit all five continents. During a pastoral visit to the Philippines in 1970, Paul narrowly escaped an assassination attempt when a man in the crowd, a Bolivian surrealist painter dressed as a priest, lunged at him with a dagger.

POPE JOHN PAUL I

Paul VI suffered a heart attack at the papal summer residence of Castel Gandolfo in 1978 and was succeeded by the Cardinal Patriarch of Venice, Albino Luciani. Taking the name of his two immediate predecessors, **John Paul I** dispensed with the age-old ceremony of coronation and began his pontificate with a simple ceremony of inauguration. Romans and visitors alike were quickly charmed by the pope's informal style and simple use of language and anecdotes. His death after only 33 days in office came as a complete shock to the world.

1978–2005	1978	1979

JOHN PAUL II	INAUGURAL MASS	VISITING AUSCHWITZ

When he stepped out onto the balcony of St. Peter's Basilica on the evening of his election in October 1978, Pope **John Paul II** introduced himself as "a man from afar." At the age of just 58, the new pope was the youngest in recent history and the first non-Italian pontiff for more than 450 years. In impromptu remarks, he vowed to dedicate himself to the See of Rome, asking the Italians in the crowd below to correct him when he "made a mistake in your— no—in *our* language." The crowd roared its approval. As the second longest reigning pope of modern times, after Pius IX, John Paul II's pontificate would prove hugely influential.

EARLY LIFE AND CAREER

Karol Wojtyla, born in the Polish town of Wadowice south of Krakow in 1920, was the youngest son of a retired army official and lost his mother when he was only nine. Interested in poetry and drama and studious by disposition, the young Karol, or Lolek as friends called him, prevaricated between a life on the stage and the priesthood.

When Karol was aged just 19, World War II broke out. These were traumatic years, as his beloved Poland became engulfed by war and the site of the slaughter of millions of Jews and other victims of the Nazi regime. Following a short period as a forced laborer, Wojtyla entered an underground seminary. After ordination in 1946, he was sent to Rome to study for a

doctorate in theology. When he returned to Poland in 1948 it was to a country under Communist control. In August 1958, Karol Wojtyla was appointed auxiliary bishop of Krakow, and he played an important role in the Second Vatican Council *(see p.75)*.

In 1963, Wojtyla was made Archbishop of Krakow and he was created cardinal four years later. Pope Paul VI was impressed with the young Pole and invited him to be a member of a committee to advise him on birth control. Wojtyla's attendance at the Synod of Bishops further extended his international contacts and, in October 1978, following the sudden death of John Paul I, he was elected as Pope John Paul II.

INTERNATIONAL MISSION

During his first public appearances, the Polish pope won over millions to his side. With his rugged good looks and his athletic physique, John Paul combined charisma with an iron-willed determination to lead the Church through the stormy waters of encroaching secularization. Over the next 26 years, interrupted only briefly by an assassination attempt in St. Peter's Square in 1981, John Paul crisscrossed the globe, making 104 international trips to 129 countries. Already a competent linguist, he learned several new languages, and was as much at home celebrating Mass in Central Park in New York as in the favelas of Brazil or the shanty towns of South Africa.

ʌ **THE TRAVELING POPE**
A bronze statue of Pope John Paul II stands outside the basilica of Our Lady of Guadalupe in Mexico. The pope visited the shrine during his first trip outside Italy in 1979.

1993

2000

2000

WITH GORBACHEV AT THE VATICAN   MEETING JORDAN'S KING ABDALLAH   VISITING THE HOLY LAND

In the political arena, John Paul led an intellectual assault on Communism. The pope backed the Solidarity movement in Poland, meeting the banned union leader and future president, Lech Walesa. He gave his support to free elections in Poland in June 1989, an event that set in motion the collapse of Communism across the Soviet bloc. The former Soviet president, Mikhail Gorbachev, noted in 1993 that "everything that took place in Eastern Europe in recent years would have been impossible without the pope's efforts." John Paul was equally vocal in his criticisms of other abuses of power, pointing out the failures of both capitalism and consumerism.

RELATIONS WITH OTHER RELIGIONS

Influenced by his strong childhood friendships with Jews, John Paul was anxious to improve relations between the Catholic Church and the Jewish community. He established diplomatic relations between the Vatican and the State of Israel in 1993, and in a poignant pilgrimage to the Middle East in 2000 he visited the Holocaust Museum at Yad Vashim and placed a note in the Wailing Wall in Jerusalem, asking for forgiveness for the behavior of past generations of Christians towards the Jewish people. He also visited a Palestinian refugee camp and offered support for their aspirations for peace following years of political upheaval.

Islam was another concern of John Paul II. At the Vatican he regularly welcomed Muslim authorities, and visited Muslim communities when in Islamic countries, although he was critical of the growth in fundamentalist Islam.

ʌ ASSASSINATION ATTEMPT
In May 1981, John Paul was shot and seriously wounded by a Turkish gunman claiming to be acting on behalf of the Bulgarian Government.

Because of his sensitivities with regard to Islam and Judaism—both monotheistic religions that have common roots with Christianity, John Paul was highly supportive of peace initiatives in the Middle East, and was a bitter and vociferous opponent of the Gulf War of 1991 and the invasions of Afghanistan and Iraq in 2001–2003.

LEADERSHIP OF THE CHURCH

The years following the Second Vatican Council saw dramatic divisions within the Church between liberals and conservatives. John Paul set himself the goal of establishing a bridge between the two camps. The delicate task did not always meet with success. His charm often failed to placate the liberals, who resented his unstinting defense of traditional sexual ethics, while his unbending will sometimes failed to win back conservatives who moved further to the right.

John Paul II had many critics both within and outside the Church. His opposition to abortion, homosexual practice, genetic research, and artificial contraception earned him both opprobrium and praise. Yet his charm and ability to hold an audience's attention ensured that people listened, even if they did not always heed the message. John Paul developed Parkinson's disease in the 1990s, although he made pastoral visits abroad as late as 2004. His funeral in April 2005 was attended by 500,000 people, the largest televised religious event in history. It was a fitting farewell to a pope who had challenged the hearts and minds of his contemporaries.

2005–2013	2005	2005
BENEDICT XVI	INAUGURAL MASS, ST. PETER'S SQUARE	CANONIZATION, ST. PETER'S SQUARE

ʌ INAUGURAL MASS
Pope Benedict XVI celebrates Mass to begin his ministry as Bishop of Rome at St. Peter's Basilica on April 24, 2005, in a ceremony broadcast throughout the world.

Cardinal Joseph Ratzinger was elected pope on April 19, 2005, after a conclave of just two days. He had turned 78 two days earlier. Choosing the name **Benedict XVI**, he presented himself to the people gathered in St. Peter's Square as a "humble worker in the vineyard of the Lord."

Joseph Ratzinger was born in 1927 in Marktl am Inn in southern Bavaria. World War II broke out in 1939, and the horrors of the war dominated his teenage years. Shortly after the war ended in 1945, Joseph and his brother, Georg, enrolled in a seminary at Traunstein. In 1951, both brothers were ordained priests together at the cathedral of Freising. After a year spent working in a parish in Munich, Ratzinger started post-graduate theological studies. Having successfully completed his doctorate, he remained in the world of academia for almost 20 years, teaching at universities around Germany. Ratzinger participated as theological advisor at the Second Vatican Council between 1962-65. In the spring of 1977, Ratzinger reluctantly left the world of teaching when Paul VI appointed him Archbishop of Munich. He was made a cardinal later that year. In 1981, John Paul II appointed him Prefect of the Congregation of the Faith in the Vatican, the office overseeing theological publications and all matters pertaining to doctrine. It was in this capacity that he supervised the publication of the Catechism of the Catholic Church, a compendium of the Church's teaching, especially in the light of the Second Vatican Council.

HOLY TEACHER

With Benedict's election in 2005, for the first time in centuries, a professional theologian occupied the Holy See. Although by nature somewhat reserved, Benedict clearly appreciated opportunities to teach; at his Wednesday audiences

> To protect creation, to protect every man and woman,
> to look upon them with tenderness and love, is to
> open up a horizon of hope.

POPE FRANCIS, MARCH 17, 2013

2013 **2013** **2013**

POPE FRANCIS' INAUGURAL MASS   PASTORAL VISIT TO BRAZIL   WEEKLY AUDIENCE, ST. PETER'S SQUARE

the pope explained the scriptures and the teachings of early theologians. He published a three-volume set entitled *Jesus of Nazareth*, sharing the depth of his learning with a much wider audience than he had previously enjoyed.

Benedict opposed the intolerance of philosophies that seek to banish religion to the private sphere. As with comparable world religions that place faith at the center of daily life for their believers, he encouraged Christians to live out their faith with pride and reject relativism (the belief that ethics and moral values are not absolute but can vary, depending on the situation). Citing reasons of age and health, Benedict XVI resigned the papacy on February 28, 2013—the first pope in some 600 years to do so. He continued to live in a house in the Vatican gardens.

POPE FRANCIS

Jorge Mario Bergoglio succeeded Pope Benedict following a two-day conclave. The first pope from Latin America, he was the first to take the name of Francis, the patron saint of Italy. A native of the Argentinian capital Buenos Aires, Jorge Bergoglio was the son of an Italian migrant and his mother was second-generation Italian. Following studies in chemistry, the 21-year-old Jorge decided to join the Jesuit Order. After years of administration and teaching, he was appointed auxiliary bishop of Buenos Aires in 1992, becoming archbishop of the capital in 1998. These were politically turbulent years following a violent military dictatorship. Bergoglio was an outspoken critic of government policies following an economic crisis in the early 2000s.

Elected pope on March 13, 2013, Francis continues the simple life style he was used to in Argentina, and he has decided against living in the Apostolic Palace in favor of a functional residence shared with other priests and bishops.

But Francis also embraces change, and, shortly after his election, he set up a commission of eight cardinals from each continent to assist his administration of the Church. In particular, he wishes to reform the workings of the Holy See to make it more transparent and efficient.

As archbishop of Buenos Aires, Francis regularly visited the people who lived in the vast, unnamed slums on the outskirts of the city. His genial demeanor and warm smile won him many friends among the poor. As pope, he is continuing the habit of years, regularly visiting prisons, hospitals, and drug rehabilitation centers. Having learned Italian from his grandparents, Francis speaks the language fluently and his use of colloquial phrases catches the attention of his listeners.

Three months after his election, the pope's day trip to the island of Lampedusa illustrated the importance that he places on meeting and helping the poor. Lampedusa lies between the coast of northern Africa and Sicily and, over decades, thousands of African migrants have perished at sea in the attempt to land on Italian territory and begin a new life in Europe. The pope's visit brought solace to the migrants and inhabitants of the island, and shone international light on the shameful situation. When Francis returned to Latin America for World Youth Day later in July he was once again in the spotlight. When some three million people went to see him celebrate mass on Copacabana beach the popularity of the new pope and the central role he plays in the lives of believers was clear to all.

> PALM SUNDAY
Pope Francis holds a woven palm frond at the beginning of Palm Sunday Mass, which observes Jesus' triumphal entrance into Jerusalem in the week before his death.

ARCHITECTURE

BUILDING THE VATICAN

Despite the small size of Vatican City, almost two thousand years of architectural history can be found within its walls. The end result of several popes' patronage, its buildings do not form a homogeneous whole—the Vatican is a mixture of various architectural styles that go back as far as ancient Rome. Some of the earliest architecture can be found underground, such as the 2nd- to 4th-century necropolis that once lay on the banks of the Tiber. The small churches of the city exemplify the simplicity of Romanesque buildings, while the magnificent St. Peter's Basilica, begun in the Renaissance period by Pope Julius II, was completed in the High Baroque era, with its plays on light, form, and scale. Preserved over hundreds of years—with very little building in the last century—Vatican City must be regarded as an incomparable treasure of Western architecture.

AERIAL VIEW

St Peter's Basilica
dome
minor cupola
colonnade
St Peter's Square
obelisk

PLAN VIEW

pier supporting dome
pier supporting dome
apse
Door of Prayer
left transept
right transept
papal altar
Chapel of the choir
nave
Chapel of the Blessed Sacrament
left aisle
right aisle
Porta Santa (Holy Door)
bronze doors
portico
entrance
façade
raised platform

∧ THE COLONNADE

There are 288 Doric columns and 88 pilasters. From two points on the ellipse, which measures 260 yards (240 m-) across, the columns line up one behind the other in an optical illusion.

> ST. PETER'S FAÇADE

Designed by architect Carlo Maderno, the façade of St. Peter's is decorated with eight Corinthian columns and four pilasters. A flight of travertine steps leads up to the basilica.

Constantine, Rome's first Christian emperor, built an imposing basilica over the tomb of St. Peter on the Vatican Hill. By the reign of Pope Nicholas V (1447–55), the structure was unsound, with the walls of the central nave more than 3 ft (1 m) off the perpendicular. Moreover, the old basilica was out of step with the Renaissance spirit of the times.

Pope Nicholas commissioned a new choir to be built in the apse behind the high altar. Work ceased with the pope's death in 1455. About half a century later, Pope Julius II (1503–13) decided to place his tomb in the unfinished choir, demolishing the old basilica in favor of a new one. The first architect, Donato Bramante (1444–1514), proposed a circular Greek-cross shape, at the center of which lay St. Peter's tomb. After Bramante's death, the project was given to Raphael (1483–1520), Baldassare Peruzzi (1481–1537), and Giuliano Sangallo (1443–1516). This triumvirate changed the shape to a Latin cross, with the central nave

longer than the side arms. The new St. Peter's was not completed until 1626, during which time many of Italy's greatest architects had worked on the building, including Michelangelo (1475–1564), Giacomo della Porta (1533–1602), Carlo Maderno (1556–1629), and Gian Lorenzo Bernini (1598–1680).

Under Pope Alexander VII (1655–67), Bernini built an elliptical square, the Piazza San Pietro, in front of the basilica between 1656 and 1667. The area around the Vatican was a warren of buildings and chapels. Bernini used this to stunning effect, so that as the pilgrims turned a corner, they found themselves emerging from the maze of streets into a vast, open space. In 1936, the Italian dictator Mussolini (1883–1945) had the buildings in front of the basilica demolished. A new road, Via della Conciliazione, was built to commemorate the Lateran Treaty of 1929, which normalized relations between the Holy See and the Italian state.

∧ CLOCK TOWER

Two clocks, flanked by angels, adorn the two corners of the façade. The papal coat of arms sits atop each clock with a small lightning conductor to prevent storm damage.

> BELL TOWER

A set of bells hang in the bell tower. Operated electronically, they chime every quarter of an hour. A single bell is tolled upon the death of the pope.

> OBELISK

The granite Egyptian obelisk from the 13th century BC originally stood in the Circus of Caligula. Pope Sixtus V moved it to its present location in the middle of the piazza in 1586. The obelisk is adorned by the star and mountains of the pope's crest.

ST. PETER'S
CENTER OF THE CATHOLIC FAITH

⋀ CREST ON THE COLONNADE
The crest of Pope Alexander VII, who commissioned Bernini's colonnade, consists of his family coat of arms, that of the Chigi of Siena, capped with the papal tiara and keys.

⋀ SAINTS ON THE COLONNADE
Some 140 saints carved in travertine, the stone used by the Romans to build the Colosseum, crown the colonnade. They need constant repair from damage caused by pollution.

< DETAIL OF FAÇADE
Pope Paul V of the Borghese family dedicated the façade in 1612. The eagle, part of his family coat of arms, stands astride a decorative garland of pomegranates, which are symbols of eternity.

⋀ DECORATIVE CAPITAL
This capital, atop one of the four pilasters of the façade, imitates the architecture of imperial Rome.

< ST. PETER
This 19th-century statue of St. Peter holding the keys of authority is one of a pair flanking the façade.

< GATE HEAD
A wrought-iron grill stands above the gates at the main entrance to the basilica. The gates were commissioned by Pope Pius VI (1775–99) whose coat of arms decorates the center of the grill.

ΛST. PETER'S SQUARE
The obelisk casts a shadow across Bernini's
piazza, while statues of Christ, John the Baptist,
and the Apostles look down from the top of
St. Peter's façade on early morning visitors.

⋁ SWISS GUARDS AT THE ARCH OF THE BELLS
Swiss Guards stand on duty at the external entrances to the Apostolic Palace, namely the Petrine Gate at the Arch of the Bells, the Bronze Door, and St. Anne's Gate.

⋁ SQUARE OF THE FIRST MARTYRS
The square takes its name from the fact that it is built over the ruins of the Circus of Nero where, according to tradition, St. Peter and other early Christians were killed.

⋀ SACRISTY WINDOWS
The windows of the sacristy, built in the late 18th century by architect Carlo Marchionni (1702–86) for Pope Pius VI (1775–99), have decorative iron lattice work that protects the glass.

⋖ CUPOLA LANTERN
The lantern of Michelangelo's cupola took 600 builders and 22 months to complete.

⋗ VIEW TO THE SACRISTY
The 18th-century, dome-covered sacristy is dwarfed by Michelangelo's basilica. To its right is the residence of the Archpriest of the Basilica.

⋀ DOME FROM VATICAN GARDENS
Michelangelo intended his cupola to be visible from all sides, as in this view from the gardens; however, from the front, it is largely hidden by the tall façade.

> **NEW SAINTS FOR ST. PETER'S**
Set into niches in the 17th-century façade of St. Peter's, these modern, white marble statues contrast with the weathered stone around them.

< BASILICA DRUM
When Michelangelo died in 1564, only the drum of the dome had been erected. The rest of the cupola was not completed until 1590.

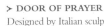

∧ **ST. PETER'S FROM THE SOUTH**
This view emphasizes the immense size and massive construction of St. Peter's. Many of the building materials used came from the ruined buildings of ancient Rome.

> **DOOR OF PRAYER**
Designed by Italian sculptor Lello Scorzelli, the door panels depict four prayers: the Our Father, the Hail Mary, the Benedictus, and the Creed. The detail shows a lion, an ox, a man, and an eagle—symbols of the Four Evangelists.

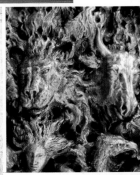

< RENAISSANCE DESIGN
Michelangelo's design, inspired by the architecture of ancient Rome, employs typical Renaissance elements, such as columns, pediments, and statuary.

⋁ ➤ PORTICO AND ARMS
In the center of the portico's stucco ceiling are the arms of Paul V (1605–21), in whose reign the façade was completed.

⋁ NAVE
The nave is 611 ft (186 m) long and 145 ft (44 m) high. The wall inscriptions include Jesus's words to Peter: "I have prayed for you."

➤ COFFERED CEILING
The nave's barrel-vaulted, gilt stucco ceiling, dating from 1780, was commissioned by Pope Pius VI (1775–99).

⋁ ➤ HOLY DOOR
Made in 1949 by Ludovico Consorti (1902–97), the Holy Door's bronze panels recount mankind's salvation, from the Fall to the Resurrection.

➤ ST. PETER'S KEYS
Under the tread of millions of feet, the white marble paving stone has worn more rapidly than the red porphyry keys.

➤ HOLY WATER FONT
On entry to the basilica, visitors encounter large holy water fonts. These marble cherubs, which date from 1725, would be 6 ft (1.8 m) tall if they were to stand up.

< ˅ BAPTISMAL FONT
Two cherubs sit atop the bronze lid of the porphyry basin. Above them is the Lamb of God, representing Jesus. The basin came from the mausoleum of Emperor Hadrian.

> ORGAN IN CHAPEL OF CANONS
There are five organs in St. Peter's. This one stands in a chapel intended for the use of the canons of the basilica.

˅ TOMB OF INNOCENT VIII
This tomb by Antonio del Pollaiuolo (c.1429–98) was dismantled when the old St. Peter's was demolished, and rebuilt a century later.

˄ LEFT AISLE
In the distance is the Altar of the Transfiguration, behind which is a mosaic copy of the last painting by the great artist Raphael. The aisle's architecture embraces much of the vocabulary of Classical Rome and Greece.

> POPE ALEXANDER VII
This magnificent polychrome monument by Bernini was a final tribute to his patron, Pope Alexander VII (1655–67). Bernini placed the pope between the virtues of Truth and Love. Truth stubs her toe on Protestant England.

⋏ MICHELANGELO'S DOME
The great dome was finished in 1590, 26 years after Michelangelo's death. Its completion is marked by an inscription around the opening at the top: "To the glory of St Peter, Sixtus V, 1590, the fith year of his reign."

⋁ MEDALLION OF ST. MARK

Four mosaic medallions, each representing one of the Evangelists who composed the Gospels, decorate the area between the main cupola of the basilica and the massive piers underneath.

⋀ THE CROSSING

The crossing beneath the center of the dome is the heart of the basilica, where the Papal Altar stands directly above the Tomb of St. Peter.

⋁ ETERNAL SHRINE

Behind the ornate balustrade a pair of staircases lead down to an altar, below which lies the *Confessio Petri*, or Tomb of St. Peter.

➤ BERNINI'S BALDACCHINO

The *baldacchino*, a great altar canopy over the Papal Altar and St. Peter's Tomb, took 9 years to build and was completed in 1633. Most of its 90 tons of bronze came from the portico of Rome's Pantheon.

< APSE
At the end of the central nave, the apse is dominated by Bernini's imposing Altar of the Chair of St. Peter.

V ALTAR OF THE CHAIR
Completed in 1666, the altar contains the relics of a chair St. Peter used to preach from. It symbolizes the teaching authority of the papacy.

< HOLY SPIRIT
The Altar of the Chair is illuminated by this alabaster sunburst around the Holy Spirit in the form of a dove.

> PAPAL TIARA
Above the Chair are two putti bearing the papal tiara and St. Peter's keys—symbols of the Roman pontiff's authority.

< STATUE OF ST. PETER
Attributed to the sculptor Arnolfo di Cambio (c.1240–1310), this 13th-century bronze statue is based on a 4th-century marble statue of a Roman senator. St. Peter's hands are raised in the act of blessing. The mosaic "curtain" behind the statue dates from 1871.

> FEAST-DAY ATTIRE
On the Feast of the Chair of Peter (February 22), the statue is dressed in a red and gold cope. A tiara from the Papal Sacristy is placed on its head.

∧ SAINT'S FOOT
The custom of touching or kissing the foot of the statue of St. Peter has, over seven centuries, almost obliterated its features.

93

ᴧ RIGHT TRANSEPT CUPOLA

Eleven cupolas punctuate the roof of St. Peter's, with windows letting in light from above. The domes are all decorated with mosaics and gilded stucco.

ᴠ ᐳ GREGORY XIII

This monument, completed in 1723, celebrates the pope's reform of the calendar in 1582, depicted in relief on the casket. The pope is flanked by the figures of Fortitude (*right*) and Religion (*left*).

ᴧ POPE PIUS XII

This bronze statue of Pius XII (1939–58), whose pontificate spanned World War II, was a gift from the cardinals that he created.

ᐸ HERALDIC DRAGON

The monument was commissioned by Cardinal Ugo Boncompagni, the pope's great grand-nephew. The heraldic dragon is part of the Boncompagni family crest.

ᐳ COLUMN BASES

The carved bases of the columns in St. Peter's are often of differing depths. This masks any unevenness in the heights of the pillars.

◁ DOVE OF PEACE

To mark the Jubilee of 1650, the pilasters were decorated with marble reliefs. The dove, the symbol of the Pamphili family of Innocent X (1644–55), graces the pilasters.

∨ RIGHT AISLE

This view toward the Altar of St. Jerome shows the Baroque delight in playing with light and shade. Begun in the Renaissance, St. Peter's was finished in the High Baroque.

∨ ALTAR OF ST. JEROME

The altar front is decorated with mosaics. These were installed on the altars in St. Peter's in the 18th century using new techniques developed in the mosaic studio.

◁ BRONZE CHERUB'S HEAD

Cherubs decorate the door that leads to the elevator connecting St. Peter's with the Apostolic Palace.

▷ BRONZED GRILLE

A series of grilles set into the floor provide light and ventilation to the crypt below where over 100 popes are buried.

∧ PIETÀ

Michelangelo was just 25 years old when he carved this statue of Mary and the dead Jesus in 1499. Mary has the face of a young woman and is considerably taller than her son. The statue was carved from a single block of Carrara marble.

▲ ETERNAL SYMBOL OF THE FAITH
Illuminated throughout the night, St. Peter's awaits the next day's influx of pilgrims and tourists. Many come to pray, while others are drawn by the magnificent art and architecture.

> POPE PIUS XI COAT OF ARMS
Above the academy's main entrance is the coat of arms of Pope Pius XI. It is based on the crest of his own Ratti Opizzoni family.

∨ ACADEMY ENTRANCE
Four marble columns support the porch over the main entrance to the Pontifical Academy of Sciences. On either side are statues depicting Faith and Science.

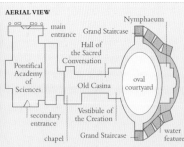

AERIAL VIEW

main entrance · Grand Staircase · Nymphaeum · Hall of the Sacred Conversation · Pontifical Academy of Sciences · Old Casina · oval courtyard · secondary entrance · Vestibule of the Creation · chapel · Grand Staircase · water feature

In the spring of 1558, Pope Paul IV (1555–59) decided to build a villa in the Vatican gardens, a stone's throw from the Papal Palace. He entrusted the project to the famous Neapolitan architect, painter, and antiquarian, Pirro Ligorio (1510–83). After the pope's death the following year, the Medici pope, Pius IV (1559–65) approved Ligorio's design, and the building was completed in 1563.

Situated around a picturesque oval courtyard, the villa complex comprises the Pontifical Academy of Sciences, a Nymphaeum (a monument to the mythological entities called nymphs), two arched gateways, and the villa itself—the Casina, or "little house." The architecture of the Casina embraces the ideals of the Renaissance, while its pictorial decorations illustrate both the Christian iconography of the Counter-Reformation and Classical, pagan themes.

Set close to a wood (now largely destroyed), the Casina evokes the suburban residences that were popular among the aristocracy of ancient Rome. The decorative frescoes inside the Casina illustrate religious themes, notably from the lives of Moses and Christ. These paintings are principally by Federigo Zuccaro (1542/3–1609) and Santi di Tito (1536–1602/3).

When the Casina was first built, it was the venue for literary events hosted by Pius's nephew, Cardinal (and later, Saint) Charles Borromeo (1538–84). Here, the leading intellectuals of the day gathered to discuss topics as diverse as astrology and Church reform.

In 1931, Pope Pius XI (1922–39) commissioned the Italian architect Giuseppe Momo (1875–1940) to design the Aula Magna (Great Hall) adjoining the original Casina. This newer building, which elegantly harmonizes with Ligorio's original design, now houses the Pontifical Academy of Sciences. The academy is made up of some 80 scientists—drawn from several nations and faiths—who contribute to the Catholic Church's social teaching and the ethics of science.

A VIEW FROM ENTRANCE
Looking east from the academy's main entrance, the Nymphaeum is just visible in the courtyard below.

> COURTYARD GATEWAY
Each of the two grand stairways leads to an arched gateway with oak doors, which open onto the oval courtyard.

∨ CARVED PEDIMENT
The upper parts of the courtyard gateways feature intricately carved figures depicting the Four Seasons.

CASINA OF PIUS IV
16TH-CENTURY PAPAL VILLA

‹ NYMPHAEUM LOGGIA
Seen here from below the oval courtyard, the Nymphaeum's *loggia* (columned walkway) overlooks an ornamental fish pond.

› YOUTH
Two classical statues, representing Youth and Grace, flank the statue of Cybele (*see below*).

⌃ FLORAL MOSAIC
Delicate polychrome mosaics, from the early part of the 19th century, recall the glories of Roman art in antiquity.

⌄ SECONDARY ENTRANCE
Originally the pope's entrance to the academy, this doorway is framed on either side by Doric pilasters. The crest of Pope Pius XI is repeated on the pediment above the door.

LEO.XII.PONTIFEX.MAXIMVS.FRONTEM.HANC.RENOVAVIT.PONT.AN.I.

PIVS·IIII·MEDICES·MEDIOLANEN·PONTIFEX·MAXIMVS·
IN NEMORE·PALATII·VATICANI·PORTICVM·
APSIDATAM·CVM·COLVMNIS·NVMIDICIS·FONTIBVS·
LYMPHAE·IMMINENTEM·ET·REGIONE·AREAE·
EXTRVXIT·ANN·SAL·MDLXI·

⌃ CYBELE STATUE
In the central niche at the Nymphaeum's base is the fertility goddess, Cybele, seated on a raised throne.

‹ WATER FEATURE
A sunken channel around the pond allows water to overflow, creating an effect like a modern infinity pool.

‹ GRAND STAIRWAY
One of two stairways leading up to the oval courtyard, this staircase is flanked by two small obelisks and paved with volcanic stone.

⌄ OVAL COURTYARD
Sculptor Niccolò Bresciano designed the geometric marble paving in the courtyard, which links the four sections of the Casina and is richly decorated with fountains and statuary.

⟩ NYMPHAEUM FRIEZE
In the center of this high relief over the Nymphaeum's entrance, Calliope, the muse of poetry, sits beneath the Medici papal crest.

⌃ FOUNTAIN FIGURE
This is one of two marble putti that are shown playfully balancing on water-spewing dolphins in the oval fountain at the center of the courtyard. The putti hold seashells to their ears, evoking images of the faraway ocean.

⟨ VESTIBULE FAÇADE
Directly opposite the Nymphaeum is the Vestibule of the Creation, with its ornate façade, which serves as the entrance to the villa.

⟩ FOUNTAIN IN NYMPHAEUM
This low fountain bears a papal coat of arms, with the six balls of the Medici crest, and the words "Pius IIII Pont [ifex] Max [imus]."

< MEDUSA HEAD
On the Nymphaeum's wall, the serpent-haired Medusa recalls the quest of Perseus, who beheaded her.

> COURTYARD GATEWAYS
This scallop shell motif appears in the arches of the two almost identical gateways that stand on either side of the Oval Courtyard.

^ COURTYARD SEATING
Large vases line the wall above a row of marble seats, where guests would sit during literary evenings and court concerts.

< ROOSTER MOSAIC
The art of mosaic dates back to antiquity. Here, using tiny pieces of colored glass, a rooster's head, with its bright red crest, is depicted.

^ THE NYMPHAEUM
A shrine not only to the nymphs, but also to the Classical muses, the Nymphaeum was a place for the discussion of the arts and sciences.

< FOUNTAIN NICHE
The fountain shown in detail on the left is set into this niche and flanked by two statues.

> ORNATE NICHE
Inside the two gateways to the courtyard are four elaborately decorated niches that are entirely covered with mosaic. The images, such as the Horn of Plenty, or cornucopia, are of Classical origin.

> CEILING STUCCO WORK
The stucco work that decorates the spaces between the frescoed panels on the ceiling features garlands of fruit.

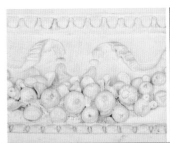

∨ VESTIBULE FOUNTAIN
Two oval fountains stand in opposite niches in the Vestibule, which opens onto the oval courtyard. Winged griffins from Classical mythology flank the pope's coat of arms.

∨ CEILING FRESCOES
While the frescoes on the Vestible ceiling depicting the Creation are Christian, there are also semi-pagan images, such as this putto driving a chariot drawn by a goat.

∧ > CLIO STATUE
In Greek mythology, Clio is the muse of history. She is often represented with a parchment scroll, as here in this statue in the Vestibule. On the vault above her, the story of the Bible unfolds.

< BARREL-VAULT
The barrel-vault of the Vestibule shows Adam and Eve and the creation of the world. Decorated by Venetian Giovanni Schiavone in 1561–63, it is a superb example of the symbiosis of Christian art and pagan iconography.

V ARTEMIS FIGURE
A marble statue depicts Artemis, the Greek goddess of hunting, and the daughter of Zeus and Leto. She stands on a plinth beneath a stylized seashell in one of four ornate niches, framed by a diamond-trellis mosaic.

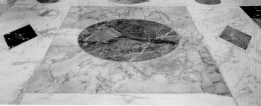

A MARBLE FLOORS
The marble on the floors was taken from Classical-era buildings that had fallen into disrepair by the 16th century. Renaissance artists regularly recycled these fine pieces of marble.

< MOSAIC DOORWAY
Surrounded by a stone frame is a false door, its panels created out of mosaic. The circles and diamonds mirror those on the Vestibule's marble floor (*above*).

A TEXTURED SURFACE
In order to give the villa a rustic feel, artists used small pebbles, shells, and pieces of cut mosaic glass in their wall decoration. The use of these materials was novel in the 16th century.

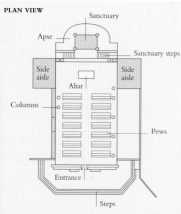

PLAN VIEW

Sanctuary

Apse

Sanctuary steps

Side aisle

Side aisle

Altar

Columns

Pews

Entrance

Steps

The Church of Santo Stefano degli

Abissini lies to the southwest of St. Peter's Basilica. The building we see today dates from the mid-9th century, although it was built on an earlier structure that formed part of a complex set up in the 5th century to serve the needs of pilgrims.

Among the buildings of the complex were two churches to St. Stephen, the first Christian martyr, another to St. Peter and St. John, and a fourth to St. Martin of Tours. In addition, there were several *diaconia*, where food was distributed to the poor and to pilgrims to St. Peter's shrine. By the early 8th century, a monastery had also been established, although it was rebuilt a century later by Pope Leo III (795–816). The year after Leo's death, Pope St. Paschal (817–24), who had been the abbot of the monastery, expanded the complex further to accommodate the growing number of pilgrims.

In the mid-9th century, Pope Leo IV (847–55) rebuilt Santo Stefano as a direct model of St.

Peter's, reusing old brick salvaged from earlier buildings in the area. There were further modifications in the 12th century, when a new transept was added and a decorative frieze placed around the door. Another restoration took place under Pope Sixtus IV (1471–84) to mark the Jubilee Year of 1475. The sobriquet, degli Abissini ("of the Abyssinians") dates from this period and refers either to the Ethiopian monks who cared for the church or the African pilgrims who came to Rome.

Santo Stefano underwent a Baroque remodeling in 1703, but in the 1930s many of the features added at this time were removed, restoring the church to its 9th-century simplicity. Some of the objects found during the 1930s restoration were placed on the walls. The adjacent Monastery of the Abyssinians was demolished, and a new college built. Today, the Pontifical Ethiopian College, founded in 1930 by Pope Pius XI (1922–39), houses student priests who attend Rome's pontifical universities.

Most Catholic churches have a cross above the entrance. Santo Stefano's wrought-iron cross is of a design popular during the 18th century.

∨ TILED ROOF
This view of Santo Stefano's roof, from a window in St. Peter's Basilica, shows the clay roof tiles. They are typical of the type of traditional roof tile that has been produced in Rome for 2,000 years.

∧ BAROQUE FAÇADE
During the restorations and Baroque remodeling that took place in 1703, the church's brickwork was covered with plaster. The interior plaster was removed in the 1930s, but the church's exterior still retains its plaster façade.

> WINDOW OPENING
The window openings, which date from the 9th century, are small compared to the windows of older Roman buildings. The marble window frames and their glazing were part of the 1930s restorations.

> BROKEN PEDIMENT
Santo Stefano's broken pediment—the "incomplete" triangular gable end—is typical of Baroque-period styling. The pediment bears a coat of arms.

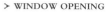

SANTO STEFANO
CHURCH IN THE VATICAN GARDENS

S·STEPHANO·PROTOMARTYRI

⋏ COAT OF ARMS ON PEDIMENT
Rather than a family crest, the coat of arms has a shell—the symbol of a pilgrim. It refers to the shells given to pilgrims who visited the shrine of St. James in Santiago di Compostella, Spain.

⋏ LAMB AND CROSS
At the center of the lintel over the doorway, the marble frieze is broken by a carving of the Lamb of God, which refers to John the Baptist's description of Jesus.

⋏ MARBLE FRIEZE
The main doorway of the church is surrounded by a superbly carved marble frieze. Part of the 12th-century modifications, the frieze features a design of swirling foliage and flowers.

> MARBLE WINDOWS

The designs of the 1930s marble windows are based on those of early Christian churches, although the originals would not have been glazed like those in Santo Stefano.

∨ AUSTERE APSE

The apse, where the clergy sat during the liturgy, was originally richly frescoed. The frescoes have since been removed, exposing the austere 9th-century brickwork.

> SANCTUARY CROSS

The crucifix is always given a place of prominence in the sanctuary. This wooden crucifix is a particularly fine example of 17th-century craftmanship. It may have been originally carried aloft in processions.

∨ SANCTUARY STEPS

Marble steps lead up to the sanctuary, which is separated from the main body of the church. The crypt, where martyrs' relics were once placed, is through the window.

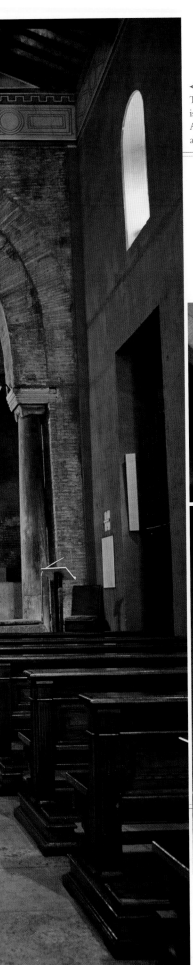

⟨ A SIMPLE PLAN
The church has only one nave and is lit by a number of small windows. A marble *baldacchino* (canopy) stands above the altar in the sanctuary.

⟩ CLEMENT XI
The church was embellished during the pontificate of Pope Clement XI (1700–21), who is commemorated in this marble monument.

⟩ STONE CROSS ON WALL
This stone Greek cross of uncertain date was unearthed during the restorations in the early 20th century.

⋎ CORINTHIAN COLUMNS
These fluted columns date from the Roman period. Along with the architrave, they were utilized in the 9th-century rebuilding.

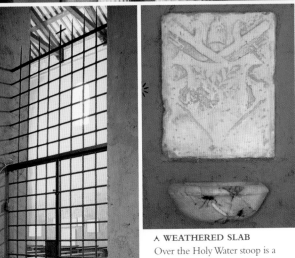

⋏ WEATHERED SLAB
Over the Holy Water stoop is a marble slab bearing the papal tiara and keys, and the oak tree of popes Sixtus IV and Julius II.

⋏ MARBLE COAT OF ARMS
A rare marble high relief of exquisite workmanship bears the coat of arms of Pope Pius III, whose brief reign lasted just two months in 1503.

⟨ IRON GRILLE
A grille separates the left side aisle from the main nave. The aisles were sectioned off during modifications carried out in the 12th century.

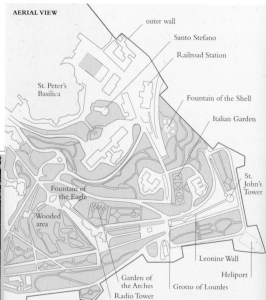

AERIAL VIEW

outer wall

Santo Stefano

Railroad Station

St. Peter's Basilica

Fountain of the Shell

Italian Garden

St. John's Tower

Fountain of the Eagle

Wooded area

Leonine Wall

Heliport

Garden of the Arches

Grotto of Lourdes

Radio Tower

<> PAPAL CREST
Trees surround the papal coat of arms of Pope Benedict XVI (2005–). Made of flowers and hedges, it sits in front of the Governatorato.

∨ STONE FOUNTAIN
This elegant stone fountain, to the side of St. Peter's Basilica, was built by Pope Pius XI, and is surrounded by a copse of trees.

On the western side of the Vatican, rising on the hill behind the apse of St. Peter's Basilica, lie the Vatican gardens. The year before he died, Pope Nicholas III (1277–80) landscaped the gardens behind the basilica as a ceremonial area for enacting pageants and receiving ambassadors to the papal court. Around 200 years later, Pope Nicholas V (1447–55) made a new formal garden, with hedges and fountains in the area now occupied by the Courtyard of St. Damascus, in front of the Apostolic Palace.

During the 17th century, horticultural artists, including Antonio Tempesta (1555–1630), Giovanni Maggi (1566–1618), and Giambattista Falda (1648–78), laid out the gardens in a Baroque style, combining subtle plays of light, shade, and perspective. The Vatican gardens cover some 40 acres (16 hectares). Comprising both formal gardens and more rustic woodland, the gardens contain 97 fountains, which are fed by water from Lake Bracciano, 25 miles (37 km) north

of Rome. The original aqueduct that brought water from Bracciano was built during the reign of Trajan in the 2nd century. It was one of 13 aqueducts that daily pumped one million liters of water into the city during the days of the Roman empire. In 1930, a vast reservoir was built under the gardens by Franco Ratti, a nephew of Pope Pius XI (1922–39).

The gardens house a number of buildings, including the church of Santo Stefano (*see pp.104–07*), a train station, and a convent. The most imposing structure is the Palazzo del Governatorato (the Governor's Palace) built in the reign of Pope Pius XI (1922–39) to celebrate the Lateran Pact. Originally intended to be used as a seminary, it houses the central administration for the Vatican City.

On three sides the gardens are bounded by defensive walls built in the 17th century. There is also a stretch of the 9th-century Leonine Wall, and a section of the Berlin Wall, given to Pope John Paul II.

∧ TRAIN TRACKS
The Vatican railroad, opened in 1930, connects with the main line from Rome to Viterbo. It is now only used for freight.

> FOUNTAIN OF THE SHELL
This typically Baroque fountain, located in the Italian Garden, is surrounded by an elaborate pattern of double-row box hedges.

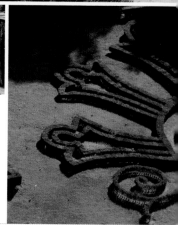

VATICAN GARDENS

THE NATURAL LANDCAPE OF THE VATICAN CITY

∨ SEATS

A number of stone seats are dotted throughout the gardens. The grounds are deceptively large and the terrain can be steep in places; the benches provide a welcome relief for visitors.

> GARDEN STATUES

The Vatican gardens are decorated with a number of pieces of statuary. These range from ancient statues and busts dating from the time of the Roman Empire to more recent sculptures depicting Christian saints and other important figures in the history of the Church.

∨ ROADSIDE WALL

Cut into the hillside and topped by neatly clipped box hedges, this decorative wall runs along the side of the main road that winds its way through the Vatican gardens.

< JUBILEE BELL

In a clearing called *capanna cinese*, or Chinese hut, hangs a bell that is a memento of the Great Jubilee of the Year 2000. The bell bears the coat of arms of Pope John Paul II.

⋏ ENCRUSTED FOUNTAIN

Rome's water is notoriously high in calcium. Over the years, many of the fountains in the gardens have become encrusted with limescale, deforming their original shapes and creating mini-stalactites that hang from their rims.

⋏ POPE'S WALKWAY

This small, tree-lined path was much favored by Pope Pius XII (1939–58), who would stroll along it on a daily basis, reading documents as he walked or taking the opportunity for quiet personal prayer.

⋎ ST. JOHN'S TOWER

Part of the 9th-century Leonine Wall, built to protect St. Peter's tomb, St. John's Tower was erected in the 1400s to defend the city from attack. Pope John XXIII (1958–63) used it as a retreat, and today it houses VIP guests of the Vatican.

⟩ WINDOW IN THE WALLS

Narrow windows served as firing posts for archers in the 17th-century outer wall that surrounds the Vatican City. Their wide bays enabled side-to-side movement.

⋎ STATUE SURROUNDINGS

Set on a plinth, the larger-than-life Madonna of Guadalupe statue stands on a lawn amid flowerbeds, clipped shrubs, and ancient cedar, yew, and pine trees.

⟩ MADONNA AND CHILD

This mosaic is reminiscent of the iconic style of the Orthodox Church. The Virgin Mary holds the child Jesus in her arms and both are attended by angels.

⋎ OUTDOOR SHRINE

Several images of the Virgin Mary adorn the gardens, such as this mosaic in honor of the Madonna of Divine Love, close to the external wall of St. John's Tower.

⟩ HELIPORT

The heliport, at the northern end of the gardens, was built in 1976 under Pope Paul VI (1963–78). The pope often uses helicopters when leaving Rome to minimize disruption on the city's roads.

ᴀ MADONNA OF GUADALUPE

This monumental sculpture, by A. Ponzanelli, commemorates the appearance of the Virgin Mary on a cloak to St. Juan Diego, a Mexican Indian, at Guadalupe, in 1531.

< FOUNTAIN OF THE FROGS
This simple fountain features four bronze frogs, one on each side, which spout water at an amphora in the center of the pond.

> STONE TABLET
This stone tablet marks the 1996 visit of Catholicos Karekin I of the Armenian Church to Pope John Paul II (1978–2005).

< ʌ ITALIAN GARDEN
Mature pine, cypress, and chestnut trees surround the centerpiece of the gardens—a pattern of boxwood hedges, typical of 16th-century Italian garden design. Among the trees are miniature palms, popularly known as "St. Peter's Palms," and at each end of the Italian Garden is a circular fountain.

< ʌ AT THE ROADSIDE
A number of roads, marked by stone signs, connect the different sections of the gardens. Numerous antique gas lamps—introduced in the latter half of the 19th century—illuminate the roads at night.

ᴠ LINKING STEPS
As the Vatican Hill rises steeply from St. Peter's, the gardens are staggered on different levels and linked by flights of steps.

⟩ GARDEN OF THE ARCHES

Located almost at the highest point of the Vatican gardens, and close to the Leonine Wall, this area comprises neatly trimmed lawns, box hedges, impressive jasmine arches, and rose trellises.

⟨ GARDEN GATEWAY

The wooded areas of the Vatican gardens—reached via an elegant gateway—are dotted with fountains and secluded benches. In contrast to the open formal gardens, this area offers cool, dappled shade.

∧ JASMINE ARCH

The Garden of the Arches is graced by decorative arches covered with sweet-smelling jasmine. This view through the arches shows one of the garden's two siren fountains, with the Leonine Wall visible beyond.

⟩ SIREN FOUNTAINS

Each siren statue is surrounded by a shallow pool. With heads raised and bodies arched, these mythical sea nymphs blow water into the air through seashells.

∧ IMPERIAL BUST

A bust of emperor Marcus Aurelius nestles in a copse of trees. In Rome, the practice of displaying statuary in gardens has been popular since imperial times.

⟨ MADONNA

Made during the pontificate of Pope John Paul II (1978–2005), this depiction of an apparition of the Virgin Mary is formed from baked, terracotta-glazed tiles.

◄ OVERGROWN FOUNTAIN
The spout of this fountain has been engulfed by moss. Water for supplying the fountains and irrigating the gardens is stored in an underground reservoir.

▼ CHERUB HEADS
These two cherubs once formed part of a monument to commemorate the First Vatican Council, which was held between 1869 and 1871.

▲ LITTLE TEMPLE OF OUR LADY
This small shrine was a gift from the Roman Catholics of Genoa to their fellow citizen, Pope Benedict XV (1914–22). The statue recalls a vision of the Madonna by a peasant.

▲ FOUNTAIN OF THE EAGLE
In 1612, Pope Paul V (1605–1621) commissioned Dutch sculptor Jan van Santen (1550–1621) to create this fountain. Above the pool is an eagle—part of the coat of arms of the pope's Borghese family.

◄ STATUE OF ST. PETER
This aerial view from the cupola of the basilica shows the statue of St. Peter that stands in front of the Fountain of the Eagle. The statue was originally designed for the Janiculum Hill, opposite the Vatican.

► URN AND CUPOLA
A decorative urn is framed by Michelangelo's towering dome, which stands majestically over St. Peter's tomb in the basilica.

A CONTRASTING VIEW
In the evening light, a modern bronze sculpture contrasts with the Casina of Pius IV in the mid-ground and Michaelangelo's magnificent cupola of St. Peter's Basilica beyond.

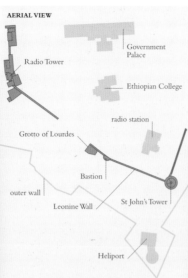

AERIAL VIEW

Radio Tower

Government Palace

Ethiopian College

radio station

Grotto of Lourdes

Bastion

outer wall

Leonine Wall

St John's Tower

Heliport

> ST. JOHN'S TOWER
One of the two surviving towers, St. John's Tower is seen here with a stretch of the Leonine Wall.

∨ SMALL DOOR
This is one of three doors into St. John's Tower, which today contains guest rooms for special visitors to the Vatican.

In 847, a year after a devastating Saracen attack on Rome (*see p.48*), Pope Leo IV (847–55) erected a defensive wall to protect the Vatican and St. Peter's tomb from further incursions. Much of the Leonine Wall, as it is now known, has since been demolished, but the surviving stretch gives an idea of how impressive the original construction must have been. This massive, high wall was built of concrete and rubble, and dressed with brick. The wall successfully warded off many attacks. During the turbulent late medieval period, though the popes still resided at the Lateran Palace, they would occasionally take refuge near St. Peter's during periods of civil unrest.

In the 15th century, the wall was strengthened by a number of circular defensive towers, only two of which have survived intact. One of the towers, which is dedicated to St. John, was a favorite retreat of Pope John XXIII (1958–63). Today, it provides lodgings for important visitors to the Vatican.

The second tower—home to the Vatican Observatory from 1919 until 1933—now houses part of Vatican Radio. Founded by the inventor Guglielmo Marconi (1874–1937), Vatican Radio was originally located in the nearby palazzina of Leo XIII. Today, the Radio Tower, as it is known, serves as the station's administrative center; radio programs are made in a building on Via della Conciliazione and transmitted from a site close to Lake Bracciano 25 miles (37 km) north of Rome.

The two towers are immensely thick and are capped by a set of windows from which soldiers had a sweeping view across the low-lying plains surrounding the River Tiber. Throughout the medieval period, such towers were constructed all over Rome by aristocratic families. Those at the Vatican are the best preserved examples of their kind.

The Leonine Wall became redundant when further walls— still surrounding the Vatican— were built in the 16th century.

∧ MAIN ENTRANCE
At the front of the tapering base is the main entrance to the tower. A third of the way up are two windows with small balconies.

> CREST OF POPE JOHN XXIII
Above the tower's main entrance is the insignia of Pope John XXIII, along with the Lion of St. Mark—the symbol of the city of Venice.

THE LEONINE WALL

DEFENDING THE CITY FROM ATTACK

WATCH TOWER
The upper section of the circular tower of St. John is entirely ringed by windows, giving a 365-degree view of the surrounding area.

LEONINE WALL
The huge bulk of the crenellated wall provided a superb defense against advancing enemies, allowing archers to attack while providing vital protection.

PASSAGEWAY THROUGH WALL
As can be seen from this low, tunnel-like passageway, the Leonine Wall was a truly formidable defensive barrier, more than 12 ft (3.5 m) thick and around 40 ft (12 m-) high.

SUMMER SHADE
Parts of the Leonine Wall are swathed in climbing plants, while the area immediately surrounding the wall is shaded by tall trees.

SEMICIRCULAR BASTION
The Leonine Wall was punctuated with bastions like this one. Slit-like windows allowed archers to fire on attackers as they approached the wall.

RADIO TOWER
The so-called "Radio Tower" has housed part of Vatican Radio since its inception in the 1930s. An antenna and satellite dishes stand incongruously astride the old tower.

GROTTO OF LOURDES
Near the bastion is a replica of the Grotto of Lourdes, where the Virgin Mary is said to have appeared to St. Bernadette.

BISHOP OF TARBES
This mosaic roundel depicts the Bishop of Tarbes, who, in 1902, presented the Grotto of Lourdes to Pope Leo XIII (1878–1903).

AERIAL VIEW

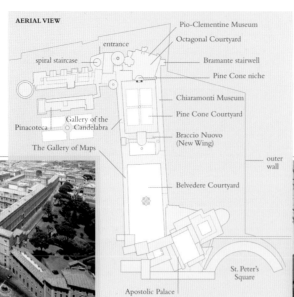

- entrance
- Pio-Clementine Museum
- Octagonal Courtyard
- spiral staircase
- Bramante stairwell
- Pine Cone niche
- Chiaramonti Museum
- Pine Cone Courtyard
- Gallery of the Candelabra
- Braccio Nuovo (New Wing)
- Pinacoteca
- The Gallery of Maps
- outer wall
- Belvedere Courtyard
- St. Peter's Square
- Apostolic Palace

Each day, thousands of people visit the Vatican Museums, designated by UNESCO as the most important museum complex in the world. In 1506, Pope Julius II (1503–13) bought a recently discovered statue of the Trojan priest, Laocoon, which had lain buried under the garden of the Roman emperor, Titus, for 1,000 years. Placed in the Octagonal Courtyard of the Apostolic Palace, it had a great influence on the artists of the Renaissance. People flocked to see the statue, as well as other works of art in the care of the popes.

Successive pontiffs enriched the Vatican's collections, building special galleries to house the artifacts. Shortly after the discovery of Pompeii in the mid-18th century, Clement XIV (1769–74) and Pius VI (1775–99) built galleries to house items recovered from archaeological digs in Rome and in the Papal States. Pope Gregory XVI (1831–46) built other galleries to display objects unearthed in excavations in Egypt, Tuscany, and Umbria.

The first painting collection was established in 1790 by Pope Pius VI to house 118 of the Vatican's most precious works. A proper art gallery, where the public could view the paintings, was only founded in 1817 after the fall of Napoleon and the return of works removed from the Vatican by French troops. Only in 1932 did the collection find a permanent home in the Painting Gallery, or Pinacoteca Vaticana, a dedicated building designed by the architect Luca Beltrami (1854–1933) for Pope Pius XI (1922–39).

The importance of the Vatican Museums goes beyond the artifacts they house: the buildings themselves are masterpieces of Renaissance art. Today, parts of the Apostolic Palace have been given over to the public, including the Sistine Chapel, the Borgia apartments, and the Raphael Rooms (the apartments of Julius II). Space is limited, but the museums continue to extend their opening hours to give all visitors to the Vatican a chance to appreciate its treasures in incomparable settings.

∨ WALLS OF VATICAN CITY
The museums lie within the walls of Vatican City. Every day, long lines of visitors can be seen snaking round the base of the walls.

⟩ DOOR OF BENEDICT XVI
This bronze door by Italian sculptor Gino Gianetti was inaugurated by Pope Benedict XVI in 2005.

∨ CREST OF POPE PAUL III
After the sack of Rome in 1527, Pope Paul III (1534–49) raised defensive walls to protect St. Peter's Tomb. His crest adorns this corner of the walls.

∧ JUBILEE DOOR OF 2000
The bronze door by the Italian artist Cecco Bonanotte (b.1942) consists of 208 panels. At the top are the arms of Pope John Paul II (1978–2005).

⟩ PRINCIPAL ENTRANCE
The staff entrance to the museums was opened during the pontificate of Pius XI, whose coat of arms surmounts the stone door lintel.

VATICAN MUSEUMS
A 500-YEAR-OLD COLLECTION OF ART

< PINE CONE COURTYARD
The bronze pine cone in this courtyard was once part of a 1st- or 2nd-century Roman fountain.

˅ ARMS OF PIUS XI
High on a wall are the arms of Pius XI (1922–39), who was instrumental in the modernization of the Vatican Museums.

< PINACOTECA VATICANA
Pius XI built this gallery to house 249 oil paintings returned to the Vatican after the Napoleonic era.

˅ PINACOTECA GATEWAY
The art gallery was built in the Square Garden, set apart and surrounded by avenues to ensure excellent lighting.

< PAPAL INSIGNIA
Pope Gregory XVI (1831–46) was founder of the Gregorian Egyptian and Gregorian Etruscan galleries. His coat of arms is carved in relief on this fountain in the Square Garden.

< MARBLE BUST
Statues from antiquity provide a Classical atmosphere to the museums' surroundings.

˄ COURTYARD NICHE
The Pine Cone Courtyard was largely the work of Bramante (1444–1514), but the niche was by Pirro Ligorio (1510–83).

‹ SKYLIGHT

An octagonal window of blue and gray glass illuminates the spiral stairwell (*below*) by Giuseppe Momo (1875–1940). The staircase ascends from the atrium of the main entrance.

⌄ SPIRAL STAIRCASE

Momo's bronze spiral staircase, designed in 1932, has two intertwined flights of steps, one for ascending and the other for descending.

⌃ OCTAGONAL COURTYARD

The courtyard was built in 1772–73 by Michelangelo Simonetti (1724–81) on the site of the Antiquarium, where Julius II (1503–13) had once housed the nucleus of the Vatican's collection.

› CORRIDOR IN CHIARAMONTI WING

Set into the northern wing of the Belvedere Courtyard is this corridor containing ancient Roman statuary. The corridor was designed by the sculptor Canova (1757–1822) for Pope Pius VII (1800–23)

◁ BRAMANTE'S STAIRWELL
The wide spiral stairwell was designed by Bramante for Julius II. Its especially high dimensions enabled the pope to ride his horse to the top of the tower without dismounting.

◮ GALLERY OF THE STATUES
The hallway in the Pio-Clementine Museum was designed by Alessandro Dori (1702–72) in order to house a number of important free-standing statues from Classical antiquity.

ᵛ GALLERY OF THE CANDELABRA

Once a *loggia* (open-sided corridor) built by Pope Clement XIII (1758–69), this gallery of Greek and Roman sculpture has a fine view of the Vatican gardens.

˃ BRACCIO NUOVO

Set amidst Roman statues in the Braccio Nuovo (New Wing), this 1st-century marble personification of the Egyptian river god was first displayed in the museums in 1513.

ᴬ SIMONETTI STAIRWAY

Built in the 1780s, the stairs were part of the conversion of the Belvedere Palace into the Pio-Clementine Museum.

ᴧ NEW WING
The Neo-Classical theme of architecture was
continued in the Braccio Nuovo by Raffaele
Stern (1784–1820). The floor here contains
pieces of mosaic floors from Roman buildings.

< ROOM AT THE GREEK CROSS
The centerpiece of this room in the Pio-
Clementine Museum are the two huge stone
coffins of the emperor Constantine's mother and
daughter, moved here in the 18th century.

ᴧ THE GALLERY OF MAPS
This gallery takes its name from the 40 maps frescoed on the
walls which represent the Italian regions and the papal properties
at the time of Pope Gregory XIII (1572-1585). The maps form
an important record of 16th-century history and cartography.

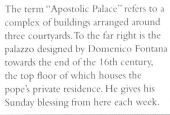

> APOSTOLIC PALACE
The term "Apostolic Palace" refers to a complex of buildings arranged around three courtyards. To the far right is the palazzo designed by Domenico Fontana towards the end of the 16th century, the top floor of which houses the pope's private residence. He gives his Sunday blessing from here each week.

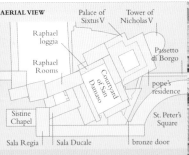

AERIAL VIEW — Palace of Sixtus V — Tower of Nicholas V
Raphael loggia
Raphael Rooms
Courtyard of San Damaso
Passetto di Borgo
pope's residence
Sistine Chapel
St. Peter's Square
Sala Regia — Sala Ducale — bronze door

The Apostolic Palace, northeast of St. Peter's, is a complex of buildings constructed largely between the 13th and 16th centuries. In the 4th century, emperor Constantine I gave the Lateran Palace to the papacy, and it became the principal residence of the popes. The palace was enlarged by Pope Innocent III (1198–1216), and the turbulence of the Middle Ages prompted other popes to continue expanding and fortifying it. Innocent IV (1243–54) added a new wing, which was further enlarged by Nicholas III (1277–80), who also included an enclosed garden, the Belvedere.

The Lateran's days as the official papal dwelling ended in 1307, when the papacy moved to Avignon in southern France. For 70 years, the Lateran was deserted, and much of it was destroyed in a fire. With the restoration of the papacy to Rome, Pope Martin V (1417–31) decided to return to the Vatican.

Nicholas V (1447–55) laid the foundations of a new palace. In the succeeding decades, this Apostolic Palace was decorated by the great artists of the Renaissance. In the last year of his reign, Sixtus V (1585–90) commissioned Domenico Fontana (1543–1607) to undertake the last major remodeling of the Apostolic Palace complex.

Because the Vatican was located in a low-lying area close to the Tiber that was humid and prone to malaria, Pope Gregory XIII (1572–85) built a new palace on the Quirinal Hill. Pope Clement VIII (1592–1605) made the Quirinal Palace the usual residence of the popes, and it remained so until 1870, when Pope Pius IX (1846–78) was obliged to vacate it in favor of the Apostolic Palace at the Vatican. This move was intended to be temporary, but the popes never returned to the Quirinal, which is now the residence of the president of the Italian Republic.

Today, the Apostolic Palace is occupied by the Secretariat of State and other offices. The pope resides in the Papal Apartments on the third floor of the Palace.

∧ ∨ COURTYARD ENTRANCE
The Courtyard of San Damaso was begun by Bramante (1444–1514) and finished by Raphael (1483–1520). It is closed on three sides by a *loggia*.

> BRONZE DOOR
The Bronze Door from the colonnade of St. Peter's into the palace is 25 ft (7.6 m) high and weighs 6 tons. It was designed by Bernini (1598–1680).

APOSTOLIC PALACE
OFFICIAL RESIDENCE OF THE POPE

< ʌ SCALA REGIA
This royal staircase was designed by Bernini between 1663 and 1666 to connect the Apostolic Palace to St. Peter's. On the left is Bernini's statue of Constantine I.

IN 1508, POPE JULIUS II (1503–13) COMMISSIONED A YOUNG UMBRIAN, RAPHAEL DA URBINO (1483–1520), TO DECORATE HIS APARTMENTS. WORK ON THE FOUR ROOMS (THE ROOM OF THE SEGNATURA IS SHOWN HERE), OCCUPIED THE REST OF RAPHAEL'S LIFE. THE FRESCOES COMBINE CHRISTIAN THEMES WITH MYTHOLOGICAL AND HISTORICAL EPISODES FROM ANTIQUITY. THE EARLY PART OF JULIUS'S REIGN HAD BEEN TURBULENT, AS HE TRIED TO BRING ORDER TO THE PAPAL STATES, AND THE FRESCOES CELEBRATE THE PAPACY'S TRIUMPH OVER ITS ADVERSARIES.

⋀ ROOM OF THE SEGNATURA
This room housed the library of Pope Julius II. In the corner is a depiction of Adam and Eve, while over the window are representations of the Four Cardinal Virtues (female figures) and the Theological Virtues (putti).

➤ DISPUTE OVER THE BLESSED SACRAMENT
Theologians on Earth debate the Church's teaching; above, in heaven, Christ is flanked by the saints, overseen by God the Father.

RAPHAEL ROOMS
APARTMENTS OF JULIUS II

< PARNASSUS
The central figure of Apollo is shown playing a stringed instrument. To his left are Homer (wearing a laurel crown) and Dante (in profile).

∨ > SCHOOL OF ATHENS
At the center of this meeting of philosophers (*below*) Plato (with the features of Leonardo da Vinci) points to the ethereal world of ideas, while Aristotle points to empirical proof on Earth. The detail (*right*) shows Parmenides, who introduced the idea of reasoned proof to philosophy.

< ∧ SEGNATURA ROOM CEILING
The medallions around the papal crest depict Theology, Justice, Philosophy, and Poetry; the rectangles depict Adam and Eve, Solomon, Astronomy, and Apollo and Marsyas.

> VIEW TO WINDOW
The muted hues of the ornate mosaic floor contrast with the vividly colored frescoes. The sepia-colored panels were painted in the 16th century to replace wooden cabinets.

POPE NICHOLAS V (1447–55), A KEEN PATRON OF THE ARTS, SUMMONED THE DOMINICAN FRIAR, FRA ANGELICO (1395–1455), FROM FLORENCE TO DECORATE HIS CHAPEL BETWEEN 1447–49. THE RESULT WAS A SERIES OF FRESCOES ILLUSTRATING THE LIVES OF ST. STEPHEN, THE FIRST CHRISTIAN MARTYR, AND ST. LAWRENCE, A 3RD-CENTURY DEACON OF ROME, ALONG WITH DEPICTIONS OF THE FOUR EVANGELISTS. THE FRESCOES ARE NOTABLE FOR THEIR USE OF PERSPECTIVE, WHICH HAD BEEN LOST FOR CENTURIES BEFORE BEING REDISCOVERED DURING THE RENAISSANCE PERIOD.

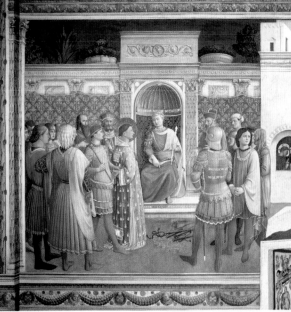

ʌ LAWRENCE ON TRIAL

Here, the deacon Lawrence is summoned by the Prefect of Rome to answer charges that he is a Christian. Emperor Valerian had initiated a persecution of the Church, during which Pope Sixtus II (257–58) was executed.

‹ ENTRANCE TO THE CHAPEL

The walls of the tiny chapel are covered with frescoes depicting the lives of the martyrs St. Lawrence and St. Stephen. In the panel above the left door, Pope Sixtus II entrusts St. Lawrence with alms for the poor.

› SIDE WALL AND ALTAR

Fra Angelico used vivid colors to brighten the chapel. He also dressed the people he painted in contemporary clothing. The images provide an important source of information on 15th-century styles.

CHAPEL OF NICHOLAS V

FRA ANGELICO'S MASTERPIECE

▼ MARTYRDOM OF LAWRENCE

Tradition holds that Lawrence was martyred by being roasted to death on a gridiron on August 10, 258; Catholics celebrate this day as a feast.

▲ THE MARTYRDOM OF ST. STEPHEN

The deacon Stephen, dressed in blue and yellow, is led out through the walls of Jerusalem, where he is stoned to death. As he dies, Stephen kneels and prays for those who are killing him.

◄ WINDOW TO CHAPEL

This small, wooden-shuttered window opens into an adjacent room. Via this window, people could participate in the Mass as it was celebrated by the pope. The window frame is frescoed, and the panel beneath is painted to imitate marble slabs.

> EVANGELIST'S CEILING

The ceiling is divided into four quarters, each devoted to one of the Evangelists—the authors of the Gospel accounts in the New Testament—Matthew, Mark, Luke, and John.

∨ SYMBOLIC CREATURES

The Evangelists are depicted with their traditional symbols: Luke with an ox; Mark with a lion; John with an eagle; and Matthew with an angel/human.

< > WINDOWS

Frescoes bearing rose shapes and busts of the saints encircle the windows. The glass disks are original, dating from the chapel's construction in the 15th century.

∨ VIEW FROM THE ALTAR

The left-hand panel shows the ordination of St. Lawrence by Sixtus II. Under the persecution of Valerian, Lawrence was given three days to collect the Church's treasure and hand it over. According to legend, he gestured to the poor, saying: "Here is our treasure."

< PAVEMENT

The slabs of the incised pavement are carved with diamond-shaped designs. The corner roundels bear the pontiff's name in Latin: *Nicolaus PP Quintus*.

> CURTAIN PANEL

It was common practice to hang tapestries in chapels. Here, painted "curtains" adorn the lower parts of the walls. In the center can be seen the papal tiara and keys.

🕇 131

THE SALA DUCALE IS A LARGE, RECTANGULAR ROOM IN THE APOSTOLIC PALACE, WHERE THE RENAISSANCE POPES RECEIVED PRINCES AND IMPORTANT VISITORS. ITS DESIGN WAS ENTRUSTED BY POPE PAUL III (1534–49) TO THE ARCHITECT ANTONIO DA SANGALLO THE YOUNGER (1484–1546). THE FRESCOES EXECUTED BY RAFFAELLINO DA REGGIO (1550–78), LORENZINO DA BOLOGNA (1530–77), AND MATTHEUS BRILL (1550–83), RECALL THOSE OF ANCIENT ROME. THE ELABORATE MARBLE FLOOR, INSPIRED BY ANCIENT ROMAN DESIGNS, MIRRORS THE TONES OF THE FRESCOES.

⋏ MYTHOLOGICAL SCENE ON CEILING
A ceiling fresco depicts Hercules slaying the giant Cacus for stealing his cattle. Cacus was a fire-breathing monster that lived in a cave on the Palatine Hill, the future site of Rome.

⋏ PAPAL COAT OF ARMS
The coat of arms of Pope Benedict XV (1914–22) is surrounded by a Renaissance-style border, with scallop shells, which harmonizes with the overall decoration of the room.

⋗ VIEW TOWARD BERNINI'S CANOPY
Sangallo intended the Sala Ducale to impress, but before Bernini (1598–1680) enlarged the room by removing a dividing wall (where the decorative canopy is now), the rear portion was very dark.

SALA DUCALE

RECEPTION HALL OF THE RENAISSANCE POPES

At the center of the elaborate ceiling, nestled in garlands of fruit and vegetables, is the coat of arms of Pope Paul IV (1555–59), who continued the program of decoration initiated by his predecessor, Paul III (1534–49).

ʌ CLASSICAL REFERENCES
With their references to ancient Greece and Rome, the designs of the Sala Ducale's ceiling were highly regarded by those who marveled at the ruins of Roman villas that were being unearthed throughout the city at the time.

ʌ THE FOUR SEASONS
These four rural scenes, one in each corner of the room, depict the seasons of the year. They were painted by Mattheus Brill (1550–83).

ʌ ANTIQUE COLORS
The ocher and red colors used in the frescoes were very popular in antiquity, especially in Rome. Their hues reflect those of the marble floor.

> CANOPY MOTIFS
The Renaissance artists who decorated the Sala Ducale employed canopy motifs and other classically influenced elements in tribute to the art of the ancient world.

A STUCCO CANOPY
Between 1656 and 1657, Bernini demolished a
dividing wall to enlarge the Sala Ducale. His
huge canopy, with putti, and stucco drapes,
disguises where the two rooms meet obliquely.

THE SALA REGIA (REGAL ROOM), COMPLETED IN 1573, WAS DESIGNED BY ANTONIO SANGALLO THE
YOUNGER (1484–1546) FOR POPE PAUL III (1534–49). ITS WALLS ARE DECORATED WITH FRESCOES SHOWING
MOMENTOUS EVENTS IN PAPAL HISTORY. THESE SCENES EMPHASIZE THE IMPORTANCE OF THE PAPACY'S
TEMPORAL (EARTHLY) POWER. THE ARTISTS GIORGIO VASARI (1511–74), TADDEO ZUCCARI (1529–66), AND
FEDERICO ZUCCARI (1540–1609) WERE RESPONSIBLE FOR MUCH OF THIS WORK. THE PAULINE AND SISTINE
CHAPELS OPEN OFF THE ROOM, AS DOES THE SCALA REGIA —THE ROYAL STAIRCASE TO ST. PETER'S BASILICA

< VIEW ALONG ROOM
The barrel vault is decorated
with magnificent plaster
decorations. Impressive
frescoes line the walls.

∨ BATTLE OF LEPANTO
This naval battle was fought
between Christian and
Muslim fleets off the Greek
coast on October 7, 1571.

∧ PAULINE DOOR FRESCOES
To the left of the chapel door is
the capture of Tunisia; to the right,
Henry IV of Germany submits to
Pope Gregory VII in 1077.

SALA REGIA
SUMPTUOUS STATEMENT OF PAPAL POWER

∨ RECONCILIATION OF POPE AND EMPEROR
This fresco depicts the reconciliation of Pope Alexander III and Frederick Barbarossa, the Holy Roman Emperor, at Venice in 1177, after a dispute over the emperor's interference in papal affairs.

∧ RECLINING NUDES
Large stucco figures recline on the top of the pediments of the great frames that outline the frescoes; these and the other ornaments were created by Daniele da Volterra in the 1540s. The details of the stucco work on the frames is picked out in gold leaf.

∨ PRE-BATTLE SCENE
With the pope's support, the Christian fleet and its fighting troops triumphed against their Muslim opponents at the Battle of Lepanto. Here, shown with symmetrical perspective, the warships line up before the battle. On the left, is a female representation of the papacy, on the right, the skeleton of Death.

∧ ASSASSINATION ATTEMPT
The attempt on the life of Gaspar de Coligny, the Huguenot (French Protestant) leader, sparked off the St. Bartholomew's Day Massacre in August 1572.

∧ ELECTORS
The electors of the empire visit Rome for a papal blessing and to pledge their loyalty.

∧ MASSACRE SCENE
The St. Bartholomew's Day Massacre saw the slaughter of French Protestants by Catholics.

KEY TO THE WALL FRESCOES

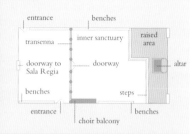

| 12 | 11 | 10 | 9 | 8 | 7 | 13 | 1 | 2 | 3 | 4 | 5 | 6 |

1. Baptism of Christ in the Jordan
2. Temptations of Christ
3. Calling of St. Peter and St. Andrew
4. Sermon on the Mount
5. Handing over the Keys to St. Peter
6. Last Supper
7. Moses's Journey into Egypt
8. Moses Receiving the Call
9. Crossing of the Red Sea
10. Adoration of the Golden Calf
11. Punishment of the Rebels
12. Last Days of Moses
13. The Last Judgement

PLAN VIEW

entrance

benches

transenna

inner sanctuary

raised area

doorway to Sala Regia

doorway

altar

benches

steps

entrance

benches

choir balcony

> **THE LAST JUDGEMENT**
At the center of the fresco, angels sound trumpets to summon the dead. Saints appear above Christ, carrying his cross and the pillar on which he was scourged.

> **CHRIST APPEARS**
Christ appears on the last day of the world as the judge of the living and of the dead. He raises his arm to summon humanity for punishment or heavenly reward. The Virgin Mary is seated on his right-hand side.

⌄ **THE MOUTH OF HELL**
Behind the High Altar and crucifix is a dramatic depiction of the entrance to Hell. As graves are opened to release the dead (*on the left*), the condemned sink down to eternal damnation. The High Altar, made of polychrome marble, is still used today.

The Sistine Chapel, in the Apostolic Palace, is famous as the site of the Papal Conclave, at which a new pope is elected. It was built in 1477 by Pope Sixtus IV (1471–84) to replace the original medieval Palatine Chapel, and was dedicated to Our Lady of the Assumption. The proportions of the Sistine Chapel correspond to those of the Temple in Jerusalem, destroyed by the Romans in 70 AD.

In 1481, Sixtus IV entrusted the work of decorating the walls of the chapel to a group of Umbrian artists, probably under the charge of Perugino (1446–1524). In addition to a series of niches between the twelve windows, with depictions of the early popes, two parallel fresco cycles were composed, one illustrating the life of Moses, and the other the life of Christ. The panels of these cycles were painted by Pinturicchio (1454–1513), Botticelli (1445–1510), Signorelli (1445–1523), and Ghirlandaio (1449–94). As well as serving a religious purpose, these fresco cycles underscored the theme of papal supremacy, which at the time was under attack from reformers.

In 1508, Pope Julius II (1443–1513) commissioned Michelangelo (1465–1574) to paint the vault of the chapel. His *Creation* consists of nine scenes from the Book of Genesis, the best known being that in which the divine spark gives life to Adam.

In 1535, Michelangelo was summoned by Pope Paul III (1468–1549) to decorate the wall above the High Altar. Two windows had to be filled in, and existing frescoes destroyed. Instructed to paint the Last Judgement, Michelangelo gave the work a clockwise motion, with the figures of the just rising up to reward, while the figures of the evil fall toward damnation. At the center is the powerful figure of Jesus as Judge, with Mary beseeching on behalf of humanity beneath his raised arm. The work, which took seven years to complete, evoked a storm of criticism at its unveiling, its nudity being considered unsuitable for such a sacred place.

> **MARBLE FLOOR PATTERN**
With contrasting shapes, the floor complements in a subdued manner the explosion of color on the walls. There are different floor patterns in the sanctuary and main body of the chapel, to separate the two areas and emphasize their different functions.

SISTINE CHAPEL

SITE OF THE PAPAL CONCLAVE

∨ MICHELANGELO'S CREATION

Starting in May 1508, Michelangelo spent four years on a scaffold as he decorated the ceiling. His famous *Creation* scenes replaced the original blue ceiling decorated with stars.

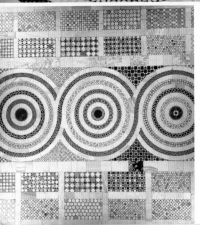

∧ COSMATESQUE DESIGN

Since the 12th century, Italian artists had excelled in intricate "cosmatesque" pavements, which were made using small pieces of marble salvaged from ruined Classical buildings.

KEY TO CEILING PANELS

A SISTINE CHAPEL CEILING
Michelangelo's masterpiece is among the most famous
works of Western art ever created. The main panels chart the
Creation of the World, and these are surrounded by subjects
from the Old and New Testament. The ceiling was returned
to its original vibrancy in 1994 following a 12-year restoration
project which revealed details not seen for centuries.

⋁ ⋗ WALL AND LAST JUDGEMENT

The brooding figure of the Biblical prophet Jeremiah dwarfs the window arches depicting the ancestors of Christ. The black patch in the right-hand corner was left by restorers in the 1990's, so that visitors can see how dark the frescoes were before they were restored. To the right is the wall behind the High Altar, which is adorned by the *Last Judgement* fresco, painted by Michelangelo (1465–1574).

⋏ FULL VIEW OF SIDE WALL

The bottom panels of this wall are painted with fictive (mock) curtains, above which stands the cycle of panels depicting the life of Moses. In between the window arches are representations of the early popes. Michelangelo's paintings begin in the upper arches.

⋏ CIRCUMCISION OF THE SON OF MOSES

Pinturrichio and Perugino worked on this panel from the life of Moses cycle. Moses, clad in green and yellow, appears several times in this one panel, which depicts a number of the key episodes in his life.

⋖ CHOIR BALCONY

The small *loggia*, or columned room, holds eight choristers. It has a coffered ceiling (made up of sunken panels), and a decorated balustrade balcony, which projects out into the chapel. In the center of the *loggia* is the music stand.

< THE LIBYAN SIBYL
The Sibyls were pagan seers whom some Christians believed prophesied the coming of Christ. Like most female figures Michelangelo painted, the beautiful Libyan Sibyl was probably modeled on a man.

∨ BAPTISM OF CHRIST AT THE JORDAN
Pinturicchio assisted Perugino with this fresco. Above Jesus, God the Father appears in a roundel supported by angels. Well-known contemporary figures appear in the crowd of onlookers.

∧ DANIEL
Michelangelo's Mannerist style distorts the figures portrayed on the ceiling. In this depiction of Daniel, a putti supports a book, while the Biblical prophet writes. A rolled up manuscript is tucked into the desk.

< ∧ TRANSENNA
A *transenna*, or barrier, with marble panels, a gilt wooden grille, and eight candles separates the inner sanctuary from the public. The oak doors date from the mid-17th century under Pope Innocent X (1644–55).

∨ CREST ON TRANSENNA PANEL
Two putti support a garland of acorns. In the center is an oak tree, the family symbol of Pope Sixtus IV (1471–84) and his nephew, Pope Julius II (1503–13), under whom much of the chapel's decoration was carried out.

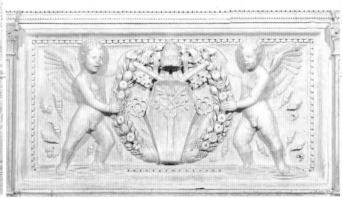

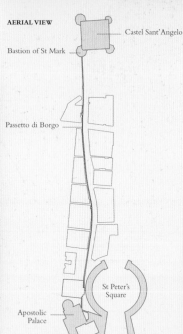

AERIAL VIEW

Castel Sant'Angelo

Bastion of St Mark

Passetto di Borgo

St Peter's Square

Apostolic Palace

> MOAT CROSSING
Close to the moat surrounding Castel Sant'Angelo, the tunnel opens to become a bridge, which was built by Antonio da Sangallo the Younger in the 16th century.

Medieval Rome was a shadow of the city that once lay at the heart of a great empire. Cows and sheep grazed in the ruined buildings. Beggars and vagabonds accosted the pilgrims who visited the shrines and churches. Aristocratic families feuded with each other for control of the city, while several dynasties fought for the papacy—a position as lucrative as it was prestigious.

During his reign, Pope Nicholas III (1277–80) of the Orsini family built a raised tunnel, or *passetto*, to link the Vatican with the fortress of Castel Sant'Angelo, originally the mausoleum of the 2nd-century AD emperor, Hadrian. The mausoleum had played an important part in the defence of Rome since 403, when Emperor Honorious incorporated it into a set of city walls. Several Roman families had occupied the mausoleum and when Nicholas was elected pope, the fortress was in the hands of his family. He therefore judged it prudent to maintain the family property, since it offered a secure haven in times of unrest.

Pope Nicholas's tunnel was in part raised on the foundations of an earlier defensive wall, built in the mid-6th century by the Ostrogoth king, Totila, who had conquered much of central and southern Italy during the Gothic War. The tunnel's slightly bow shape was determined by the pre-existing wall, while the materials, mostly rubble and tiles, were reclaimed from earlier buildings. For most of its length—some 2,600 ft (800 m)—the tunnel is covered, giving users shelter from the elements, and lit by windows of varying sizes.

In 1527, German troops under the flag of the emperor Charles V laid siege to Rome. Pope Clement VII (1523–34) escaped along the tunnel to the fortress, as soldiers shot at the fleeing pontiff.

In the 16th century, Antonio da Sangallo the Younger (1484–1546) was commissioned to provide military defences, which were later amplified by Francesco Laparelli (1521–70). By the late 17th century, the tunnel had fallen into disuse.

⋀ > BASTION OF ST. MARK
The tunnel enters the fortress of Castel Sant'Angelo at the Bastion of St. Mark, one of four bastions constructed between the pontificates of Nicholas V (1447–55) and Urban VIII (1623–44).

PASSETTO DI BORGO
TUNNEL TO A SAFE HAVEN

< ROOFTOP

The crenellated roof of the tunnel allowed soldiers to take refuge while resisting attack from below.

> ARCHES

A number of archways were cut into the *passetto* to allow easy access to the warren of streets in the surrounding Roman districts of Saint Pius and Borgo.

ᐯ COAT OF ARMS

The coat of arms of Pope Pius IV (1559–65) stands over an archway to the Borgo district.

ᐯ FOUNDATION SUPPORT

The 13th-century *passetto* of Pope Nicholas III was raised on the foundations of a 6th-century wall.

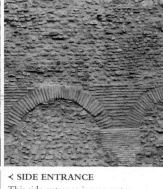

< SIDE ENTRANCE

This side entrance incorporates parts of the 6th-century wall and the medieval wall. Below the square window is the coat of arms of Pope Alexander VI (1492–1503).

ᐱ WALL SHRINE

Many walls in Italy are decorated with simple shrines of the saints. This devotional station depicts Mary, the Mother of Sorrows, and is set into the wall of the *passetto*.

ᐱ HANGMAN'S HOUSE

The Hangman's House is unique, since it has no front door. For his own safety, the city's executioner could only access his home from the upper level of the Passetto di Borgo.

ᐯ VATICAN LINK

With the colonnade to the left, the *passetto* arrives at the Vatican beneath the Apostolic Palace. The battlements were added during the pontificate of Pope Urban VIII.

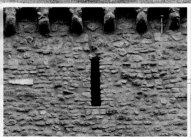

ᐱ > TUNNEL WINDOWS

The small windows in the upper level of the enclosed tunnel allow light in and provide ventilation. The size of the windows made access by anyone scaling the walls impossible.

AERIAL VIEW

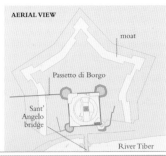

moat

Passetto di Borgo

Sant' Angelo bridge

River Tiber

DETAIL

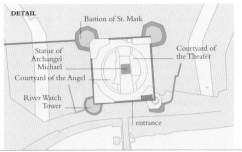

Bastion of St. Mark

Statue of Archangel Michael

Courtyard of the Angel

River Watch Tower

Courtyard of the Theater

entrance

> **BRONZE ANGEL**
Atop the fortress is a statue of Archangel Michael designed by Flemish sculptor Peter Anton von Verschaffelt (1710–93) and cast in 1753 by Francesco Giardoni (1692–1757).

CROSS-SECTION VIEW

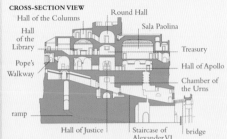

Hall of the Columns

Hall of the Library

Pope's Walkway

ramp

Round Hall

Sala Paolina

Treasury

Hall of Apollo

Chamber of the Urns

Hall of Justice

Staircase of Alexander VI

bridge

> **PASSETTO DI BORGO**
The *passetto* (passage) leading from the Vatican enters the fortress at the Bastion of St. Mark, one of four watchtowers built by Antonio da Sangallo under Pope Alexander VI.

ˇ **BASTION OF ST. MARK**
The octagonal defensive tower was ringed with projecting galleries for dropping rocks and hot liquids on attackers, and holes through which cannon could fire.

Between 123 and 138 Emperor Hadrian built a large mausoleum for himself and his family on the banks of the River Tiber. In 403, Emperor Honorius incorporated it into the city's defenses.

According to medieval legend, Pope Gregory the Great (590–604) ordered a procession to pray for the end of a plague in Rome. The story goes that Pope Gregory then had a vision of Archangel Michael over Hadrian's mausoleum, In the vision, Michael sheathed his sword as a sign that the plague was at an end.

In the 13th century, the mausoleum was transformed into a papal fortress. Pope Nicholas V (1447–55) considered moving the papal court to the monument and initiated a set of defensive ramparts. Pope Alexander VI (1492–1503) commissioned Antonio da Sangallo the Elder (1455–1535) to build further defenses. Between 1492 and 1495, Alexander also added a set of sumptuous apartments for his family, which were decorated by the artist Pinturicchio (1454–1513).

Nothing remains of Alexander's residence; it was demolished under Pope Urban VIII (1623–44) in 1628 to make way for more fortifications. Pope Julius II (1503–13) spent the first year of his pontificate at the castle, while Pope Leo X (1513–21) kept political prisoners in the dungeons of Castel Sant'Angelo.

On May 6, 1527, Rome was sacked and pillaged by the troops of Charles V, the Holy Roman Emperor. The reigning pope, Clement VII (1523–34), took refuge in the fortress, but after a month-long siege, the castle fell and Pope Clement was held prisoner there for six months.

The next pope, Pope Paul III (1534–49), ordered a refurbishment of the papal apartments. He also installed the papal treasury and archives in the central drum of the mausoleum—possibly on the site of Hadrian's original burial chamber. For the following three centuries, however, Castel Sant'Angelo was used chiefly as a prison. Today, the castle is a prized museum.

CASTEL SANT'ANGELO
FORTRESS OF THE POPES

∨ PAPAL LOGGIA
The upper *loggia* (columned walkway) of the apartments of Pope Paul III (1534–49) looks out over the Tiber River. The papal crest was effaced following Italian Unification in 1870.

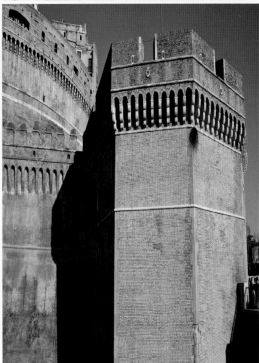

∧ HIGH-LEVEL RESIDENCE
In antiquity, a statue of a chariot and horses crowned the mausoleum. During the Renaissance, a papal residence was built on the summit.

< RIVER WATCHTOWER
From this 16th-century tower, sentries would keep watch for ships sailing up the River Tiber from the Port of Ostia.

∧ VIEW FROM MOAT
Seen from the moat, which was often flooded by the nearby Tiber, the sheer scale of the mausoleum becomes evident. Both Pope Alexander VI and Clement VII were obliged to take refuge in Castel Sant'Angelo.

∧ THE CASTLE AND ITS ANGELS
In addition to the statue of St. Michael that
crowns the castle, there are a further ten angels,
designed by Bernini in the 17th century, that
flank the bridge leading to Castel Sant'Angelo.

149

> VIEW OF RAMPARTS

The ramparts were built onto the bare walls of the mausoleum, which can just be seen to the extreme right. The ramparts ran around the entire building, ensuring comprehensive surveillance.

< RAMP THROUGH MAUSOLEUM

This circular ramp rises up through the interior of Hadrian's mausoleum into the chamber where the ashes of the emperor and his family were interred.

⌄ COURTYARD OF THE ANGEL

Despite restrictions of space, Renaissance architects managed to construct an adequate apartment for the pontiffs, which included this open, yet secure, courtyard.

⋀ DECORATED GLOBE

The globe beside the courtyard stairway is decorated with carved bees, the emblem of the Barberini family, in honor of Urban VIII, who carried out renovations in the 17th century.

⋀ MARBLE ANGEL WITH COPPER WINGS

The Courtyard of the Angel is named after this statue of Archangel Michael—dressed as a Roman soldier with a Hellenistic face—created in 1544 by the sculptor Raffaello da Montelupo (1504–66).

> FLEUR-DE-LYS ARCH

This arch over a stairway from the Courtyard of the Angel to the upper terraces bears the fleur-de-lys, the family emblem of Pope Paul III, who carried out renovations in 1542–49.

∨ CATAPULT DEFENSE
In the medieval period, catapults, firing stone missiles and torches doused in oil, were used to protect the castle. The apparatus is not unlike that used by the Roman army in antiquity.

∧ FRESCOES OF THE GODS
Now faded, or damaged with time, frescoes of Classical gods adorn the walls of the Courtyard of the Theater.

∧ COURTYARD OF THE THEATER
This semicircular courtyard was laid out in the early 16th century. It is thought that plays were performed here in the reign of Leo X (1513–21).

< ARTILLERY
Cannons have been used in Europe since at least the 13th century. The ones in the Courtyard of the Theater are a stark reminder of the building's military purpose.

∧ STAIRCASE TO TOMB
Known as the Staircase of Alexander VI, this stairway leads to the Chamber of the Urns, which housed the ashes of Hadrian's family. The walls and ceiling were once covered with marble, but this was stripped off in medieval times.

⟩ POPE'S WALKWAY
The uppermost level of the castle was created in the mid-16th century for Pope Paul III (1534–49). This arched walkway offered impressive views over Rome and of the River Tiber below.

⋎ DEFACED CREST

The papal crest on the ceiling of the pope's walkway (*see facing page*) was obliterated by 19th-century nationalists, who were glad to see the end of the Papal States.

⋗ SALA PAOLINA

The impressive frescoes in the Sala Paolina recall the military glory of ancient Rome, with which the Renaissance papacy felt great affinity.

⋏ TREASURY ROOM

This specially constructed strongroom deep in the heart of the fortress was built for Pope Paul III. Its four iron-clad chests, which were always kept under lock and key, contained money and precious vessels.

⋖ DOOR WITHIN A DOOR

This studded oak door opens into the soldiers' quarters and one-time barracks. The defensive doorway had a smaller door in the center, for use when individuals needed to pass through.

⋏ CLASSICAL INFLUENCE

The ceiling of this large room decorated for Pope Paul III is covered with stucco work and frescoes that hark back to the Classical age. Renaissance artists often copied designs and techniques used 1,500 years earlier in ancient Rome.

PLAN VIEW

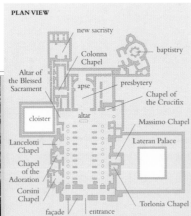

new sacristy
Colonna Chapel
baptistry
Altar of the Blessed Sacrament
apse
presbytery
Chapel of the Crucifix
altar
cloister
Massimo Chapel
Lancelotti Chapel
Lateran Palace
Chapel of the Adoration
Corsini Chapel
Torlonia Chapel
façade
entrance

⌄ **ACANTHUS-LEAF CAPITAL**
The columns flanking the main door and the pilasters along the facade have Corinthian capitals. The carving of the acanthus leaves is finely detailed.

⌄ **FACADE**
Alessandro Galilei (1691–1736) designed the travertine façade. The new pope delivers his first blessing from the open *loggia*.

The Basilica of St. John Lateran (San Giovanni in Laterano) was the world's first Christian basilica, and the mother church of the Catholic faith. Since the 4th century, it has served as Rome's cathedral and the seat of the Bishop of Rome.

The basilica was constructed on land given to Pope Miltiades (311–14) by Emperor Constantine I in c.313. Dedicated to the Savior, the church, one of the first to be built under imperial patronage, followed the traditional layout of a Roman basilica, with a nave separated by rows of columns. The emperor endowed the church with many precious silver and gold vessels and elaborate altars, and, in the mid-5th century, an octagonal baptistry was added to the side of the basilica by Pope Sixtus III (432–440).

In the same century, the Vandals sacked Rome, plundering much of the church's liturgical treasure. After a severe earthquake in 896, the church was largely rebuilt on its original foundations. Pope Lucius II (1144–45) dedicated the new basilica to St. John the Evangelist. Fires in 1307 and 1360 reduced the building almost to ruin. When Pope Martin V (1417–31) restored the papacy to Rome, he renovated the cathedral, but moved the papal residence from the Lateran Palace to the Vatican.

At the end of the 16th century, Pope Sixtus V (1585–90) remodeled the basilica, entrusting the project to his favorite architect, Domenico Fontana (1543–1607). To mark the Jubilee Year of 1650, Innocent X (1644–55) instructed the architect Francesco Borromini (1599–1667) to embellish the interior.

In 1878, Pope Leo XIII (1878–1903) had the apse torn down to facilitate ordination and liturgical ceremonies. Its 4th-century mosaics were removed and remounted in the new, extended apse.

The inauguration ceremonies surrounding the beginning of each new pontificate formally come to an end when the pope visits the Lateran basilica to "take possession" of his cathedral.

⌃ **EMPEROR CONSTANTINE I**
This 4th-century statue of Constantine I was placed in the atrium in 1737. Dressed in military uniform, he carries the scroll of authority in his hand.

⊁ **LATERAN INSIGNIA**
The open umbrella and crossed keys are a symbol of both the papacy when it is vacant, and also of the Lateran basilica itself.

ST. JOHN LATERAN
CATHOLICISM'S MOTHER CHURCH

CHURCH DOCTORS
Twelve statues representing the Doctors of the Eastern and Western Churches stand along the top of the balustrade.

MAIN DOORWAY
In 1660, Pope Alexander VII (1655–67) installed these doors, which had formerly stood in the old Roman senate house.

TOUCHING TRADITION
This sculpture on the Jubilee door includes an image of the baby Jesus whose foot has been worn away by the faithful.

PAVEMENT ROSETTE
This rosette is made of *giallo antico* marble, which the Romans imported in large quantities from mines in Tunisia.

ENTRANCE
Classical architecture used large, ceremonial doorways, such as the one seen here. A small entrance to the basilica is set into the door.

> CEILING AND CREST OF PIUS IV
This gilt wooden ceiling, begun in 1562, is attributed to Pirro Ligorio (1510–83). The crests of various popes bearing the name Pius appear on the ceiling.

∨ BLESSED SACRAMENT ALTAR
Designed by Pier Paolo Olivieri (1551–99) to celebrate the Jubliee Year of 1600, this altar is flanked by gilt bronze pillars thought to be from the Temple of Jupiter built by Augustus.

> DRAMATIC SCULPTURES
In the 18th century, huge marble statues depicting the Apostles and Evangelists were inserted into niches in the nave.

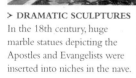

< HIGH ALTAR BALDACCHINO
The Gothic marble altar canopy dates from c.1367. Silver busts in the canopy contain relics of St. Peter and St. Paul.

> TOMB OF INNOCENT III
In the lunette over this sculpture of the pope's catafalque (funerary bier), Christ appears between St. Francis of Assisi and St. Dominic.

∨ NAVE AND HIGH ALTAR
Borromini encased the nave's marble pillars in massive supporting piers set with niches for the statues of the Apostles and Four Evangelists.

∧ ORGAN
The wooden organ case, which dates from the 16th century, is decorated with representations of musical instruments and a figure of King David.

∨ BRONZE LECTERN
The basilica has a plain, unadorned lectern. The *Lectionary*, or book of the Scriptures, is placed on the lectern during the liturgy.

∧ ORGAN GALLERY
Two organs are set into the apse. Dating from 1866, they were made by Morettini of Perugia.

< APSE
When the apse was lengthened under Leo XIII (1878–1903), its 4th-century mosaics had to be dismantled and reassembled.

∧ COLUMN OF MARTIN V
Pope Martin V (1417–31) of the Colonna family restored the basilica. The column of his family crest decorates the pavement.

⌄ CUPOLA OF CHAPEL
The stucco ceiling of the Lancelotti Chapel's cupola depicts episodes from the life of St. Francis of Assisi in frames supported by putti.

> LANCELOTTI CHAPEL
The wealthy Lancelotti family had this chapel dedicated to St. Francis refurbished in High Baroque style in the late 17th century.

> STUCCO FRAME
The lively stucco decoration around the painting of St. Francis receiving the Stigmata was the work of Filippo Carcani. It shows angels and putti at play.

⌄ ALTARPIECE
This gilt altarpiece in the Lancelotti Chapel, which has a tabernacle set into its center, is decorated with saints connected to the Franciscan order.

> SYMBOL OF POPE MARTIN V
Throughout the basilica are signs of the restoration work carried out by Pope Martin V. The restoration celebrated the end of the Avignon papacy.

< THE CREST OF POPE INNOCENT X
Innocent X, whose crest appears throughout the building, commissioned Borromini to embellish the basilica.

ⴷ SIDE AISLES
On the orders of Innocent X, Borromini's alterations preserved the nave and four aisles of the original basilica. The arches are decorated with putti heads.

< CHERUB HEAD
One of the hallmarks of the Baroque remodeling was the preponderance of cherubs and putti in elaborate stucco.

ⴷ WROUGHT-IRON GATE
The bronze gate and cross, designed by Quintiliano Raimondi (1794–1848), contrasts with the coffered stucco ceiling, which is reminiscent of Classical Rome.

ⴷ PALM FRONDS
The palm is common in Christian art. It symbolizes martyrdom, and recalls when crowds waved palm branches on Christ's entry into Jerusalem before the Crucifixion.

> TORLONIA CHAPEL
Over the altar of the Torlonia Chapel is the *Deposition from the Cross* by Pietro Tenerani (1789–1869). The rich marble work is decorated with lapis lazuli, alabaster, and malachite.

< 17TH-CENTURY PAVING
When Borromini modified the interior of the basilica in the 17th century, parts of the old pavings were replaced with this striking marble pattern, with its almost 3-D appearance.

∨ 13TH-CENTURY CLOISTER
Only the cloister survives of the great monastery that once served the basilica. Monks meditated and prayed in its garden and corridors.

< ORNATE PILLAR
Several of the columns in the cloister are decorated with intricate designs that were executed using glass tesserae.

∨ COURTYARD WELL
The well in the centre of the courtyard, from which monks would have drawn their water, dates from the 9th century.

> MEDIEVAL COLUMNS
Decorated with acanthus leaves, the capitals of the the monastery cloister imitate the styles of antiquity.

∧ CROUCHING LION
This lion appears crushed by the weight of the pillars that flank the opening into the garden.

> INCENSE HOLDER
The cleric carrying the thurible in Cardinal Annibaldi's funeral cortege anxiously opens the lid and blows inside to keep the charcoal alight.

∧ TOMB OF CARDINAL ANNIBALDI
This was the first major work in Rome by Arnolfo di Cambio (c.1240–1310); the procession shows the emerging artistic interest in movement and expression.

> PAPAL THRONE
The walls are covered with items found during archaeological excavations. This throne may have been used by the popes, and was originally inside the basilica.

⌃ ∨ CUPOLA OF BAPTISTRY
The upper interior of the cupola is decorated with oil paintings. In the center is a depiction of a dove, symbol of the Holy Spirit.

⌃ ∧ BAPTISMAL AREA
The baptistry's eight porphyry columns were taken from the residence of Fausta, Constantine's wife. Seventeenth-century frescoes depicting the life of Constantine adorn the walls. The font is carved from green basalt.

⌃ LOGGIA OF SIXTUS V
The northern entrance to the basilica, with its double-tiered *loggia*, was built during the reign of Sixtus V (1585–90).

∧ EXTERIOR OF BAPTISTRY
The octagonal baptistry, founded by Constantine I, was rebuilt in the mid-5th century. A number of side chapels were added later.

˅ › LOGGIA DETAIL
Built between 1271 and 1276, the palace's *loggia* bears the eagle crest of Pope Gregory X beneath the crossed keys symbol—the first time this appeared in papal iconography.

˅ THE PAPAL PALACE
The main entrance to the Papal Palace was completed in 1266. The buildings were built entirely of locally sourced volcanic *pepperino* stone. A lion, the symbol of Viterbo, stands proudly over the palace doorway.

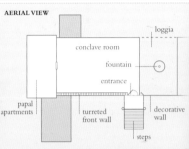

AERIAL VIEW

conclave room

loggia

fountain

entrance

papal apartments

turreted front wall

decorative wall

steps

The papacy gained possession of Viterbo, an ancient Etruscan town, in the 8th century. Lying 37 miles (60 km) north of Rome, in what is now the Lazio region, the city and its Papal Palace intermittently played host to the popes for several centuries, becoming known as the "City of the Popes." The historic center of the city—which is one of the best preserved medieval towns of central Italy—is surrounded by walls, still intact, which were built during the 11th and 12th centuries.

In late medieval times, when the popes had difficulties asserting their authority over Rome (*see p.54*), Viterbo was chosen as a residence by several popes, as it offered security and yet was close to Rome.

Pope Eugene III (1145–53) took shelter at Viterbo when the citizens of Rome refused him residence. It was from here that he launched the Second Crusade. A century later, with political turmoil in Rome, Pope Alexander IV (1254–61) spent his whole pontificate in Viterbo, where he remained until his death.

Pope Clement IV (1265–68) also resided in the city for two years while the bitter conflict between the Hohenstaufen dynasty and the papacy was at its height (*see p.54*).

Five popes were elected in Viterbo: Gregory IX (1227–41), Urban IV (1261–64), Gregory X (1271–76), John XXI (1271–76), and Martin IV (1281–85). The practice of locking the cardinals in conclave to elect a pope began at Viterbo in 1271, when the French and Italian cardinals were unable to choose a candidate for 33 months. When the French cardinal, Simon de Brie, was elected as Martin IV in 1281, he was ousted by the Viterbese, who were outraged at the choice of a foreigner.

In the 14th century, when the popes resided at Avignon, Viterbo's importance declined. Pope Sixtus IV (1471–84) restored the palace, and Pope Paul III (1534–49), who hailed from nearby Camino, patronized the city. By the 16th century, its days of prestige were over. It became part of the new Kingdom of Italy in 1871.

PALAZZO DEI PAPI

THE PAPAL PALACE AT VITERBO

> COAT OF ARMS

> COAT OF ARMS
This stone slab bears the coat of arms of Boniface VIII (1294–1303). Only after Urban IV (1261–64) did papal crests incorporate family insignia.

< ∨ RECYCLED FOUNTAIN
Within the *loggia* is a 15th-century fountain made using pieces of older medieval monuments during the reign of Pope Sixtus IV (1471–84).

∧ MONUMENTAL FAÇADE
The Audience Hall (*left*) is illuminated by mullioned windows and rectangular attic windows. To the right is the surviving side of the wide, roofless *loggia*, a seven-bay arcade supported by doubled columns.

< FOUNTAIN HEAD
Above the arms of the diocese and the ruling Viterbese Gatti family is a basket of acorns, the symbol of Sixtus IV's family.

∧ LION SPOUT
Water spills from the upper basin through lions' mouths. The city's fountains once provided fresh water for its citizens.

∨ **LION SYMBOL**
The crowned lion, the symbol of Viterbo, represents the mutually beneficial alliance of the civil powers and the papacy. The fresco was once part of a larger mural.

∧ **CONCLAVE ROOM**
The cardinals were locked in this room during the 33-month conclave of 1268–71. Their food rations were eventually reduced and the roof was taken off to "encourage" them to reach a decision. They eventually elected Pope Gregory X (1271–76).

➢ **MARBLE TABLET**
This 19th-century tablet commemorates the five popes who resided at Viterbo in medieval times. The papal court brought prestige and prosperity to the town.

QVOD. FELIX. FAVSTVMQ. SIT.
AEDES. VETVSTA. MOLITIONE.
ET VRBANI. IV. CLEMENTIS. IV. GREGORII. X.
IOANNIS. XXI. NICOLAI. III. MARTINI. IV.
DOMICILIO. INSIGNES.
CVRANTE
G. BERNARDO PIANETTI. CARD. EPO.
III. NON. SEPTEMBRES.
PATENT
PIO. IX. PONT. MAX.
VT. ANTIQVAM. POPVLI. FIDEM.
OPTIMO. INDVLGENTISSIMO. PRINCIPI.
PERSPECTAM. FIERI. COMMENDATAMQ.
CONTINGAT

> FAMILY CREST
The papal apartments were renovated under
Pope Clement VIII (1592–1605). His family
crest, with its serrated bar between six stars,
decorates the painted wall frieze.

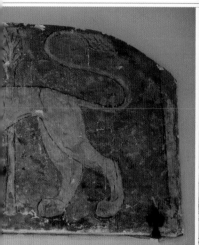

< OIL PAINTINGS
By the 17th century, oil paintings were
preferred to frescoes. Oils predominate
in the papal apartments; frescoes are
reduced to architectural decoration.

^ FRESCO DETAIL
This detail of a putto astride a vegetable-
and-fruit garland shows artichokes, onions,
bay leaves, grapes, pears, and eggplants—all
still key ingredients of the regional cuisine.

< PAPAL APARTMENTS
The 17th-century fresco frieze around
the upper walls of the papal apartments
depicts scenes of the local countryside.

DAILY LIFE

 ## INSIDE THE VATICAN

Though it is located in the heart of Rome, Vatican City forms its own state, with all the attendant trappings of nationhood. It retains its own citizenship and diplomatic corps, its own security and financial system, and also its own postal and media network. From here the popes have led the Catholic Church for almost two millennia as the Bishops of Rome, the successors to St. Peter. Although the pope is the sovereign of the city state, the day-to-day running of the Vatican is entrusted to a variety of governing bodies and individuals, who oversee the Vatican's relationship with the rest of the world and also make decisions that will affect the lives of the world's 1.2 billion Catholics. The Vatican administration must also rely on many lay workers to keep the small nation running, and to provide maintenance work, security, clerical assistance, and a host of other services.

The Vatican City State is all that remains of the Papal States—a group of Italian territories that were under the political control of the pope from the 8th century until 1870. Today, this tiny state is both the spiritual home of the world's one billion Catholics, and one of the greatest repositories of Western art in the world. The Vatican is the oldest non-hereditary monarchy in the world, and the head of this sovereign state is the pope, or pontiff. He is at once the Bishop of the diocese of Rome as well as a head of state, and is elected by the College of Cardinals.

The popes have resided in Rome for most of the 2,000 years of Christian history, and Italy plays a large part in the life of the Vatican. Most of the workforce responsible for running the Vatican comes from Italy, and the state relies on the Italian government for such basic commodities as electricity and water. This is a relationship based on mutual respect; the Vatican cannot survive without Italy's help, and Italians readily acknowledge the important part the Vatican plays in Italy's lucrative tourist market.

✖ THE VATICAN STATE

On February 11, 1929, the Italian government and the Holy See signed an agreement that established the Vatican City State. Known as the Lateran Treaty, the agreement resolved almost 60 years of tension that followed the capture of Rome by the armies of Victor Emmanuel II of Italy. The Treaty recognized the international status of the Holy See, and established the pope's authority within the Vatican City. It made financial restitution for properties confiscated from the Church, and granted various buildings in Rome extraterritorial status. For its part, the Vatican recognized the legitimacy of Italy's government.

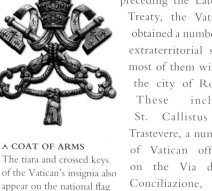

∧ COAT OF ARMS
The tiara and crossed keys of the Vatican's insignia also appear on the national flag

VATICAN TERRITORY

Vatican City is the world's smallest sovereign state. Nestled close to the banks of the River Tiber in Rome, the area within its walls comprises roughly 109 acres (44 hectares) and includes St. Peter's Square. Almost half of the Vatican site is occupied by gardens. The borders broadly follow the defensive walls erected in the 16th century. A granite line forming the outside edge of St. Peter's Square marks the boundary between the Vatican City and the city of Rome.

During the negotiations preceding the Lateran Treaty, the Vatican obtained a number of extraterritorial sites, most of them within the city of Rome. These include St. Callistus in Trastevere, a number of Vatican offices on the Via della Conciliazione, and the Congregation for the Evangelization of the Peoples, located close to the Spanish Steps. The Vatican also has three major basilicas in Rome—St. John Lateran is the cathedral of Rome, where the Vicar appointed by the pope resides; St. Mary Major is a significant 5th-century basilica that welcomes a constant stream of pilgrims; and St. Paul-Outside-the-Walls is built over the tomb of St. Paul, who along with St. Peter is the co-patron of Rome. The villa at Castel Gandolfo, to the south of Rome, also belongs to the Vatican; purchased in the 16th century, the Pontifical Villa is the summer residence of the pope and is occupied by him for almost three months of the year.

WITHIN THE CITY WALLS

LIVING AND WORKING IN THE VATICAN

> The Vatican, the spiritual home of the world's billion Catholics, covers an area no bigger than 109 acres (44 hectares).

NATIONAL SYMBOLS

Despite its small size, the Vatican has most of the trappings of nationhood found in other states in the world. It has its own flag and coat of arms, and a constitution to guide internal affairs and its relations with other states. The Vatican also has a tuneful national anthem, the Pontifical March. It was composed by Charles Gounod in honor of Pope Pius IX (1846–78); such was its popularity that it was adopted as the Vatican City anthem by Pope Pius XII in 1949. The anthem is played at Christmas and Easter, as well as during other solemn occasions at which the pope is present.

The Vatican City maintains a postal service, issues its own stamps, and prints its own money (the euro). Since the Vatican does not have a mint, it pays the Italian state to produce its coins and notes. The first Vatican euro coins were minted in 2002, bearing the image of Pope John Paul II. It is almost impossible to get the new coins; people line up for hours before the coins are released and they are quickly snapped up by enthusiastic collectors.

The State of the Vatican City has issued stamps every year since 1929 to commemorate events and anniversaries. These are much prized by philatelists, fetching high prices at auction—especially the first-day issues. A section in the Vatican Museums is dedicated to the development of philately at the Holy See, and holds examples of all the issued stamps, as well as artists' preparatory sketches.

The Vatican City also has its own media services, with a radio station, a television studio, and a daily newspaper, *L'Osservatore Romano*.

RUNNING THE CITY

The day-to-day administration of the Vatican is entrusted to the President of the Pontifical Commission of Cardinals for Vatican City and is housed in the Palazzo del Governatorato, a large building situated behind St. Peter's Basilica. A number of cardinals are appointed by the pope for a five-year period to serve on the board of this commission. The office oversees all the internal functions of the Vatican City State.

Although the Vatican does not maintain an army, the state is protected by the Hague Convention

⋀ THE VATICAN FROM ABOVE
From the air, there is no visible boundary between the Vatican and the surrounding city of Rome. Visitors are often surprised that half the area of the Vatican is taken up by gardens.

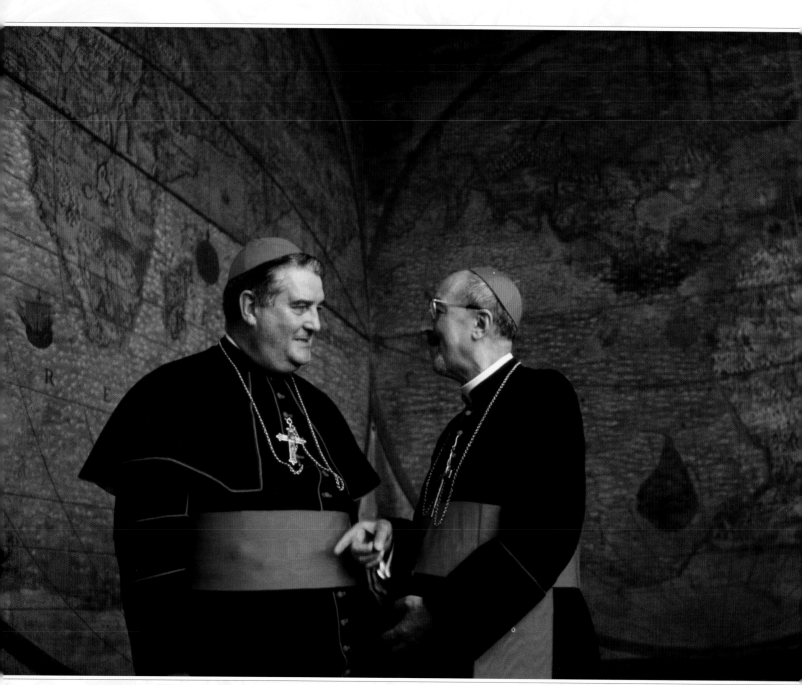

▲ CATCHNG UP ON EVENTS
Two bishops pause in The Gallery of Maps
in the Vatican Museum. Most of the world's
5,000 bishops live in their dioceses and travel
only occasionally to the Vatican for meetings.

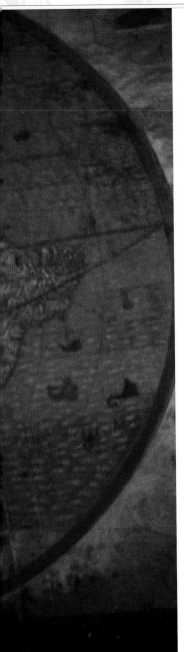

of May 14, 1954, which safeguards the Sovereign State in case of armed conflict. Equally, though the Vatican has no direct access to the sea, it enjoys the right to maintain a fleet under the terms of the Convention of Barcelona, signed in 1921, which it has no need to exercise.

FINANCE

As an independant state, the Vatican receives no financial assistance from the Italian Government. Running the city state and maintaining the wealth of art within its walls is very costly. The Vatican, however, survives on relatively few sources of income. A certain amount of revenue is generated from tourism, the sale of art reproductions, and museum entrance fees. A small income is also derived from the sale of Vatican publications, stamps, and coins. A number of organizations assist the work of the pope; Friends of the Holy Father donate large sums, as do The Knights of Columbanus, a group of Catholic lay people, founded in the US, who financed the cleaning of the facade of St. Peter's.

Each year, the various dioceses offer financial assistance to the Vatican. A large contribution is also made to the pope's charities by the world's Catholics. The practice of collecting for papal charities, known as Peter's Pence, originated in Medieval England when a yearly tax was imposed on households in favor of the pope. Today, the practice is strictly voluntary and each year, on the last Sunday in June, Catholic churches all over the world hold a collection. The funds raised are delivered personally to the pope, who then distributes them to the various charities that call on his aid.

> Throughout the course of modern world history, leaders from Stalin to Reagan have acknowledged the influence of the world's oldest diplomatic corps—the Holy See.

INTERNATIONAL AFFAIRS

The Vatican boasts one of the oldest diplomatic services in the world. The earliest record of a papal representative occured at the Council of Nicaea (present-day Iznik in Turkey) in 325 to which Pope Sylvester (314–35) sent two presbyters (local Christian leaders).

Today, the Vatican has strong diplomatic ties, with many nations around the world maintaining an embassy to the Holy See. With a Catholic presence in so many countries, international links are vital and nuncios (ambassadors) are appointed by the pope to act as mediators between the Holy See and local Catholic communities. Nuncios keep the Holy See informed of events in the country to which they are appointed and act as mediators on the ground. They also maintain close links with the Episcopal Conference (assembly of bishops of a given territory) and nurture links with both Christians and members of other world faiths. Future diplomats train at the Pontifical Ecclesiastical Academy in Rome, taking courses in canon law, diplomacy, and languages.

The Holy See also plays its part in various international organizations. Its status as a Permanent Observer of the United Nations means that it has the right to participate in debate but not to vote, thus maintaining its neutrality. Permanent Observer status is also held for such bodies as the World Food Program, the World Health Organization, and the International Organization for Migration, among others. The Holy See is also a member of the United Nations High Commission for Refugees and the United Nations Conference on Trade and Development where it plays an active role.

⌃ **WORKMEN ON SITE**
A team of workers regularly maintain
the Vatican buildings. Many of the
structures are hundreds of years old and
in constant need of attention and repair.

 LIVING IN THE
VATICAN

Inside the world's smallest sovereign
state is a thriving community:
citizens of the Vatican who live and
work in this unique environment.
Ordinary life here is rarely seen by
the outside world, yet beyond the
public ceremonies and mass
audiences, behind the lavish riches
of the papal treasures and priceless
art, the city functions like any other.
The Vatican's employees work
tirelessly, cleaning and maintaining
the buildings, tending to the gardens,
and carrying out an ambitious
program of restoration. Food is
prepared daily in the staff canteens,
and clothing is washed and made
ready for all papal ceremonies. At
the end of the working day,
employees shop, cook, play, and rest.

Very few people know what it is
like to live and work at the Vatican.
To most who visit, this is an awe-
inspiring, sometimes intimidating,
place. To those who live and work
here, there is an easy familiarity.
Some refer to it as "the village"—
indeed, there is a certain informality
in the way a Swiss Guard salutes a
passing cleric, or a housewife hastens
by with a basket of goods from the
Anonna, the Vatican supermarket.
Nuns exchange friendly greetings as
they pass each other, cardinals stand
in courtyards locked in discussion,

and a seminarian cycles to the Post
Office. From time to time, an
entourage of cars carrying officials
and other guests sweeps through St.
Anne's Gate, heading for the
Apostolic Palace behind St. Peter's
where the pope waits to greet them.

Some 800 people work in the
city state, of which about 450 hold
citizenship. Since citizenship is
conferred by virtue of one's office, it
must be surrendered upon resignation
or retirement. Most, therefore, hold
dual citizenship, that of the Vatican
and their own native country.

Those who visit the Vatican on
official business are subject to
stringent security measures, put in
place to protect the Vatican and its
residents. For all who live and work
within these walls, there is a strong
sense of devotion and loyalty
to the person of the pope, the
successor of St. Peter.

POWER AND
MAINTENANCE

Given the Vatican's small size within
the sprawling city of Rome, it is not
surprising that it should rely heavily
on amenities provided by the Italian
State. Electricity, water, gas, and
other utilities have to be imported,
as do almost all foodstuffs, building
materials, machinery, and other
goods needed to run the city state.
The Vatican's location in the heart
of Rome means that everything has

⌃ **MAINTAINING THE STONEWORK**
Air pollution caused by carbon emissions
is a constant threat to St. Peter's Basilica
and the colonnade. Cleaning the facade
is therefore necessary and ongoing.

to pass through the city to get to the
Vatican. Fortunately, most of the
heavy goods can be transported by
train, via a small section of track
that links the Vatican with Rome.

The historic buildings and
sprawling grounds within the
Vatican walls are in constant need of
attention, and maintenance work is
ongoing. A dedicated team of
builders and restorers work tirelessly
on the repair and upkeep of the
buildings, while the gardens are
cared for by a specialist team of
horticulturalists and gardeners who
maintain the grounds.

SECURITY

The Swiss Guard, young men in colorful, striped Renaissance uniform, guard the entrances to the Vatican City and patrol the Apostolic Palace that houses the papal apartments. These guards also accompany the pope at all public appearances within the Vatican. Although the service they provide today is largely honorary, the Swiss Guard is made up of highly trained, fit individuals capable of defending the pontiff should the need arise.

The Vatican also has a second, more elaborate security system in place, the Central Security Corps of Vatican City State, who police the Vatican. These guards, comprising some 130 members, protect the entrances to the Vatican and provide surveillance throughout the city state. Their uniform is navy blue with a white shirt and navy tie; in winter they wear a navy coat with a cape lined with red. The Central Security Corps co-operates closely with the Italian police force and is responsible for all matters relating to internal security, including border control, crime investigation, and traffic control.

Visitors who do not work in the Vatican on a regular basis have to file through the Permissions Office, where they show a form of identity and collect a badge. Discreet, closed-circuit television is in place to help ensure that visitors do not wander off their permitted course. Tourists visiting St. Peter's Basilica are also required to pass through a security screen located at the colonnade.

EMERGENCY SERVICES

The Vatican employs a number of highly trained emergency service personnel. The fire department, the

> In 2007, the Vatican became the first carbon-free state in the world, installing solar panels and planting trees to offset carbon emissions.

most costly, is in place to protect the citizens, visitors, and buildings of the Vatican, and, given the number of artistic treasures held here, it would be unthinkable to have anything less than the best possible defense against fire. Installed throughout are expensive anti-fire devices that protect the priceless works of art as well as important documents.

There is also a First Aid service on hand to tend to the thousands of people visiting the Vatican daily. First Aid teams are located in the museums and to the side of St. Peter's Square and there is also an emergency service in place for the

pope and senior members of the clergy whose duties oblige them to remain in the Vatican. Ambulances are kept on standby in case there is a need to transport someone to the hospital, and a small suite at the Gemelli Polyclinic, north of the Vatican, is retained should the pope need attention in the hospital; Pope John Paul II had several stays in the hospital, quipping that it should be known as the alternative Vatican.

TRANSPORTATION

Given the size of the city, there is little need for anything more than a bicycle for transport. Most people get around on foot, and access to various buildings and areas is controlled by the Swiss Guard and Central Security Corps. Employees can, if they wish, bring their cars into the Vatican, but parking spaces are difficult to come by. In 2003, a new car park was built underneath the Vatican—during the excavation work, archeological artifacts were unearthed from an underground cemetery.

At the northern end of the Vatican gardens stands a heliport, which houses helicopter transport for the pope when he needs to leave

< SWISS GUARDS ON DUTY
Dressed in their blue, yellow, and red Renaissance uniforms, the Swiss Guards provide security in the Apostolic Palace, directing visitors to their destination.

Vatican City; with Roman traffic so chaotic, the pope causes less fuss and disruption when he leaves by air.

A railroad station, built in 1933 in the Neo-Classical style by architect Giuseppe Momo, is today used only for transporting heavy commercial goods into the Vatican. There is also a small pool of cars available for use by senior members of the pope's household, cardinals, and distinguished visitors. Vatican cars carry the number plate SCV (*Stato della Città del Vaticano*) while the pope's car bears the plate SCVI.

COMMUNICATIONS

The Vatican postal service is one of the most efficient in the world. Letters sent internally for delivery within the city do not require stamps and are delivered on the same day. Documents destined for outside Italy are sometimes dispatched in diplomatic pouches to *nunciatures* (embassies of the Holy See), where they can be forwarded to the addressee by local mail.

The Vatican telephone service is administered by a group of religious sisters. The sisters are fluent in several languages and are well-equipped, therefore, to assist callers from all over the world. The telephone service deals with hundreds of calls everyday from the various dioceses around the globe and from members of the public.

The Vatican also operates its own website (www.vatican.va) where visitors can download pictures and documents free of charge. The site is expressly maintained for the benefit of the public and is a useful tool that allows Catholics all around the world to keep abreast of developments within the Vatican and the Roman Catholic Church.

SHOPPING AND BANKING

Employees' wages are marginally lower in the Vatican than in Rome or the rest of Italy. However, the Vatican enjoys tax-free status (agreed in the Lateran Treaty) and since the price of groceries, toiletries, and medicines is lower, Vatican employees benefit from this arrangement.

Within the Vatican walls is a supermarket, the *Anonna*, which stocks everything from basic groceries, meat, fish, and fruit to alcohol and tobacco. In order to shop here, customers are required to show a residence or work permit. A limit is imposed on the amount of alcohol and tobacco that can be purchased in any one month. This is to prevent such goods being bought and then resold outside the Vatican. The milk and other dairy products stocked in the supermarket come from a farm that is part of the pope's country residence at Castelgandolfo in the Alban Hills south of Rome.

The Vatican also has a store in the old Train Terminal where clothes, both lay and ecclessiastical,

⋀ THE VATICAN POST OFFICE
The Post Office provides a reliable service for Vatican staff who use it for processing both official and personal mail. Visitors can also buy stamps and postcards here.

are sold. Also stocked here are electrical goods, jewelry, and other gift items. These goods are available exclusively to Vatican employees and other people with close connections to the Vatican; for example, staff at embassies and diplomatic missions.

The Vatican pharmacy stocks many medications from all around the world not easily found in Italian pharmacies. The pharmacy was founded in 1874 by the St. John of God Brothers on the Tiber Island and is located close to St. Anne's Gate. As well as dispensing medication to Vatican employees and residents, the pharmacy distributes medicines to missions throughout the world.

The Institute for the Works of Religion is otherwise known as the Vatican Bank. Established in 1944, the bank functions like a commercial bank for the employees of the Holy See, providing ATMs and other services. ATM cards and checks are not valid outside the Vatican. The bank also provides ethical investment options for charitable organizations, and many religious orders keep their money here.

LEISURE TIME

Given the purpose of the Vatican, and its small area, there is little room for recreational facilities. The gardens provide the largest area for walking in and there are tennis courts and a small space for games. Many of the colleges attended by trainee priests have their own sports facilities, which are informally used by groups in the Vatican such as the Swiss Guard.

A few small canteens within Vatican City operatate a lunch and dinner service, providing meals to employees of the various offices. The canteens are reserved for workers and not accessible to tourists. There are no restaurants or bars in the Vatican but given the plethora of cafés and restaurants in the immediate vicinity, this does not pose any

inconvenience and employees are able to take advantage of the amenities on offer outside the gates.

FAMILY LIFE

A small number of families live in the Vatican. Some senior Swiss Guard, for example, occupy family apartments on site, though these tend to be small. There are no schools in the Vatican and the children who live here are educated outside the city state, in various schools throughout Rome. No restrictions are imposed on visiting those who live in the Vatican and the children often invite school friends to come and play within the grounds. Other regular visitors include the boys of the Sistine Choir, which attracts children from Rome and further afield. The choir has a practice room in the Vatican where it rehearses prior to singing at papal liturgies in the Vatican.

A PLAYING BALL
This photograph, taken in the 1950s, shows a group of African seminarians making the most of their free time in the grounds of the Vatican.

From the early broadcasts of Vatican Radio in 1931 to the Vatican website today, the pope's voice is heard far beyond St. Peter's Square.

 VATICAN MEDIA

The Vatican uses every form of media available to communicate the Gospel to the world—from radio to television, newspapers, books, the Internet, and new digital technologies. Though Latin remains the official language of the Holy See, from which all official documents are translated, the ability to use a multitude of languages is crucial to the Holy See's ability to communicate with the faithful around the world. Therefore, a significant proportion of the Vatican's media employees are fluent in a variety of languages, and documents are also published in several languages.

VATICAN RADIO AND TELEVISION

Pope Pius XI (1922–39) inaugurated Vatican Radio on February 12, 1931, when the first Vatican broadcast was made to the world. An important expansion took place in 1957 when Pope Pius XII (1939–58) opened a new transmission center at Santa Maria di Galera, 15 miles (25 km) north of Rome. Today, the main radio center is located on Via della Conciliazione, within Vatican territory. The management of the center has been entrusted by the Holy See to the Society of Jesus, otherwise known as the Jesuits. The service is almost entirely funded by the donations of the faithful and other benefactors.

The station's principal function is to broadcast information about the pope's activities and teaching. It specializes in Church and religious news as well as offering in-depth analysis of moral and religious issues. The station also transmits information on secular world events, addressing youth and social justice issues, as well as running news and music programs.

Vatican Radio transmits continuous programming 24 hours a day and is available on short wave, medium wave, FM, and satellite frequencies. Broadcasts are also accessible on the Internet and are available as downloads.

Vatican Radio plays an important role in countries where the Catholic community is small, or persecuted. Listeners are able to keep abreast of developments at the Vatican and within the Church and can follow liturgical events and the Angelus Prayer on Sundays, or the pope's General Audience on Wednesdays. The programs are broadcast in 34 languages, making them accessible to audiences all across the globe.

The Vatican Television Center was established in 1983, initially to broadcast papal liturgies and ceremonies. In recent years, the center has broadened its horizons and now assists television stations around the world in obtaining footage of papal events. The center does not transmit as an independent television channel.

∧ **FOLLOWING THE NEWS**
A bishop takes a moment to catch up on the daily news in *L'Osservatore Romano*, the official newspaper of the Holy See, before a meeting begins.

ᐁ IN THE VATICAN MUSEUMS
A number of stalls in the galleries of
the Vatican Museums sell guide books,
posters, and other souvenirs.

ᐁ THE POPE ON AIR
In March 2006, the pope visited the Vatican
Radio offices on Via della Conciliazione
where he was interviewed by broadcasters.

THE VATICAN IN PRINT

In 1587, the Vatican Printing Press was inaugurated by Pope Sixtus V (1585–90) to print books for use in the Roman Curia and the papal court. Administered by the Salesian Brothers of Don Bosco, the press is still in operation and is located in a building dating back to 1908, which was extended in 1991.

The Vatican Publishing House was made independent of the Vatican Press in 1926 and is the official publishing house of the Vatican. Located close to St. Anne's Gate, it publishes all the documents produced by the Holy See, including the pope's writings and official documents from the various Vatican offices. The publishing house also produces a range of promotional and other material, including posters for the Vatican Museums, museum guide books, and prayer books. The John Paul II International Book Center on St. Peter's Square stocks all Vatican Publishing House material, and many of the publications are available in up to 30 languages.

The Vatican's quarterly journal, *Acts of the Apostolic See*, is an official publication of all documents published by the Holy See and is available to the public. In circulation since 1909, the journal contains works composed by the pope, as well as documents published by the departments of the Roman Curia.

The daily *L'Osservatore Romano* (The Roman Observer) is the official newspaper of the Holy See. The original aim of the paper was to give voice to the Church's grievance over the rise of the Italian Independence movement, which threatened the temporal power of the Church. The first edition was published on July 1, 1861 and today it is a valuable resource for disseminating daily news with a broad religious scope. The paper is published every day in Italian, with weekly editions available in English, Spanish, German, Portuguese, Polish, and French. The newspaper also offers a photographic service, located on the Via dell Pellegrino. Available here are images of papal events for use in magazines, newspapers, and books; images are also on sale to the public and can be purchased either at the Vatican or over the Internet.

THE PRESS

Located in the Palazzo dei Propilei in front of St. Peter's Square, the Vatican Information Service is a press office that provides information to journalists who are accredited by the Holy See. Official bulletins, printed in several languages, are issued daily at noon and via email each afternoon. The bulletins give information on the pope's audiences, as well as his speeches and papal appointments. The service also holds press conferences concerning issues relating to the Holy See and the Church, which are simultaneously published on the Vatican Information web page. The Holy See employs a Press Officer to act as a spokesperson for the pope when required.

The enormous task of assisting the world's media, both religious and secular, is managed by the Pontifical Council for Social Communications. Set up in 1988, the Council provides information on the activities of the Holy See and is responsible for granting permissions to photograph and film within the Vatican. The Council also promotes studies in mass communication, sponsoring seminars to examine the impact of new means of communication, such as the Internet and digital technology, and ways in which this new media can be used to disseminate information.

< CIBORIUM OF POPE SIXTUS IV
This 15th-century marble monument, which once stood over the tomb of St. Peter, is now being painstakingly restored in the attic area of the basilica.

✺ CULTURAL HERITAGE

There are few places on earth where so many artistic masterpieces are gathered together. Given its modest size, the Vatican has an astonishing range of precious art and artifacts, as well as architecture of great historical importance. The awe-inspiring St. Peter's Basilica, priceless frescoes, paintings and sculptures, the Secret Archives, and papal treasures make up one of the finest repositories of art in the world. Much of the collection is a result of papal commissions made over the centuries; it is also made up of the popes' own private acquisitions, as well as generous bequests and donations by wealthy benefactors.

THE SECRET ARCHIVES

From as far back as the fourth century, the popes of Rome have kept careful archives, recording their decisions and enterprises. Early documents were preserved on papyrus, and later, on vellum; by the 11th century, however, much of this early material had been destroyed in political upheavals.

In 1612, Pope Paul V (1605–1621) founded what was to become the Vatican Secret Archives, which he housed in the specially constructed Pauline Library located in the Belvedere Court. After World War I, the amount of bureaucratic paperwork tripled, and during the 1940s, underground galleries were built beneath the immense Belvedere courtyard to house the increasing amount of important documents and correspondence.

The Archives hold documents and papal bulls dating back over a thousand years and include the English King Henry VIII's request for annulment of his marriage to Catherine of Aragon. Every document of note is kept here, although documentation emanating from curial offices is kept within the respective offices.

Because of the delicate condition of many of the documents, and their sensitive content, the Secret Archives are only open to scholars with prior permission. However, as a security measure, the Vatican stores all documentation in electronic format, which is housed in five secret centers around the world.

RESTORATION WORK

The Vatican's priceless collection of treasures requires constant restoration work. The vast collections of books, ancient manuscripts, paintings, sculptures, frescoes, mosaics, and tapestries, as well as the buildings themselves, are looked after by a team of dedicated specialists whose expertise ensures their very survival.

During the Middle Ages and the Renaissance, it was common practice to hang tapestries on walls as impressive displays of power and wealth. The Vatican possesses a number of these works of art, including a series by the Italian Renaissance artist Raphael Sanzio (1483–1520), created to cover the lower walls of the Sistine Chapel on feast days. Sadly, many tapestries that hung in the Vatican perished during the Sack of Rome in 1527. Today, a team of specialists undertakes the painstaking work of restoring the delicate woollen and silk tapestries, which were often embroidered with gold and silver threads.

Much of the Classical statuary in the Vatican Museums was discovered in the 16th and 17th centuries, on archaeological digs that took place among the ruins of ancient Rome. Restoration of the statuary is on-going; Michelangelo's *Pietà* was repaired after it was damaged in 1972. Broken pieces were glued on with marble dust from Cararra, which had been ground and mixed with a paste.

Rooms inside St Peter's two cupolas store ancient archives dating to when the basilica was built (1506–1626). These archives, along with ancient manuscripts and the Vatican's store of books, are extremely fragile and require specialist bookbinders who can restore the articles that have fallen into disrepair.

Vatican City is home to the greatest
concentration of art in the world.

▲ ST. PETER'S ARCHIVE
The rooms behind this internal cupola house
the archives of St. Peter's Basilica. Over 500
years old, these archives contain accounts of
the works carried out by artists and architects.

⋀ RESTORING A MOSAIC
The painstaking work of restoring mosaics is carried out by a team of experts. By tapping the surface of the mosaic, this restorer can hear where the plaster beneath has dried up.

All but one of the oil paintings that adorned the walls of St. Peter's Basilica were replaced by faithful mosaic copies in the 17th and 18th centuries. As a result, a large part of the interior of the basilica is covered with mosaic. In order to restore these mosaics, the individual pieces of glass must be removed. This is an extremely difficult process, since moving the delicate pieces can destroy them, and a team of specialist mosaic restorers is on hand to carry out the work.

In 1983, a group known as the Patrons of the Arts in the Vatican Museums was founded to provide finance for the restoration of works of art. The restoration work carried out on the Sistine Chapel was also made possible by an agreement between the Japanese firm Nippon and the Holy See.

THE VATICAN MUSEUMS

Home to the largest repository of Western art in existence, the Vatican Museums are among the finest in the world. This vast collection of Classical statuary, religious artifacts, paintings, mosaics, and friezes is housed in a complex comprising four main museums: the Gregorian Egyptian Museum with monuments and artifacts of ancient Egypt, including finds from Mesopotamia; the Gregorian Etruscan Museum displaying objects from the ancient cities of southern Etruria (today the region of Lazio and Tuscany in Italy); the Pinacoteca (Art Gallery) housing Italian paintings from the 12th to the 19th centuries, including works by the masters of the Renaissance; and the Missionary-Ethnological Museum with religious artifacts and items of anthropological importance from Asia, Africa, and the Americas.

The various buildings that house these treasures are works of art in their own right. Visitors can wander through the private apartments of Pope Alexander VI to look at the fine wall-paintings, or through the apartments of Pope Julius II and Pope Leo X to see frescoes by Raphael. Throughout, exhibits are presented in ornate wooden cabinets that line the walls of beautifully frescoed corridors and galleries. The Sistine Chapel and the public part of the Papal Apartments known as the *Stanze di Raffaello* (Raphael rooms) are on the visitor route through the museums.

Other exhibits on display in the museums include uniforms and weapons formerly used by the papal guards prior to their dismantlement in the early 1970s, modern religious art, tapestries, and maps. A contemporary art museum, founded in 1973, demonstrates the Church's continuing interest in art, while donations of art works by philanthropists add to the collections.

VISITING THE VATICAN

Each year, some four million people are estimated to visit the Vatican. The pilgrims are drawn by the tomb of St Peter, underneath the high altar of the basilica, and the chance to see the pope. The tourists flock to see the stunning architecture and wealth of art conserved within the Vatican Museums.

The museums are closed every Sunday except for the last Sunday of each month, when entry is free. This is an extremely popular time to visit; the lines begin early in morning and can be several hours long. It is not unusual for lines to stretch from the entrance of the museums, along the city walls and back toward St. Peter's Square. Other than the last Sunday of the month, an entry fee is charged to all visitors and it is this fee that funds the day-to-day running of the Vatican Museums. In 2000, a new entrance was inaugurated to facilitate the ever-increasing number of visitors to the museums and all entrances are now wheelchair accessible.

The Vatican Museums are supported by a comprehensive website that provides visitors with all the neccessary information needed for their visit. The collections on display in the four main museums can be viewed online and there are also virtual tours of the highlights of each of the museums.

ʌ INSIDE THE VATICAN MUSEUMS
A Vatican Museums' tour guide accompanies a group of visitors around the museums, stopping in The Gallery of Maps to explain the history of this famous corridor.

˄ POPE BENEDICT XVI
The pope, one of the most photographed people in the world, is greeted by a sea of cameras upon his arrival at a General Audience in St. Peter's Square.

Of the world's religious leaders, the pope is arguably the most easily recognized. The world's billion Catholics look to him as their spiritual father, while many other Christians who are not in full union with Rome respect that he is the successor of St. Peter. The teachings of the Catholic Church address not only questions of morality but also deal with political, social, and scientific issues. Given the pontiff's vast audience, expanding rapidly with the availability of new media, these teachings can, and do, have far-reaching effects. In recent years, papal trips to all areas of the globe have been undertaken by popes John Paul II, Benedict XVI, and Francis. These apostolic journeys have done a great deal to raise the global profile of the papacy.

THE ROLE OF THE POPE

As the head of the Roman Catholic Church, the pope has supreme authority over the Universal Church (the Catholic Church throughout the world). The title "pope" (Greek for "father") is the most readily recognized of all the pontiff's titles; others include Bishop of Rome, Vicar of Jesus Christ, Successor of the Prince of the Apostles, Primate of Italy, Sovereign of the State of Vatican City, and Servant of the Servants of God. The most important of these titles is the first, for it is from his ministry as bishop that he governs as the universal pastor. The law of the Church confirms that the pope is "the head of the College of Bishops and has supreme, full and immediate and universal ordinary power in the Church and is free to exercise this power". Exercising power does not mean that the pope can invent or introduce new teachings. According to the dictum of the 5th-century monk, St. Vincent of Lerins, bishops can only teach *ubique, semper, ab omnibus*—that which has been held everywhere, always, and by everybody. The pope must teach in

> **PAPAL BULL**
These charters, issued under the authority of the pope, carry lead *bulla* (seals) that authenticate the document.

harmony with other bishops and can only teach that which has been handed on in tradition. This concept is termed "collegial authority".

The papal role is a monumental one. The pope is called upon to address problems affecting the Church, be they issues of poverty, injustice, or challenges to the Catholic faith. He must maintain contact with the dioceses around the world, dealing with problems that arise on a daily basis. It is also the pope's responsibility to settle matters of Church practice and doctrine, which he does through Ecumenical Councils, a conference of all the bishops of the world, and, every two or three years, through a Synod of Bishops, a meeting of the pope's advisory body made up of elected bishops from around the world. The pope must publish and promulgate the proceedings of all Ecumenical Councils and, following a Synod of Bishops, must compose an Apostolic Exhortation, a document reflecting on the issues raised during the synod. As bishop of one of the oldest dioceses in the

THE PAPACY

THE LIFE OF THE PONTIFF

world, the pope is highly regarded, not only by Catholics but by many other Christians; it is his task to unify these Christian Churches and communities. The pope must also make his own contribution to seminars and addresses, present his own writings, celebrate papal liturgies, and hold public audiences.

As well as spiritual authority, the pontiff also exercises temporal power. For centuries, popes governed territories that provided both income and security in central Italy. Since 1929, the pope has been the sovereign of Vatican City State and is, as such, a Head of State. He is responsible both for guiding the world's Catholics and for overseeing a complex administration made up of various congregations, commissions, tribunals, and secretariats.

AT WORK

In practical terms, the pope cannot govern both the Universal Church and the diocese of Rome. A chief deputy, normally a cardinal, is appointed to look after matters of state, while the various departments of the Roman Curia, a body similar to a civil service, are in place to assist the pontiff in his work.

A never-ending round of engagements may see the pope greet heads of state, politicians, cardinals, bishops, and pilgrims who visit the Vatican. There are speeches and

discourses to prepare, and visits outside Rome and overseas to undertake. A small group of religious sisters looks after the pontifical wardrobe, ensuring all the garments that are to be worn on specific occasions are ready when they are needed. The pope is the most readily recognized of all Christian leaders, in part due to the distinctive clothes he alone may wear. Everyday attire consists of a white, ankle-length garment, known as a *scimar*, which is worn with a caped gown that buttons at the front. A silk waistband embroidered with the papal coat of arms hangs to one side. The pope wears a gold pectoral cross on a chain around his neck and a white silk *zucchetto*, or scull cap, on the crown of his head. He may also wear a burgundy red *mozzetta*, or elbow-length cape. During Mass, he dons a long white *pallium* (a woollen stole embroidered with crosses, and the symbol of his office as pastor), which is worn over his chasuble (a long cloak). The pope no longer wears the tiara, the traditional ceremonial headdress worn by popes for centuries.

In today's world of rapidly expanding media development, the pope's profile is heightened and his image spread across television, radio, the Internet, and print. This constant exposure puts an enormous amount of pressure on the Vatican to respond

A MASS IN ST. PETER'S BASILICA
Pope Francis incenses a statue of Mary, the Mother of Jesus. Pope Francis, like many Catholics, has a tender devotion to Mary.

quickly to the diverse issues affecting the Church and the secular world. The Roman Curia, with its various departments, is in place to help the pope meet this increasing pressure, preparing documents, gathering material, and helping to diffuse the pope's teaching. The pontiff must, above all, be a man of prayer, and reserve time each day to celebrate Mass and recite the Divine Office, the public prayer of the Church. Each Lent, in preparation for Easter, the pope retreats to his private quarters and for one week all public audiences and meetings are suspended. During this time, the pope invites a preacher to give brief meditations each morning and evening on spiritual themes.

As Bishop of Rome, the pope is responsible for the liturgical and prayer life of the people in his diocese. As universal pastor of the Church, he has an enormous influence on Catholics throughout the world. Pilgrims travel from across the globe to participate in papal liturgies and to attend the public audiences. Every Wednesday morning, the pope holds a General Audience, either in the Paul VI Audience Hall or, when large numbers demand, in St. Peter's Square. The pontiff greets pilgrims and distinguished visitors, usually in a number of languages, and offers a brief meditation on a passage from the Bible. At midday on Sundays, and on some other feast days, he addresses the crowds that gather in St. Peter's Square from his study window. On these occasions, the pope prays the Angelus, a prayer in honor of Mary, mother of Jesus, as well as giving a brief address.

In recent years, popes have taken advantage of improved means of transportation to reach a wider audience. Pope John Paul II (1978–2005) was the most widely traveled pope in history, visiting almost every country in the world over his 27-year papacy.

In the past, the papacy was a much sought-after office. Today, the reality is that few would seek the position, and most would accept it

Every Sunday and during various feast days, the pope addresses the crowds from his study window.

the pope does not tender his resignation to the cardinals or any other designated body, nor is anyone empowered to accept the resignation. The law of the Church decrees, "if it should happen that the Roman pontiff resigns his office, it is required for validity that he makes the resignation freely and that it be duly manifested, but not that it be accepted by anyone" (Canon 332).

Even if a pope becomes incapacitated, he cannot be forced to resign. Once his decision to abdicate is final, his renunciation must be made publicly to the whole world. There are no provisions in law as to where a retired pope may go once he leaves office.

Faced with an abdication, the Dean of the College of Cardinals and its chairman, the Camerlengo, are obliged to arrange a conclave in order to elect a new pope. There have been few abdications. The first pope to resign from office was Pontianus, in the middle of the third century. The resignation of Pope Benedict XVI in 2013 was the first abdication in nearly 600 years. One pope, John XII (955–63), was deposed, but died the following year, thus allowing a valid election of his successor to proceed.

reluctantly. Writing of his successor, John Paul II urged, "God who imposes the burden, will sustain him with his hand, so that he will be able to bear it. In conferring the heavy task upon him, God will also help him to accomplish it and, in giving him the dignity, he will grant him the strength not to be overwhelmed by the weight of his office."

The pontiff, if he so chooses, may abdicate. In the event of such a retirement, the pope must make his decision known to the whole Church and the decision must be given of his own accord, not under compulsion from any quarter. Although he may resign from the Bishopric of Rome,

< GENERAL AUDIENCE
Thousands of followers crowd into St. Peter's Square to listen to the papal address during the pope's General Audience, held every Wednesday.

One must shield the pope from a monstrous
mass of mail and documents so that he can do
what he needs to do with necessary calm.

THE POPE'S PRIVATE SECRETARY

⋏ THE SYNOD OF BISHOPS
The opening ceremony of the XI Ordinary
General Assembly of the Synod of Bishops
begins with a celebration of Holy Mass
with Pope Benedict XVI.

 THE PAPAL FAMILY

In the past, the Papal Household had all the trappings of an ancient court, with a large variety of attendants. Among some of the colorful titles were Master of the Sacred Palace and Prefect of the Bedchamber. Following reforms by Pope Paul VI in 1970, the number of aids was greatly reduced and today the pope's team of immediate staff, when compared to other heads of state, is surprisingly small.

THE PRIVATE SECRETARIES

In all his work, the pontiff's two private secretaries are fundamental. These priests administer the pope's immediate schedule, facilitating correspondence and arranging appointments. It is also their role to filter requests to the pope, preventing him from being inundated. Officially called Chaplains to His Holiness, the priests are seconded from the Secretariat of State and are entrusted with a variety of tasks, some personal, others official. They co-ordinate the pope's diary with the Prefect of the Papal Household and look after the pontiff's personal life, arranging phone calls or preparing correspondence with his friends and acquaintances. There must always be one private secretary attending the pope at all times.

THE PREFECTURE

The Prefect of the Papal Household, normally a bishop, is responsible for the pope's timetable. His office, in collaboration with the pontiff's private secretaries, the Secretariat of State and the Office for Liturgical Ceremonies, oversees the pope's daily appointments. The care of the papal apartments also falls under the remit of the Prefecture, who sees to all the domestic needs of the pope in his private quarters. The pontiff does not receive a salary, or even have a bank account, and it is the prefect's job to look after any financial matters on his behalf. He also arranges seating for the pope's public appearances, including the Wednesday General Audiences and liturgies celebrated at the Vatican. The prefect oversees all the pope's travel arrangements in Rome and throughout Italy; papal trips are organized in close collaboration with the Secretariat of State who also liaises with the local authorities and governments.

THE SYNOD OF BISHOPS

Following the Second Vatican Council held between 1962 and 1965, Pope Paul VI established the Synod of Bishops. This group consists of members of the Roman Curia and delegate bishops from around the world. The synod meets in Rome every two or three years to discuss contemporary issues facing the Church, and the pope either presides over the synod himself or appoints a president to act on his behalf. The synod is essentially an advisory body to the pope. It cannot pass binding legislation but rather offers suggestions to the pontiff on various issues. Following the synod, the pope composes an Apostolic Exhortation, which reflects on issues that may have been raised during the sessions.

ATTENDANTS

In times gone by, the papal court consisted of a complex nobility, each member of which played an elaborate part in the protocol that surrounded the pope. Nowadays, few such groups survive. One, the *sediari,* looks after visitors to the pope's audiences, presenting those greeted by the pontiff with a rosary or medal as a memento. Another body, the Gentlemen of His Holiness, attends the pope when he is receiving public dignitaries and escorts the dignitaries to and from papal audiences.

The pope's personal attendants include a confessor, appointed by the pope himself, who visits the Vatican once a week to hear his confession. The pope also has a permanent private physician and a medical team on call to deal with any health issues.

▲ MOURNING THE DEATH OF A POPE
Crowds gathered in St. Peter's Square during
the final hours of Pope John Paul II's life.
Thousands prayed for the pontiff who died
in the late evening of April 2, 2005.

PAPAL ELECTIONS

The elaborate rituals surrounding
the death of a pope and the subsequent election of a new pope go
back centuries. The pope's funeral
rites last for nine days, during which
time people from all over the world
come to Rome to pay their respects
to the deceased pontiff and assist in
the funeral obsequies. Meanwhile,
the Vatican's cardinals prepare the
conclave, the closed session in which
the College of Cardinals elects a
successor to the papacy.

THE DEATH OF A POPE

As soon as he is infomed of the pope's
death, the Cardinal Camerlengo
(Chamberlain) must verify the death
in the presence of the Master of
Pontifical Liturgical Celebrations.
The Fisherman's Ring, the pope's
personal seal, is then removed and
ceremonially defaced to ensure that
it is not used again; the ring is later
buried with the pope. The Cardinal
Camerlengo takes responsibility for
the Church during the *sede vacante*—
the period until the next pope is
elected. It is the job of the Cardinal
Vicar of Rome, who administers the
diocese of Rome on the pontiff's
behalf, to announce the death of the
pope to the world. All but three
members of the Roman Curia then
cease their activities. These are the
Camerlengo, the Master of
Liturgical Ceremonies, and the
Major Penitentiary, the cardinal
responsible for issues relating to the
forgiveness of sins.

In preparation, the body of the
pope is clothed in red liturgical
vestments with a simple white mitre
on his head. Assuming that the pope
has died in the Apostolic Palace, his
body is exposed for veneration in
the Sala Clementina, close to the
entrance of the papal apartments.
On the second day, the body is
transferred to St. Peter's Basilica so
that the public may pay their respects.
At the funeral of Pope John Paul II
in 2005, some four million people
filed past his body.

THE CONCLAVE

On the morning of the conclave,
the College of Cardinals celebrate a
public Mass in St. Peter's Basilica.
In the afternoon, the cardinal-
electors, those cardinals who are
under 80 years of age, assemble in
the Hall of Benedictions in the
Basilica. From here, the cardinals
proceed, in procession, across the
Sala Regia to the Sistine Chapel.
The Sistine Choir lead the prelates,
singing the hymn *Veni Creator
Spiritus* (Come Holy Spirit, Creator
blest) to invoke God's blessing.

The 120 cardinal-electors take
their places in the limited space
inside the Sistine Chapel. On

entering the chapel, they are required to take the oath of the conclave laid down by Pope Paul VI in 1975, promising to maintain confidentiality and impartiality. When the cardinals have taken their positions, the Master of Liturgical Celebrations orders, *Extra omnes!* (All must leave!). The choir and all media personnel depart and the doors to the Sistine Chapel are locked and sealed from both inside and out with ribbon and wax. Among the few non-cardinals who remain in the conclave are the Master of Liturgical Ceremonies, who looks after the prayers recited during the conclave, the delegate for the Pontifical Commission for the Vatican City State, the legislative body of Vatican City, and other essential staff. A great deal of secrecy surrounds the conclave and at all stages, even after the process has ended, the cardinals are prohibited from speaking about it except to other cardinals and a confessor.

THE ELECTION PROCESS

Inside the chapel, each cardinal is provided with a chair and a small desk. There are two ballots cast in the morning and two in the afternoon; each cardinal must therefore cast a vote four times each day. At each ballot, the cardinal sits at his desk and completes a card inscribed *Eligio in summum pontificem...*

▲ INSIDE THE CONCLAVE
At the beginning of the conclave, the cardinals solemnly vow to elect the person they believe to be the best candidate for the papacy and swear to serve him loyally.

(I elect as Supreme Pontiff...), adding the name of the person he believes to be suitable. The cardinals go to great lengths to disguise their handwriting and once they have completed the ballot paper they proceed, one by one, to the High Altar on which an urn has been set. Holding up his folded paper, each cardinal says aloud, "I call as my witness Christ the Lord who will be my judge that

my vote is given to the one who before God I think should be elected." He then places his ballot in the urn. If a cardinal is unable to attend the session due to illness, three cardinal delegates collect his vote for him.

The votes are counted by three cardinal-scrutineers, calling the names out loud as they go along. If the voting session proves inconclusive, the cardinals gather the ballots and pass them to the Master of Liturgical Celebrations, who takes them to a stove at the back of the Sistine Chapel where they are burned. A chimney leading from the stove

protrudes from the chapel roof. The crowd waiting below in St. Peter's Square can gauge by the color of the smoke if a pope has been elected: white smoke indicates an election, while black confirms that the pope has not yet been chosen. In the past, if the voting did not produce a pope, damp straw was put in with the ballots to make the smoke black. Since 1978, chemicals have been used to ensure the clear differentiation of the colors.

If after three days the cardinals fail to find a candidate to be pope, they are required to suspend the

The old Roman saying, "One pope dies, we elect another" underlines the importance of the office rather than the person.

▲ ENTERING THE CONCLAVE
The cardinals file from the Hall of Benedictions, through the Sala Regia, where the Swiss Guard form a guard of honor, and into the Sistine Chapel, where they will elect a new pope.

< URBI ET ORBI
The newly elected Pope Francis blesses the crowds from the balcony of St. Peter's. This blessing is called *Urbi et Orbi*—to the City (of Rome) and to the world.

At the election of Albino Luciani in 1978, he took the first double name in honor of the previous two popes, John XXIII and Paul VI, becoming John Paul I.

If the cardinal chosen by the conclave is not yet a bishop, the Dean of the College of Cardinals immediately ordains him. The new pope is led to a small sacristy located to the left of the High Altar prosaically called the Room of Tears where the Master of Liturgical Celebrations and the papal tailor wait to vest the new pontiff. The tailor will have three clothes sizes—small, medium, and large—already prepared. The new pope dons a white ankle-length *soutane* (cassock), a linen *rochet* (a liturgical garment with lace sleeves), and a red silk *mozzetta* (cape), over which is placed a red and gold stole. He exchanges his scarlet *zucchetto* (skullcap) for a white silk one. He also changes his black shoes to the red moccasins worn by the pontiff. The new pope is then led back to the High Altar positioned underneath Michelangelo's *Last Judgement* where a throne is set. The cardinals then make their obeisances to the new pope before returning to their places.

balloting for one day of prayer and meditation. While God's inspiration is sought, some cardinals may seek to promote certain candidates. Voting continues once more for seven ballots with a pause, then a further seven ballots (each cardinal must vote 14 times) followed by a pause and an address by the senior cardinal. Although it is possible for a conclave to last for a long time, it is unlikely that any modern session will be as long as those of the past. Not since 1831, when the conclave lasted an astonishing seven weeks, has it taken more than five days to elect a new pontiff. When a candidate gains two thirds of the votes plus one, he is deemed elected.

THE NEW POPE

Once a candidate for the papacy has attained the required majority, the Cardinal Dean, accompanied by two other cardinals, proceeds to the desk where the candidate is sitting and asks in Latin, "*Acceptasne electionem de te canonice factam in Summum Pontificem?*" (Do you accept your canonical election as Supreme Pontiff?). If the cardinal accedes to his election, he must declare "*Accepto*"(I accept). The Cardinal Dean then asks, "By what name will you be called?" The new pope must then choose the papal name by which he will be known for the length of his office. The first pope to change his name was John I in the sixth century. His original name was Mercury, which was regarded as unsuitably pagan.

THE ANNOUNCEMENT

When the obeisance is over, the closed session of the conclave ends. The senior Cardinal Deacon or his assistant leaves the Sistine Chapel to inform the world of the election of the new pope. Already smoke will have issued from the chimney above the Sistine roof and now the bells of all the churches of Rome peal, announcing the news that the city has a new bishop, the world a new pope. As the media flashes the news throughout the world, people hasten to reach St. Peter's Square. There is a mounting sense of excitement as the crowds wait to hear the name and nationality of the new pope. While thousands surge into the square, a procession of cardinals crosses the Hall of the Benedictions, which runs across the inside of the facade of the basilica. The windows of the main *loggia*, or balcony, open and the curtains are parted. Preceded by a golden processional cross, the Cardinal Deacon steps out onto the balcony and says, "*Annuntio vobis gaudium magnum. Habemus papam!*" (I announce to you a great joy. We have a pope!). He then proceeds to give the name of the elected cardinal and the name the new pope has chosen for himself. Shortly after the public announcement is made, the pontiff is escorted to the *loggia*, where he presents himself to the crowds and gives a brief address, acknowledging the salute of the crowds and concluding with his first Apostolic Blessing.

Returning to the Apostolic Palace, the pope consults with the Camerlengo and the Master of Liturgical Celebrations in order to fix the day for the Inauguration. The following morning, the pope concelebrates Mass in the Sistine Chapel and in his homily gives an outline of his ministry as successor of St. Peter.

THE INAUGURATION

Although the pope is recognized as soon as he accepts his nomination, there is an Inaugural Mass some days later to mark the beginning of the Petrine Ministry. During the Mass, the pope receives the Ring of the Fisherman, a newly cast gold band inscribed with an image of St. Peter. The pontiff takes possession of the private apartments, sealed following the death of his predecessor, and some days later travels to St. John Lateran, the cathedral of Rome, where he celebrates Mass for the people of his new diocese. After the Mass, the pope receives all the dignitaries and heads of state who participated in the ceremony.

ᴠ INAUGURAL MASS
The Mass of Inauguration is celebrated by the new pope in St. Peter's Square, which is filled with well-wishers.

The diocese of Rome is referred to as the Holy See, or the Apostolic See, with the pope, the Bishop of Rome, at its head. Although the Vatican is a city state, its principal role is to serve as a focus for unity of all the world's Catholics. Everything that pertains to a Catholic is addressed at the Vatican, from ethical and moral questions to more practical issues. The pope, as head of the Catholic Church, must serve the faithful by teaching and providing spiritual leadership; the Holy See and its government, the Roman Curia, provide the infrastructure to support his work.

Beyond Catholicsm, the Holy See works to foster relations between governments around the world. Papal diplomatic delegations monitor political developments, especially in the moral and ethical spheres, and the Holy See maintains a number of non-voting delegations to international institutions.

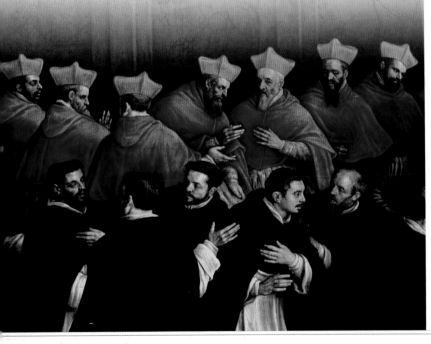

⚜ THE ROMAN CURIA

The Roman Curia, the government of the Catholic Church, is an effective organization that facilitates communication between the Holy See and Catholics throughout the world. The Curia was established in its present form in 1588 by Pope Sixtus V (1585–90). Since at least the fourth century, a number of offices had existed to assist the pope carry out his duties; the most recent reform of the Curia dates from 1988, under Pope John Paul II.

At the head of the Vatican government is the Secretary of State. This position is always occupied by a cardinal who acts as the pope's chief deputy, charged with the running of the Church. The Secretary of State is assisted by a Secretariat comprising some 70 workers, mostly clerics. Drawn from around the globe, these officials are generally assigned to represent one or more geographical areas. The Secretariat is divided into two sections; the first deals with internal relations within the Church, while the second deals with international relations, especially those with other states.

In order to cope with the enormous demands made upon the Church, the Roman Curia is divided into a number of offices called Congregations, Tribunals, Pontifical

⌃ SECRETARY OF STATE
The second highest dignitary after the pope, the Secretary of State is in charge of the Roman Curia.

Councils, and Pontifical Commissions. The Church is involved in a rich variety of works throughout the world—from education to healthcare, and from worship to relations with other faiths—and the various Vatican offices reflect this diversity.

THE CONGREGATIONS

Many of the Curia's nine Congregations were established in the 16th century. The Congregations are the equivalent of government ministries, overseeing relations between the Holy See and the local churches. Each congregation is headed by a cardinal prefect, who presides over

THE HOLY SEE
THE HEAD OF THE CHURCH

> Modeled on the Roman Empire, the Roman Curia's role is to help the pope fulfil his office as the Successor of Peter.

a small staff. There are also a number of consultants who regularly attend meetings to offer advice.

The Congregation for Bishops deals with the appointment and needs of bishops. Support of its priests is vital to the Church, and the Congregation for the Clergy looks after all priests and deacons, as well as local parishes and the personnel that staff them. All Catholic schools and universities are assisted by the Congregation for Catholic Education. The Curia's other Congregations include the Congregation for Divine Worship and the Discipline of the Sacraments, which regulates the celebration of the sacraments; the Congregation of the Evangelisation of Peoples, which cares for territories such as New Zealand; the Congregation for the Causes of the Saints *(see p. 200)*; the Congregation for Oriental Churches; and the Congregation for Institutes of Consecrated Life and Societies of Apostolic Life, which supports religious orders and some lay groups. Underpining all these areas is the Congregation for the Doctrine of the Faith, which addresses important questions of theology and issues pertaining to the Catholic faith.

PONTIFICAL COUNCILS

The Pontifical Councils were set up following the reforms of the Second Vatican Council (1962–65) and respond to issues such as ecumenism, ethics, and social justice. The Pontifical Council for Promoting Christian Unity works to foster relations and understanding throughout the whole Christian family, while the Pontifical Council for Inter-religious Dialogue fosters relations between the Catholic Church and other world faiths.

The Pontifical Council for Justice and Peace raises the awareness of justice issues, especially in poor, war-torn areas, addressing subjects such as prostitution, exploitation, and healthcare. The Pontifical Council Cor Unum oversees the charitable services organized by the Church for the underpriviliged throughout the world, while care for the sick, is the principal aim of the Pontifical Council for Pastoral Assistance to Healthcare Workers.

PONTIFICAL COMMISSIONS

A number of offices, known as Pontifical Commissions, oversee varying aspects of the Vatican and the Catholic Church. Their remit is broad, from providing for the needs of Catholics in Latin America to commissions that are more focused on the Vatican itself. The Pontifical Commission for the Fabric of St. Peter's Basilica, for example, is responsible for the maintenance of the tomb of St. Peter and the basilica, while the Pontifical Commission for the Cultural Heritage of the Church oversees the preservation of its patrimony. Other commissions include the Pontifical Commission for Sacred Archaeology, which sponsors seminars and fosters the education of archaeologists, and the Pontifical Committee for Historical Sciences, which reviews historical events pertaining to the life of the Church.

> **CARDINALS IN CONVERSATION**
The College of Cardinals comprises cardinals drawn from most countries around the world. This body advises the pope and is similar to a senate.

GUIDING THE FAITHFUL

The Catechism of the Catholic Church (1992) declares that "the task of interpreting the Word of God authentically has been entrusted solely to the Magisterium [teaching authority] of the Church, that is, to the pope and to the bishops in communion with him". According to the Catholic Church, the pontiff may err in human judgment but is defined as infallible when teaching dogma. The pope, therefore, is charged with the enormous task of guiding the faith of the world's Catholics.

In fulfilling his duty, the Roman pontiff must speak by virtue of his authority as the successor of Peter the Apostle in areas of faith and morals. The pope is not permitted to make a statement that is not supported by the world's bishops or that is in variance with the traditional teaching of the Church. Any teaching that he makes must be held by the Church as a whole and the pope must always act with respect for tradition.

There are many ways in which the pope is able to disseminate the teachings of the Church. One of the most obvious is through homilies during liturgies. Throughout the year, the pope presides over a number of liturgies, many of which are broadcast all over the world. During these liturgies, the pontiff may reflect on the Scriptural readings and expand some of the themes, offering homilies that seek to illuminate aspects of the liturgical readings. Another effective way to reach a wide audience is through the General Audiences, held each week at the Vatican. On these days, the pope addresses a variety of issues and offers meditations on passages from the Bible. The various popes have had their own individual style of address. Pope John Paul I (1978) had an inimitable and friendly approach, quoting contemporary writers and inviting people to interact during his short addresses. Over his 27-year pontificate, Pope John Paul II (1978–2005) addressed a wide range of topics, often from a philosophical point of view, while

⌃ A PAPAL LITURGY
Pope Benedict XVI celebrates Vespers, the Evening Prayer of the Church, at the magnificent St Paul-Outside-the-Walls, one of Rome's four patriarchal basilicas.

Pope Benedict XVI regularly devotes his speeches to figures from the early centuries of the Church. Private Audiences are another way in which the pope can teach. These audiences are granted to specific groups and the pope will normally give a discourse closely allied to their visit. Given the pressures of work on the pontiff, Private Audiences are both rare and highly prized.

Every year, Catholics around the world await the pope's yearly address, *urbi et orbi* (to the city and the world). This takes place on Christmas Day and Easter Sunday when millions tune in to hear his speech, broadcast live on radio, television, and over the Internet. The apostolic journeys undertaken by the pontiff are also an important aspect of the papal role. The pope travels to all parts of the globe to spread the faith and give his followers a chance to connect with their spiritual father.

Closer to home, the pontiff uses various types of formal writing to convey his teachings. An encyclical, for example, is a document that examines issues that the pope regards as important. The encyclicals are addressed to Catholics and non-Catholics alike, and are of a more personal nature and therefore less formal than papal bulls, official charters or decrees. Following a

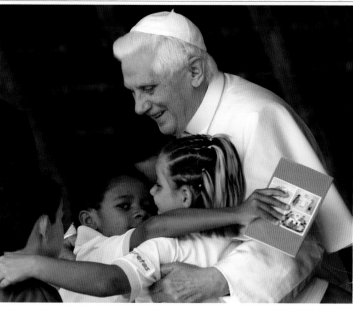

< AN APOSTOLIC JOURNEY
Pope Benedict XVI embraces children in Guarantigueta during his five-day visit to Brazil in 2007.

Synod of Bishops, a meeting of the pope's advisory board, the pope also publishes an Apostolic Exhortation, which reflects on the deliberations of the meeting. Another type of document is a *motu proprio* (literally "of his own accord"). This is often a personal document addressing a particular interest of the pope. The words *motu proprio* signify that the contents of the document were dealt with personally by the pope. Although not obliged to, the pontiff normally circulates drafts of his important writings to curial offices and to trusted advisors before these writings are published.

Various offices within the Roman Curia contribute to the life of the Universal Church. Their

deliberations are published in *Acts of the Apostolic See*, a publication of all the official documents produced by the Holy See, which is circulated to local churches. The Vatican newspaper, *L'Osservatore Romano,* is also a useful tool for keeping up to date with the decisions of various offices, as is the Vatican website.

For those guiding the faithful, help is at hand in the form of the Catechism of the Catholic Church, which was published in 1992. The Catechism is the official reference book on the teachings of the Catholic Church and is some 900 pages long. The book is used by those teaching Catholic dogma and has been translated from the original French into several other languages.

The first Roman Catechism was printed in 1566, following the Council of Trent.

Various bodies also exist within the Church to aid the pope in his work. Important questions of faith that are referred to the Holy See for adjudication are normally addressed by the Congregation for the Doctrine of the Faith. Founded in 1542, the office was originally designed to defend the Church from heresy but today the Congregation oversees all questions pertaining to doctrine and morals. The range of questions is vast, from In Vitro Fertilization to belief in heaven, hell, and purgatory. The Congregation consults with other bodies in the Roman Curia, including the Pontifical Biblical Commission, which ensures the proper interpretation and defence of Sacred Scripture, and the International Theological Commission, made up of respected theologians from around the world. Another body, the Congregation for Divine Worship and the Discipline of the Sacraments, looks after the manner in which the seven sacraments (Baptism, Confirmation, Penance, Eucharist, Matrimony, Holy Orders, and the Sacrament of the Sick) are administered.

✕ JOINING THE PRIESTHOOD

If a person feels himself called to the priesthood, the first step is to approach a bishop or a religious order. This most disciplined of professions requires conviction, dedication, and the ability to be a good judge of character. A request to enter the priesthood, therefore, is granted only after reflection on a candidate's suitability. Future clergy enter a program of training in a novitiate or seminary, where they are taught the main disciplines of philosophy and theology. Training can take up to seven years, and although there is no age limit for entering the priesthood, candidates are usually young and must be over 25 before they can be ordained.

Priests normally belong to a diocese or a religious order. Those who belong to a diocese (diocesan priests) work in a particular territory under the jurisdiction of the local bishop and are not permitted to move from one place to another without permission. They are usually assigned to a parish, a territorial subsection of the diocese, where they are responsible for the spiritual life of its inhabitants. The priest is assisted by the Parish Council, which is made up of a number of parishioners who all collaborate on the administration and development of the parish.

The roles available to trainee seminarians are many and varied. Those not assigned to a parish may be appointed to their bishop's Curia, or diocesan office. Some bishops in large dioceses may appoint a moderator of the Curia, a priest who administers certain sections in his name. Priests who belong to religious orders (religious priests) work in specialized ministries, such as education or a hospital ministry.

Clergy that go on to become bishops are given their own diocese for which they are responsible. To become a bishop, candidates must prove themselves to be wise and men of faith and prayer, and have good administrative skills. The selection process can take several months of consultation, with the pope making the final decision.

Seminarians are looked after by the Congregation of the Clergy. This body oversees the education and pastoral activities of all clerics, and ensures that a sufficient number of priests are spread across the globe to offer the most effective pastoral care.

> The Church does not "make" a saint. Rather, it "recognizes" saints.

✕ THE ROAD TO SAINTHOOD

The Vatican receives many petitions for beatification and sainthood from around the world, and a dedicated department, the Congregation for the Causes of Saints, is in place to consider these petitions and oversee the complex process of canonization.

The road to saint-hood is a fascinating one. It can begin not only with martyrdom but with an ordinary Christian whose piety is a source of inspiration to others. Already in the New Testament there was a concept of the saint, one who lived an outstanding life of holiness, and by the fourth century, Christians venerated "confessors", people whose life of asceticism or teaching was inspirational.

In the early centuries, local churches decided who was worthy of the title of "Saint", but in 1173, Pope Alexander III (1159–81) decreed that bishops should not recognize a person as a saint "without the authority of the Roman Catholic Church".

In the 15th century, the concept of beatification was developed. This allowed local dioceses to act independently and honor candidates with the title of "Blessed".

∧ A SAINT IN THE MAKING
Nobel Peace Prize winner Mother Teresa (1910–97) at the National Right to Life Convention held in Washington D.C. in 1985.

In 1588, Pope Sixtus V (1585–90) established the Congregation of Rites. This Congregation allowed certain "Blesseds" who had gained widespread devotion to be canonized, that is, recognized as saints. Today, this body is known as the Congregaton for the Causes of Saints.

The present-day procedure for recognizing saints was set out in 1983 by Pope John Paul II. It states that a diocesan bishop may formally begin to examine the life of a potential candidate for sainthood, five years after the candidate's death. The bishop must have the permission of the Holy See to establish a local tribunal in which to do this. If, after careful assessment, there is judged sufficient evidence for the person's holiness, the material is sent to Rome to the Congregation for the Causes of Saints where further investigations are made. If the application is approved, the pope will confer the honorific title of "Servant of God". In order to be beatified, that is receive the title of "Blessed", one miracle must be recognized, normally a physical healing. A medical team, made up of non-Catholics to avoid partisanship, examines the miracle according to a stringent set of requirements. The healing must be immediate and without any medical explanation. It must also be definitive and the illness must not reoccur. Full medical records before and after the healing must also be submitted.

For a canonization, proof of one further miracle is required. However, if somebody died a martyr, that is, for the faith, proof of miracles are not required. A request for canonization is always examined by the pope himself. If he is convinced of the merits of the case, the pope notifies the College of Cardinals and sets a date for the canonization ceremony. The pope is presented with a relic of a newly canonized saint, such as a lock of hair, item of clothing, or, in some cases, a piece of bone. These relics provide a tangible link with the saints and are stored in the reliquary, a large room in the Apostolic Palace.

The Catholic nun, Mother Teresa of Calcutta, is the best known "saint" of the 20th century. A native of Albania, she dedicated her life to serving the poor and the sick of Calcutta, in India, until her death in 1997. Her order, the Missionaries of Charity, work with the poor, the sick, and the dying in 124 countries throughout the world. In 1979, Mother Teresa won the Nobel Peace Prize for her humanitaran work and, following the recognition of a miraculous cure, she was beatified in 2003 and carries the title "Blessed Teresa of Calcutta".

A BLESSED SIMON OF LIPNICA
During a plague in Krakow in 1482–83, this Polish Franciscan friar cared for the dying before contracting the disease himself. He was canonized in June 2007.

> Let us avoid division, and follow the path of solidarity, of mutual trust, and of respect for diversity. POPE BENEDICT XVI

✠ UNIFYING THE CHURCH

The mission of the Holy See is to promote unity within the Church, and the Vatican's many Congregations, Councils, and Synods work to foster and maintain that unity. The Congregation for Catholic Education, for example, oversees all academic institutions where the Catholic faith is taught, offering advice and receiving information on the development of the faith in different regions. The Congregation for the Oriental Churches unites the various strands of Christians, particularly in the East, and the Holy See's diplomatic missions serve to develop these links further.

The apostolic journeys undertaken by the pope also play their part in uniting the faithful around the globe with the mission of Peter the Apostle. These trips allow the pope to investigate the conditions of Christians in far-flung parts of the world and offer a bond of unity with the Holy See. The pope also visits members of other Christian communities and religious faiths.

From the time of the apostles there have been rifts within the Catholic Church. The Second Vatican Council (1962–65) acknowledged the failures of the past and urged Catholics to improve relations with other Christians. Today, although full communion has not been achieved, it is common for Christians to work, pray, and worship together.

The Holy See, however, faces further challenges and its ability to adapt is fundamental to the very survival of the Church. The *Unitatis Redintegratio* (Restoration of Unity) decree, promulgated on November 21, 1964, stated that "Christ summons the Church to continual reformation as she sojourns here on earth".

✠ OUTSIDE THE FAITH

In the past, relations between the Catholic Church and other religions were often fraught with misunderstanding and hostility. The Second Vatican Council played a large part in changing this, helping to promote tolerance through its *Nostra Aetate* (In Our Time), the Declaration on the Relation of the Church with Non-Christian Religions. The declaration was promulgated on October 28, 1965 and stated that "the Catholic Church rejects nothing that is true and holy in these religions. She regards with sincere reverence those ways of conduct and of life, those precepts and teachings which, though differing in many aspects from the ones she holds and sets forth, nonetheless often reflect a ray of that Truth which enlightens all men." The same declaration also acknowledged the mistakes of the past, stating that "since in the course of centuries not a few quarrels and hostilities have arisen between Christians and Muslims, this sacred synod urges all to forget the past and to work for mutual understanding."

During the periods of missionary expansion, between the 16th and 18th centuries, Christians were often guilty of high-handedly dismissing indigenous faiths. While maintaining

^ TRAVELS IN AFRICA
In 1990, Pope John Paul II embarked on an apostolic journey through Africa. Upon arrival in the Republic of Mali, he was greeted by animist bird dancers.

absolute conviction of the mission of the Church to all people, the Second Vatican Council sought to eradicate the failure of previous centuries: "The Church reproves, as foreign to the mind of Christ, any discrimination against men or harassment of them because of their race, color, condition of life, or religion."

In 1986, Pope John Paul II invited Christian leaders and leaders of other world religions to Assisi, the town of St. Francis, to pray for peace. Gathered close to the tomb of St. Francis, the pope noted "with the other Christians we share many convictions and, particularly, in what concerns peace. With the religions of the world we share a common respect of and obedience to conscience, which teaches all of us to seek the truth, to love and serve all individuals and people, and therefore to make peace among nations." It was the first "summit" of its kind in history.

Today, the Vatican continues to promote unity with other faiths. The Holy See and Islamic authorities regularly exchange greetings and acknowledge each others important religious festivals. Bodies like the Pontifical Council for Inter-religious Dialogue and the Pontifical Council for Justice and Peace have also been set up to look at inter-faith questions and to foster tolerance and understanding of other religions.

▲ REACHING OUT TO MUSLIMS
Pope Benedict XVI is guided around Istanbul's famous Blue Mosque by head cleric Mustafa Çağrıcı, during a visit to Turkey in 2006.

PEOPLE

 ## A DAY IN THE LIFE

The public face of the Vatican that is typically shown to the world conjures up images of the white-clad pontiff, the multicolored Swiss Guard, and black-robed cardinals, all set against the majestic backdrop of St. Peter's Basilica. But behind this outward display of colorful pomp and pageantry, there are a whole host of employees, the performance of whose daily routine permit the Vatican to function efficiently: its security forces, museum staff, sisters and brothers, curators, art restorers, administrative staff, and many others. The Vatican has a truly international population, though some of its residents were born into Italian families who have provided generations of service. This chapter presents a day in the life of 12 workers in the Vatican, some of whom are members of the Church hierarchy, and some of whom hold responsibilities of a more secular nature.

The beginning of Pope Francis's pontificate was unusual.
For the first time in history, two popes lived side by side at the Vatican. While emeritus-Pope Benedict XVI resided in a converted convent in the Vatican Gardens, Pope Francis chose to live in a residence, the Casa Santa Marta, close to the Vatican walls. Francis has said it is "like having a grandfather at home—a very wise grandfather."

The Casa Santa Marta was built in 1994 as housing for clergy working in the Roman Curia or for guests visiting the Vatican on business. It is used by the Cardinals during papal conclaves. After his election, Pope Francis decided to continue living at the Casa Santa Marta where he has a small bedroom and study.

Each morning, the pope rises at around 5:00 a.m. The earlier hours are his private time before going to the chapel, where he celebrates Mass at 7:00 a.m. with guests and often invites them to join him for breakfast.

Shortly after 8:00 a.m. the pope attends to correspondence and official documentation, and also meets privately with visitors. With Pope Francis it is common to see not only Heads of State but also soccer players or sick children and their carers. He salutes each person individually, offering a blessing, exchanging a joke, or a word of encouragement. His spontaneous and extrovert style are in contrast to the reserved demeanor of the scholarly Benedict XVI. On Wednesday mornings, the pope holds a General Audience, during which he greets as many people as possible, especially the needy or disabled.

Meals are taken in the refectory where he lives. Not standing on ceremony, the pope sits down wherever he finds a space and enjoys the Italian food prepared in the kitchen. After a short siesta, the pope holds meetings from 5:00 p.m. until 7:00 p.m. with Curial officials, followed by an hour of prayer. After a light supper in the refectory, the pope meets people for discussions and often phones family or friends. The day ends with prayers in the chapel before the pope retires for the night.

While the pope welcomes hundreds of thousands to the Vatican, he also travels throughout the world and uses the press and social media to reach a global audience, too—whether via an impromptu press briefing on a plane or through a message on his twitter account.

POPE FRANCIS
HEAD OF THE CATHOLIC CHURCH

◄ TWO POPES MEET
Pope Francis and emeritus Pope Benedict embraced at Castelgandolfo on March 23, 2013, the first time the two men had met since the conclave.

∨ TALKING WITH CARDINALS
Following a cannonzation ceremony at St. Peter's, the cardinals greet the pope and exchange pleasantries.

∨ PRIVATE AUDIENCE
The pope regularly engages with other religious leaders. In May 2013, he met with the Coptic Orthodox leader Tawadros II.

∧ PRESS CONFERENCE
Pope Francis gave an impromptu press conference for more than an hour on the flight to Rome after World Youth Day in July 2013.

∨ GENERAL AUDIENCE
Children embrace the pope during a General Audience. Pope Francis is relaxed in crowds and enjoys greeting people from around the world.

A MASS CELEBRATION
More than three million young people,
from 178 countries, joined Pope Francis
in the celebration of Mass at Copacabana
beach in Rio de Janeiro on July 28, 2013.

Dear young friends, the Church needs you, your enthusiasm, your creativity, and the joy that is so characteristic of you.

❯ THE WEDNESDAY AUDIENCE

The pope emerges for the weekly General Audience, which in warmer weather takes place in St. Peter's Square.

⋎ THE POPEMOBILE

The pope travels through St. Peter's Square in an open-top jeep—the "Popemobile"—greeting the thousands of people who attend the audience.

❯ GREETING THE PILGRIMS

On his journey around the square, the pope stretches from the Popemobile to touch as many hands as possible.

⋎ THE AUDIENCE PODIUM

During the audience, the pope, seated under a canopy, offers a brief spiritual meditation in several languages. After this, he blesses the visiting pilgrims.

⋏ MEETING FELLOW BISHOPS

Arriving for the General Audience, the pope takes a few minutes to welcome bishops who have traveled to see him, offering words of encouragement and support.

‹ SUNDAY ANGELUS
At noon every Sunday, the pope appears at the window of his study to pray with the crowds of people gathered in St. Peter's Square below.

› INSPIRING SIGHT
Pope Francis often banters in a good humored manner with the crowds, who enjoy his informal and exuberant style.

⌄ MUSICAL INTERLUDES
Among the crowds that gather below on these occasions are choirs and musicians. In his speech, the pope will often greet these groups by name.

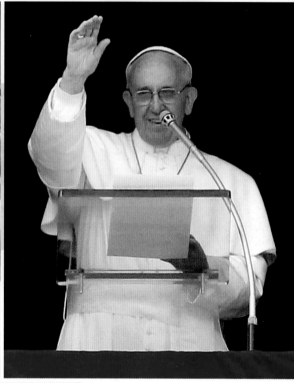

‹ ⋀ READING THE ANGELUS
Large crowds of the faithful, some of whom carry banners and flags, gather to listen to the pope as he greets the pilgrims. The pope reads his greeting and prayer from a podium; he speaks into a microphone so that his voice can be amplified to fill the whole square.

> DISCUSSING THE AGENDA
The cardinal meets his secretary each morning shortly after 8:00 a.m. to plan the activities and audiences of the day.

⌄ PAPERWORK
With correspondence from different offices within the Vatican and from all over the world, Cardinal Sandri oversees all documentation personally.

Although there are over a billion Catholics in the world, not all belong to the Roman rite. There are some 22 million members of Eastern Churches, who preserve their own ancient liturgical, theological, and disciplinary traditions, but are in full communion with the pope. Cardinal Leonardo Sandri is Prefect, or head, of the Congregation for Oriental Churches, the Vatican body that deals with the affairs of these Eastern Catholics.

The Congregation for Oriental Churches is concerned with the situation of Catholics belonging to various Eastern traditions in many countries, including Iran, Iraq, Syria, Jordan, Turkey, Egypt, and Lebanon. It works—where possible—with the governments of these countries and also cares for Eastern Catholics who have migrated to the West or other parts of the world, organizing charitable collections and funding education. Many of these Christians live in countries where practice of their faith is restricted or even forbidden. In some places they face outright persecution.

Today, Churches such as the Armenian Catholic Church and the Ukrainian Greek Catholic Church, with their ancient rites and Eastern theological heritage, act as a bridge between the Latin Catholic Church and the Greek Orthodox Church.

Leonardo Sandri was born in Buenos Aires, Argentina, in 1943. After studying philosophy and theology, he attended the Gregorian University in Rome. After his ordination he was invited to join the Church's diplomatic mission. He completed a doctorate in Canon Law at the Vatican's Academy for Diplomats, then spent many years in the diplomatic corps, serving as Apostolic Nuncio (ambassador from the pope) in Venezuela and Mexico.

In 2000, Pope John Paul II appointed him Substitute for General Affairs at the Secretariat of State, one of the most senior positions in the Roman Curia. He was responsible for the Roman Curia and dealings with embassies and nuncios. It was in this capacity that he announced the death of Pope John Paul II to the world on April 2, 2005. Sandri was appointed Prefect of the Congregation for Oriental Churches in 2007, and became a cardinal that same year.

As Prefect, Cardinal Sandri is based principally in Rome, but he travels regularly to countries under his jurisdiction as the representative of the pope. Apart from his native Spanish, he also speaks Italian, French, German, and English.

⋏ DAILY AUDIENCES
Each morning the cardinal receives several people in audience, many of them from the Middle East. Some, like this priest from India, come from even further afield.

> POLICY MEETING
The cardinal discusses Congregation projects with two priests. These include the sponsorship of an academic institute and the raising of funds for scholarships.

VATICAN DIPLOMAT
PREFECT OF THE CONGREGATION FOR ORIENTAL CHURCHES

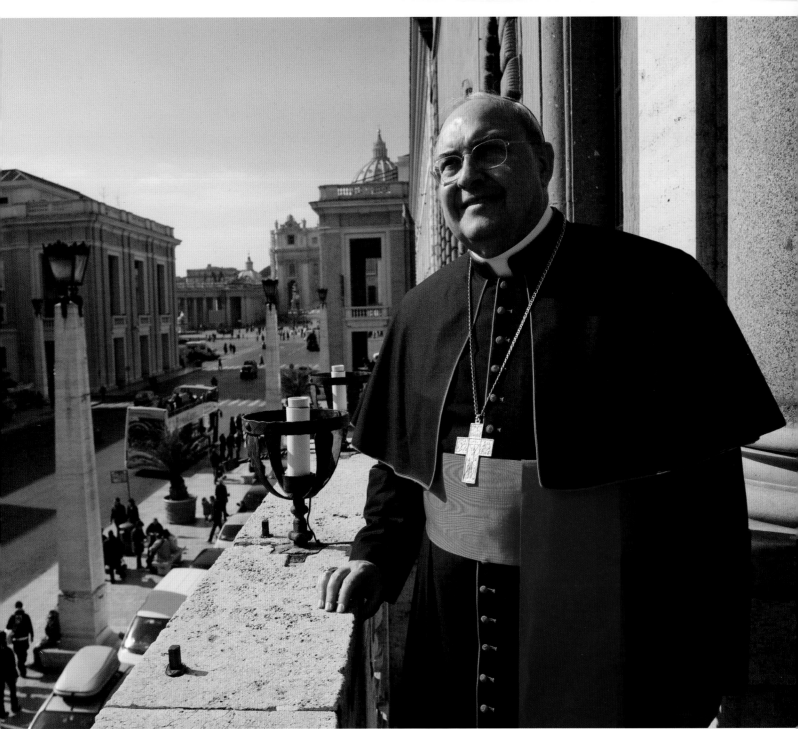

ʌ A BREAK ON THE BALCONY
The Congregation's offices overlook Via della Conciliazione, the street that leads to St. Peter's. The building, like many others in Rome, belongs to the Vatican.

< CONTINUING THE DISCUSSION
The cardinal moves with his colleagues to another part of the building, which comprises about ten rooms plus a chapel.

> A FRUITFUL MORNING
Meeting the Cardinal Prefect is greatly valued by visitors, since it gives them the chance to present their views in person.

> ACCOMPANYING A VISITING BISHOP
After talks in his office, Cardinal Sandri accompanies a visiting bishop who works for the Congregation down to the courtyard.

⌄ DEEP IN DISCUSSION
In the courtyard of the Congregation, the cardinal and bishop discuss plans for further meetings. The cardinal promises to inform the pope of their discussion.

⌃ A VISIT TO THE CHAPEL
Cardinal Sandri has invited the bishop to join him in the chapel, which is situated off the central courtyard of the office building.

< ARRIVING FOR MASS

Cardinal Sandri arrives at the church of Sant'Anselmo on the Aventine Hill, where the pope is due to celebrate Mass to mark the start of Lent on Ash Wednesday.

∧ SOLEMN PROCESSION

The procession moves from Sant' Anselmo to the nearby 5th-century basilica of Santa Sabina. Popes have followed this route for over 1,500 years.

< MEETING BEFORE MASS

Cardinal Sandri greets Cardinal Ruini, the Vicar of Rome, who administers the diocese of Rome. Behind them stand two Benedictine monks from Sant'Anselmo.

< CONGREGATION'S CHAPEL

The decoration here is quite different from what is usually found in a church of the Roman rite. The iconography and general decorative scheme reflect the Congregation's close links with Eastern churches.

∧ AT THE ALTAR

The two prelates pause for a few moments of prayer together beside the altar of the chapel. Above the crucifix behind the altar is an icon of Jesus offering bread and wine to the Apostles at the Last Supper.

< ∧ ASH WEDNESDAY MASS

The cardinals, as the most senior prelates of the Catholic Church next to the pope, walk beside the pontiff as the procession approaches the basilica of Santa Sabina. Inside, the pope takes his place on the church's magnificent episcopal throne.

The Papal Sacristy, or Treasury as it is sometimes called,
holds the liturgical items that have been given to the Vatican
over the centuries—from chalices and candlesticks to robes and
other vestments (clothing). Leonardo Marra, a native of Rome,
is one of the small group of sacristy curators who look after the
objects kept here; he also gathers and prepares the vestments and
liturgical vessels that will be used during papal ceremonies.

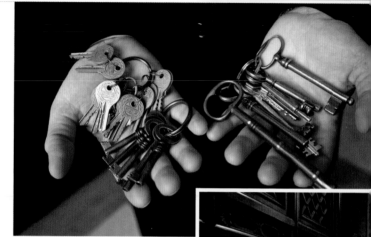

Located behind the Sistine Chapel,
the Papal Sacristy itself consists of a
combination of storerooms, display
rooms, and workrooms in which
the staff maintain and prepare the
items. The present sacristy dates
to the 15th century; however, the
treasury has existed in some form
or another since the 4th century,
when Constantine I became the
first patron of the Church, gifting
silver and gold chalices, altars, and
candlesticks for use in the liturgy.
As the power and prestige of
Christianity grew, its worshipers
produced more elaborate liturgical
objects as well as vestments of
exquisite workmanship to be
donated to the Papal Treasury.

The sacristy has been robbed
on several occasions in its history,
most notably during the final
Sack of Rome in 1527 and during
Napoleon's occupation of the city
in the 18th century. Though many
of the stolen items were returned,
a great deal of the older liturgical
vessels were never found. Thus, the
majority of the 5,000 liturgical

items now held in the Papal Sacristy
date only from the latter half of the
19th century and the 20th century.

The sacristy is administered by
Augustinian friars and a group of lay
curators. Leonardo began working
at the Vatican in the warehouse of
the Vatican Museums, but has been
a curator in the sacristy for almost
ten years. One of his first tasks was
to prepare for the celebrations of
the third millennium, assisting Pope
John Paul II during the ceremonies
that took place throughout the year
2000. Leonardo also assisted at the
papal elections of 2005, when he
and his colleagues prepared the
Sistine Chapel for the conclave of
cardinals, and also made ready all
the vestments and vessels used
during the new pope's first Mass.

As well as preparing the
liturgical objects for ceremonial
use, since 2000, Leonardo has been
responsible for transferring all of
the treasury records from the old
catalog system to a computer
database; he also writes for Vatican
exhibitions and catalogs.

∧ > KEEPER OF KEYS
Many of the cabinets and doors around
the sacristy are several centuries old, and
some are still secured by their original
locks. Leonardo is in charge of the keys,
and therefore the security, of the sacristy.

∨ PAUSE FOR THOUGHT
Changed out of his motorcycle gear,
Leonardo stops to ponder the frescoes
in the Sistine Chapel, which he passes
on the way to the Papal Sacristy.

TREASURY CURATOR
PRESERVING THE VATICAN'S LITURGICAL HERITAGE

< ⌄ PREPARING FOR A MASS
With his colleague Stefano, Leonardo collects
a number of liturgical objects that will be used in
the morning's papal Mass. The removal of each
item from the cabinets is carefully recorded.

⌄ TRANSPORTING THE LITURGICAL ITEMS
Once the items are individually packed, they are
placed in a large case. Leonardo and a colleague,
Luca, transport the box to the chapel in which
the Mass will be celebrated.

⋀ ⊁ PACKING THE TREASURES
The items are chosen according to a list drawn
up by the Master of Liturgical Celebrations.
The treasures are then packed into boxes to
ensure their safe transit to the Mass.

⋀ ASSISTING THE FRIARS
Though the lay curators look after the older
liturgical treasures and vestments, a group of
Augustinian friars is responsible for the more
everyday liturgical items held in the sacristy.

Many of these objects are no longer used in ceremonies, but we must still maintain and care for them for the sake of posterity.

⌃ CATALOGING THE TREASURES
As part of the cataloging process, Leonardo measures the dimensions of a chalice. There are some 5,000 items in the Papal Sacristy, and the details of each one must be carefully recorded.

⋏ LUNCH TIME
At midday, Leonardo, Stefano, and Luca, who are friends as well as colleagues, remain in the sacristy to chat while they eat their home-made lunches.

⋏ > PAPAL VESTMENTS
Though many vestments are no longer used—styles change even in the Apostolic Palace—Leonardo checks them regularly to make sure they are in perfect condition.

> CLEANING JEWELS
The pope will often wear vestments gifted to his predecessors—this mitre once belonged to Pope Leo XIII. Before the pope wears it, Leonardo cleans the jewels with a cotton bud.

⋎ PAPAL STOLE AND MITRE
Leonardo examines a mitre and stole that may be worn by the pope, checking that the gems are still firmly in place and that the material is in good shape.

> SKETCHING TREASURES
Leonardo, who is a skilled draftsman, makes a sketch of the patterning found on a stole to capture its details.

< RECORDING ITEMS
Though sketches are useful for recording details, each item is also photographed for the Vatican's catalog record.

⌃ MAINTAINING THE TIARAS

Even though the pope is no longer crowned with a triple tiara, nor does he ever wear one, Leonardo must periodically check on the condition of each of these priceless historical items.

< ⌃ THE ARCHIVAL RECORDS

The details of each item were once recorded in manuscript catalogs, but the information is now entered into a new computer database.

< HELPING TOURISTS

On his way out of the sacristy, Leonardo makes a stop in the Sistine Chapel to point out some interesting features on Michaelangelo's ceiling to some of the Vatican's visitors.

⌃ LEAVING WORK

At the end of his working day, Leonardo makes his way down to the Belvedere Courtyard below the sacristy to retrieve his motorcycle.

< ⌄ BACK AT HOME

A dedicated cook, Leonardo unwinds at home by preparing the evening meal for his family. Once the food has been eaten, the day is finished off with a board game, allowing Leonardo to spend some time with his three sons.

With the construction of the large churches in Rome during the 4th century, the papal liturgies became evermore complex, and by the 8th century, a prelate was appointed to oversee them. This role continues to this day as the Master of Liturgical Celebrations. Giuseppe Passeri, who has worked in the Office of Pontifical Liturgical Celebrations for over 30 years, is assistant to the Master and helps organize liturgies in Rome and around the world.

Over the centuries, through a series of donations and commissions, a large store of vessels, vestments, and prayer books used in the liturgy were amassed. The sacristy (a room where sacred vessels are stored) and the treasury were entrusted to the care of a team who looked after the elaborate liturgical ceremonies. In 1563, Pope Pius IV established a special office with a Master of Ceremonies who oversaw all the liturgies presided over by the pope. In 1988, Pope John Paul II restructured the office, and gave it its present name, the Office of Pontifical Liturgical Celebrations.

The Master of Liturgical Celebrations is appointed personally by the pope. It is his responsibility to prepare every liturgy at which the pope and cardinals preside. These vary from functions in the chapel of the pope's private apartment to public Masses in St. Peter's. Preparations are complex. Thousands of booklets have to be printed with the text of the liturgy for the faithful who attend. The main part of the liturgy is celebrated in Latin or Italian, although prayers in other languages are also included. The Office works closely with the Master of the Sistine Choir, who chooses the liturgical music, which ranges from Gregorian Chant to modern compositions.

In addition, the Master of Ceremonies organizes all liturgies for the pope's visits outside Rome and abroad. These ceremonies also require careful collaboration with the local churches.

A native of Sicily, in southern Italy, Giuseppe Passeri spent seven years in the merchant navy marines before coming to work at the Vatican. Giuseppe works with Monsignor Guido Marini, Master of Liturgical Celebrations, and his assistants in the administration of the office. In 2007, Giuseppe married his wife, Eva, whom he first met when she visited the office to collect a ticket for a papal ceremony. Away from his day job, Giuseppe has an exciting sideline in the manufacture of fireworks.

∧ THE CORRIDOR
Giuseppe enters the Apostolic Palace and walks along the *loggia* decorated by Giovanni da Udine, a student and assistant of Raphael in the early 16th century.

> THE OFFICE DOOR
The corridor was decorated under the pontificate of the wealthy Medici pope, Leo X. The drapes on either side of the office door are an illusionistic painted fresco.

CEREMONIES ASSISTANT
CLERK IN THE OFFICE OF PONTIFICAL LITURGICAL CELEBRATIONS

< ANSWERING E-MAILS
The day begins by checking e-mails from all over the world. The Office for Liturgical Celebrations sets standards for the Catholic liturgy throughout the world.

∨ PREPARING THE DIARY
Giuseppe assists Monsignor Marini, the Master of Liturgical Celebrations, in making appointments for the large number of people who wish to see him.

< MIDDAY PRAYER
Each day, all office staff members and visitors present at midday gather with Monsignor Marini to say the Angelus, a series of prayers in honor of Mary, the mother of Jesus.

> SNACK LUNCH
Giuseppe, who gets an hour's break for lunch, meets his friend Dario for a snack in a bar directly outside the Vatican's St. Anne's Gate.

> OUTSIDE THE PRIVATE OFFICE
The rhythm of work can be intense, but there is always time to exchange pleasantries. Giuseppe pauses with Monsignor Marini before a meeting.

∨ WORKING IN THE OPEN AIR
On the terrace directly overlooking the facade of St. Peter's, Giuseppe and his boss, Monsignor Marini, discuss some of the large volume of mail that arrives daily at the office.

< RENAISSANCE PASSAGEWAY
Giuseppe follows a scenic route from his office to the Belvedere Courtyard. Passionate about history, he knows every nook and cranny of the Vatican.

> OUTSIDE THE POST OFFICE
After a full day's work, Giuseppe and Dario meet in the late afternoon to travel to the firework factory that Giuseppe runs outside Rome.

AT THE FACTORY

Giuseppe and his associates put the finishing touches to some new fireworks that will be used at the display for a celebrity wedding at the castle of Bracciano, north of Rome.

ANCIENT RECIPES

At home in the evening, Giuseppe tries out historical formulae for fireworks that he has discovered in a rare 17th-century manuscript in the Vatican Library. Giuseppe has been making fireworks since he was 16.

PAST AND FUTURE DISPLAYS

Over the years, Giuseppe has been commissioned by the Vatican to put on several displays, including a spectacular one for the millennium. At his computer (*inset*) he plans a display at the pyramids in Egypt.

EXPLOSIVE CARGO

Giuseppe and his colleagues carry the fireworks carefully to the van that will deliver them to Bracciano for the celebrity wedding.

END OF A LONG DAY

Giuseppe's wife, Eva, has cooked the evening meal. It is time to relax over a glass of wine, although there's always a danger conversation may return to the subject of fireworks.

> WALK TO SCHOOL
Each morning Stefano is accompanied on the short walk to school by his father. Some of the pupils travel as far as 18 miles (30 km) a day to attend the school.

Stefano di Benedetto is an 11-year-old chorister who lives in Rome with his parents and his younger sister. At the age of eight, he beat stiff competition to win a place to study at Rome's School of the Sistine Choir. He now sings treble in the Pueri Cantores ("the boy singers") section of the world-renowned choir who perform during liturgies attended by the pope, as well as special services such as Christmas, Easter, and Pentecost.

The history of the papal choir begins in the 6th century when Pope Gregory I (c.540–604) founded the *schola cantorum* to train boys to sing in the papal liturgies. Study lasted for nine years, and was learned by oral tradition. With the transfer of the papal see from Rome to Avignon in the 13th century (*see p.56*), Innocent IV (1243–54) did not take the *schola cantorum* with him. Instead, a new choir was formed, and when the popes returned to Rome in 1378 after seven decades, many French singers accompanied the papal court.

By the mid-15th century, boys were no longer trained as choristers and instead adult male countertenors were enlisted. During the 17th century, the papal choir regularly employed *castrati* (male singers castrated at puberty to retain their alto and soprano voices) to sing the upper parts of the music. However, as the popularity of castrati rose in the 18th century, many left the papal choir in favor of the operatic stage. The choir entered a period of

decline, halted only in the early 20th century when Pope John XXIII (1958–62) founded the present-day School of the Sistine Choir in Via Monte della Farina in central Rome.

Today, there are 55 pupils at the all-boys school, drawn from all over Rome and its surrounding areas. As places are highly sought after, competition is tough and each boy who wishes to enter the school must audition for a place at the age of eight. Successful candidates enter the school the following year and will be singing in the choir by Christmas. During the six years they spend at the school, the pupils receive a full scholarship that includes book and traveling expenses.

The experience of attending the School of the Sistine Choir is a rewarding one. Even when their voices break and they can no longer sing in the choir, many of the boys continue to further their musical education at university level and, in time, some go on to enter the adult section of the Sistine Choir.

∧ LESSONS BEGIN
As the bell rings at the start of the school day, Stefano joins his classmates as they walk down the corridor to their first lesson, which begins at 8.30 a.m.

> GEOGRAPHY CLASS
Although the school specializes in choral practice, the pupils also study the same lessons as their contemporaries—including Italian, Maths, Science, English, History, and Geography—and take the State exams.

∧ BREAK TIME
Like other Italian schools, there is a games room at the School of the Sistine Choir. During a break, Stefano joins his friends in an animated game of football.

CHOIR BOY
TREBLE SINGER IN THE SISTINE CHOIR

< ∨ DAILY CHOIR PRACTICE
Led by Master of the Choristers, Don Marcos,
the boys sing a motet (choral composition)
by Giovanni Pierluigi da Palestrina, who was a
member of the Sistine Choir in the 16th century.

< PIANO LESSON
In addition to singing, the boys learn
a musical instrument and study music
theory. Stefano has chosen the piano.

> LUNCHTIME
As the school is small, there is a family
like atmosphere at meal times. The boys
take turns each week dishing out the
lunch in the refectory.

> FORMAL DRESS
The boys change into their choir robes in
preparation for singing at the afternoon
Vespers service led by Pope Benedict.

I have two favorite composers: our Choir Master, Maestro Liberto, and Bach.

⋏ FINAL PRACTICE
The boys have a final rehearsal. At the
church they will join the tenors and
basses under Maestro Giuseppe Liberto.

ᐁ READY TO LEAVE
Don Marcos lines up the boys in the corridor. They will be singing in San Paolo fuori le Mura for the Feast of St. Paul, over which the pope will preside.

ᐱ BOARDING THE BUS
St. Paul's Basilica is several miles away so Stefano and his classmates take the bus. The choir boys also get the opportunity to travel abroad, performing all over the world.

ᐳ A QUIET DISCUSSION
The boys are encouraged to speak softly before a concert to preserve their voices. Rest is an important part of their vocal preparation.

ᐳ PREPARING TO SING
Seated in the basilica, the choir will sing the Gregorian Chant and polyphonic hymns (where two or more tones are sung) in the Vespers service.

⋎ THE ENTRANCE PROCESSION

Pope Benedict arrives at the basilica accompanied by two cardinals. Stefano and the choir begin the Gregorian Chant as the pope and the cardinals take their seats.

⋎ SOCCER PRACTICE

Stefano gets ready for his weekly after-school soccer training. The sports-gear he wears and his bag bear the papal insignia of the school club.

⋏ ON THE FIELD

The boys wait to begin their warm-up on the field of the Oratoria of St. Peter (a youth club). The dome of St. Peter's Basilica can be seen from the pitch.

⋎ BEDTIME

Stefano's mother says goodnight to her son. It is especially important for the choir boys to get enough sleep to keep their voices in peak condition.

⋏ BACK TO SCHOOL

After the Vespers service, Don Marcos leads the boys back to school to change before being collected by their parents.

⋏ EXCHANGING NEWS

Stefano's mother picks him up from school in the afternoon. Stefano checks a text message from his sister while they walk home.

> HOSTEL ENTRANCE
This small, plain door, located in the Vatican walls, leads to the *Dono di Maria* hostel. Anyone who arrives at the door in need of help will be offered a free meal.

∨ AFTERNOON PRAYERS
Each day the Sisters gather in the small chapel to pray. On Sunday, they spend an hour of prayer kneeling before the Sacred Host, which is exposed in the monstrance.

Tucked into a quiet corner a stone's throw from St. Peter's Basilica stands a small and unassuming green door. It leads into a hostel for the homeless—the *Dono di Maria* (the gift of Mary)—where seven Sisters from different countries serve the poor and other people in difficulty. The Sisters belong to the Missionaries of Charity, the order of Sisters founded by Mother Teresa of Calcutta in 1950.

Blessed Mother Teresa of Calcutta was a good friend of Pope John Paul II, and every time she visited Rome the nun called on the pontiff. During one of these audiences, she asked the pope to open a hostel close to the Vatican. Expressing his deep concern for those without work, without a home or shelter, and even without food, the pope told Mother Teresa that he too had been thinking about such a project.

Pope John Paul II entrusted some collaborators—a mixture of personnel from the Vatican and people who had long been involved in practical charitable work—to develop a project in conjunction with the Missionaries of Charity, and a small building was found at the corner of Vatican City and converted into a hostel. A door was opened in the walls of the Vatican so that people in need could gain access to the building and the adjacent courtyard.

On May 21, 1988, less than a year after work had begun, Pope John Paul II inaugurated the hostel,

naming it *Dono di Maria* (Gift of Mary). He visted the hostel on six further occasions and often arranged for gifts of food to be sent to the Sisters who care for the poor.

The Sisters, who run the hostel, exude a tranquil air at all times but are very firmly in control—both crucial qualities when running a center dedicated to helping those less fortunate in society. They deal with their "guests"—some of whom will arrive at the hostel drunk and confused—in a firm but fair manner.

Every day, the seven Sisters split their time between prayer and work in the hostel. Along with a few volunteers, they supply 58 evening meals—and a further 120 food parcels—to the homeless of Rome, and offer accommodation to a number of women. It would be true to say that, at the *Dono di Maria*, the Sisters offer a priceless gift of love and companionship to those most in need. In January 2008, Pope Benedict XVI visited the hostel to mark its 20th anniversary.

∧ IN THE STORE ROOM
Many Romans donate clothes to the hostel. Each day they are sorted and kept in a store room. The Sisters then distribute them as required.

SISTERS OF CHARITY
HELPING THE HOMELESS

< TICKETS FOR FREE FOOD
Each day the Sisters offer a free meal to 70 men. The men line up to collect their meal ticket. The food is given to all people regardless of their origin, religion, or status.

Ⅴ CHOPPING ONIONS
Trainee priests help out by spending the afternoon preparing the food and then serving dinner to the guests.

Λ HEATING THE WATER
Water is boiled to cook the pasta. Simplicity is the key here, with only the most basic utensils being used.

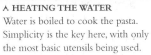

Ⅴ A STAPLE DIET
On a cold evening, a home-cooked plate of tagliatelli is very welcome, as many of the men will not have eaten all day.

< Λ VOLUNTEERS HELP OUT
Volunteers help the Sisters to prepare simple nutritious food, including *panini* (bread) for those still waiting at the door when the refectory is full.

Λ EXTRA NUTRITION
Fruit is also added to the food parcels that are distributed at the door. On Sundays the crowds are even larger than usual, as most other church-run charity kitchens in Rome close on that day.

⌄ AFTERNOON WAIT
The people lining up
outside the hostel are cold
and hungry. The world of
busy Romans and harried
tourists can be harsh for
the homeless. Inside, warm
food and welcoming
smiles make the hostel a
real refuge in the city.

< SIMPLE DECORATION
The refectory is relatively spartan, with
bare walls and simply designed tables and
chairs. The only "decorations" are a
crucifix and a picture of Pope John Paul II.

⌃ TABLES SET
The places are set in the refectory for
the arrival of the guests. It will be an
opportunity for the men who come
here to chat and relax for an hour.

> A WATCHFUL EYE
The Sisters look over the guests from the
stairs. They will call a doctor if any of the
men are ill. Many outside professionals
help the Sisters with the men's care.

DINNER TIME

The food is served by young priests. The guests who come here are grateful for the help they receive. Some are simply down on their luck, while others are immigrants trying to find their feet in a new country.

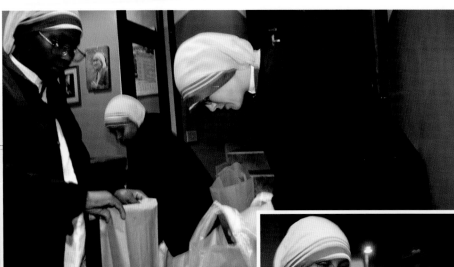

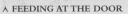

∧ FEEDING AT THE DOOR

While people inside eat, the feeding of more homeless people begins at the door. The Sisters distribute the food parcels to those who do not get a space to sit down in the refectory for this evening's meal.

∨ THE DISHES

After the food has been served, volunteers help with the washing up. To pass the time, they sing songs, those from the monastery in Taizé, France, being especially popular.

∧ SERVING THE FOOD

The guests will often clamor for food, banging plates and tin pots—none of this dampens the enthusiasm of this volunteer, a student priest from Spain.

∧ EVENING PRAYERS

In the small chapel beside the hostel, guests of the Sisters gather for evening Mass. Meanwhile, the Sisters retire to their chapel for evening prayers. Tomorrow, a new day of service awaits them.

For centuries, students have traveled to Rome to prepare for the priesthood. Here, they study philosophy and theology in preparation for life as a diocesan priest or member of a religious order. Among the many young men studying for the priesthood is Fabio Goldini. He began to think about his vocation when he was 16. "I was wondering what to do with my life," he recalls, "and I decided to try to see if this was my path."

Several countries have national colleges or seminaries where the students live together while attending classes in one of Rome's many ecclesiastical universities and other Catholic institutions. While most come before ordination, others live in Rome while they pursue graduate studies. The international aspect of studying in the Eternal City makes a deep impression on students and many lifelong friendships are forged.

Ordination as a deacon, in the year before priestly ordination, is normally celebrated in Rome. Where circumstances permit, it can be a wonderful opportunity for family and friends to travel to Italy and experience some of its delights. Most seminarians choose to be ordained priests in their home towns, although there is also the possibility of being ordained by the pope himself at St Peter's Basilica.

Fabio Goldini is a native of Brazil. He was born in 1982 and has two sisters. His mother is a Catholic, while his father, who is a military officer, is Protestant. At 19, he entered the major seminary in Brazil. His was the first vocation from his parish of some 55,000 inhabitants. When his bishop asked him to go to Rome, he was not very excited at first, but he obeyed. He was given two months to prepare for the trip. There are now three seminarians from his home diocese studying for the priesthood.

Fabio studies at the Pontificia Università della Santa Croce (Institute of the Holy Cross), close to Piazza Navona in the historic center of Rome. The seminary where he eats and sleeps is on the other side of the River Tiber—the same side as the Vatican—in the picturesque quarter of Trastevere. After his ordination, he will return home to work in Brazil. There are more than 137 million Catholics in Brazil, making this South American republic the largest Catholic country in the world. According to tradition, the first Mass there was celebrated by a Portuguese priest on Easter Sunday in the year 1500.

SEMINARIAN
STUDENT FOR THE PRIESTHOOD

< THE UNIVERSITY CHURCH
Before he leaves after class, Fabio prays in the Basilica of Sant'Apollinare, the church attached to the institute.

∨ PRAYING THE ROSARY
Every day Fabio recites the Rosary, a series of prayers in honor of Mary, the mother of Jesus, either with his fellow seminarians or alone.

∧ LEAVING THE INSTITUTE
Most classes are held in the morning, although there are often seminars to attend in the afternoon.

∨ TAKING A COFFEE BREAK
Fabio relaxes in Piazza Navona, one of Rome's most famous squares. On occasion, he will stop here for a cup of coffee on the way home.

237

> CROSSING THE TIBER

Walking is the best way to discover any city. Fabio varies his daily journey to and fro across the Tiber in order to learn more about the Eternal City.

ᴠ THROUGH PIAZZA NAVONA

Fabio catches up with some other students returning to the seminary of Sedes Sapientiae after their morning classes. There are 90 seminarians living there from 32 different countries.

ᴧ LUNCH AT THE SEMINARY

The students gather in the refectory at 1:30p.m., where they enjoy a plate of pasta and other good Italian food.

> RELAXATION

A keen musician, Fabio is an excellent guitarist. He spends an hour after lunch in his room playing guitar and singing.

⋖ ⋎ THE SEMINARY

Fabio's seminary, the Sedes Sapientiae ("Throne of Wisdom") in the Trastevere district of Rome, occupies a pleasant modern building completed in 2000.

➤ PRAYER IN THE CHAPEL

After lunch the seminarians go directly to the chapel where they pause for silent prayer. Fabio prays for his parents, his sister, and all his friends in Brazil.

⋎ AFTERNOON PRAYER

Later, Fabio pauses to recite the Rosary in the Basilica of Santa Cecilia in Trastevere. St Cecilia, the patron saint of music, was martyred for her faith in the late 2nd century.

⋀ SINGING IN THE CHOIR

On Sundays and feast days, a group of seminarians, Fabio among them, sing in the choir; they stand in the gallery at the end of the chapel overlooking the altar.

> **TOUR OF THE WORKSHOPS**
Each morning Paolo arrives at his office, then makes a tour of the Floreria's workshops and depositories. Here, he visits the furniture restoration workshop.

∨ **PAPAL COATS OF ARMS**
In the restoration workshop, a craftsman points out to Paolo the details on a crest of Pope Leo XIII; on the table is a sketch of a new crest of Pope Benedict XVI that he intends to make.

The Floreria is a small department of specialized workers who look after the valuable furnishings of the Apostolic Palace. It also provides chairs, carpets, drapes, flowers, and other forms of decoration for pontifical ceremonies in St. Peter's and on occasions when the pope visits other Vatican churches in Rome. Paolo Sagretti, who was born in Rome, has worked at the Floreria since 1988 and is now its director.

The ancient name *Floreria* is misleading. In medieval times, all the royal and noble courts of Europe had a department that provided floral decoration for their palaces. In the Vatican, the name has survived, but over the centuries, it has been extended to include the care of furniture, carpets, curtains, and a whole host of other decorative features.

For centuries, the workmen of the Floreria have cared for the decoration and furniture of the Apostolic Palace, which contains hundreds of rooms, lengthy corridors, and a number of chapels. In the past, the popes were great patrons of the arts, and their residences were as magnificent as the palaces and royal courts of Europe. From the Middle Ages, through the Renaissance, and into the Baroque era, the palace was designed as much to impress visitors as to provide comfort for its occupants. With each successive extension, new furnishings were needed for the palace. These ranged from thrones to kneelers, from dining tables to door frames, and from curtains to candlesticks. One of the main tasks of the Floreria today is the preservation and restoration of all these historic furnishings, but the department also provides the decoration and furnishings for services in St. Peter's and elsewhere.

The Floreria workshops are based in two centers. The antique furniture workshop is tucked into three rooms off the tunnel leading from the Belvedere Courtyard to the Courtyard of the Parrot, while the furniture and fabric workshop is at the end of the Street of the Four Gates near the Vatican gardens. In these workshops old techniques are passed on to new generations of furniture makers and restorers.

Paolo Sagretti studied engineering at Rome's La Sapienza University. He is very proud of the work of the Floreria. "In today's world of mass production," he notes, "it is difficult to find craftsmen capable of the specialized work we carry out here."

> ∧ **A BRONZE CASTING OF THE PAPAL CREST**
A preparatory sketch provides the outline from which a clay model of Pope Benedict XVI's crest is made. This is used to create a plaster mold into which bronze is poured. The finished crest will be gilded.

HEAD OF THE FLORERIA
DIRECTOR OF FURNISHINGS AND RESTORATION AT THE VATICAN

⟨ FURNITURE WORKSHOP
The Floreria's furniture makers use traditional 18th-century materials for upholstery stuffing, such as horsehair and a special kind of grass, over which velvet will be laid and then the chair will be gilded. It is rare to find such a level of craftsmanship in today's world.

⋎ EXAMINING A FRAME
Paolo visits the picture-framing studio to see how work is progressing on a new gilt frame for a portrait of Pope John Paul II. All the frames for the paintings that hang in the Apostolic Palace are made or restored in the studios of the Floreria.

⟨ ⋏ WOODCARVING
Craftsmen study their trade in the workshops as in the past, learning the traditional skills of restoration handed down from one generation to the next. Here, a carpenter works on the carved coat of arms of Pius XI on a cabinet that has been completely stripped for restoration.

⋏ ⟩ GILDING AND GESSO WORK
A restorer carefully applies gold leaf to an 18th-century chair from one of the reception rooms in the Apostolic Palace. The original gold leaf has worn away over the centuries. To the right, a candelabrum is being repaired. Missing pieces of wood are filled with a primer called gesso and later it will be regilded.

⋏ AFTERNOON APPOINTMENT
Paolo and a colleague walk through the colonnade around St. Peter's Square on their way to visit a church where Pope Benedict XVI is due to celebrate Mass.

⋎ LIAISON WITH OTHER OFFICES
Paolo calls the Prefecture and Office for Liturgical Celebrations to tell them how many people will fit into the church, so they can issue free tickets.

⋏⋗ LITURGICAL CHAIR
An ornate gilded chair, created for Pope Leo XIII in the 19th century, is restored for use in the liturgy in St. Peter's by Pope Benedict XVI.

⋏ CURTAIN MATERIALS
Sister Domitilla carefully cuts fabric that will be used to make curtains for the Apostolic Palace. The Floreria ensures that the Vatican is, wherever possible, self sufficient in all aspects of furniture, fixtures, and fittings.

⋖ STAFF CANTEEN
Paolo pauses for lunch in a canteen with other Vatican employees. There are several canteens for the various groups of workers inside the Vatican, such as the Swiss Guard and the security forces.

⋏ CHANCE MEETING
Cardinal Achille Silvestrini meets Paolo outside his office in the Cortile di San Damaso. The Floreria also provides furnishings for the cardinals and senior clerics who work in the Vatican.

< IN ST. PETER'S
The seating in St. Peter's and in the Square come under the jurisdiction of the Floreria. Paolo greets a workman collecting chairs used at Mass the previous day.

> CARPET STOREROOM
Since medieval times carpets have been laid for important ceremonies. When not in use they are rolled up here.

∧ PLANNING AHEAD
Paolo discusses the measurements of San Lorenzo in Piscibus, a medieval church soon to be visited by Pope Benedict XVI to mark 25 years since the foundation of the San Lorenzo International Youth Centre. The church is examined three weeks ahead of the pontiff's visit.

< THROUGH THE BRONZE DOOR
Paolo returns to the Apostolic Palace. On the way back he and his assistant have been thinking ahead to the next event.

> BACK AT HIS DESK
In the office, there is always paperwork to attend to. Paolo finishes the day with calls to various Vatican departments.

> ARRIVING AT WORK
In the morning, Paolo goes straight into the basilica to inspect the restoration of the mosaics of the evangelists under the dome.

∨ UNDER MICHELANGELO'S DOME
Paolo discusses the restoration project for the medallions with one of his colleagues, who incidentally wrote his university thesis on the mosaics of St. Peter's.

Mosaic, using small tesserae (tiles) of stone, glass, and gold, has been employed in the decoration of churches since the early 4th century. One of the hidden treasures of the Vatican is the Mosaic Studio and school, founded in the early 18th century, which is tucked away at the side of the Piazza of the First Christian Martyrs. Today, its director is Paolo di Buono, who heads a team of ten specialists in charge of all restoration at St. Peter's.

In the heyday of the Roman Empire, the art of mosaic was raised to high levels by skilled craftsmen. After the fall of the Roman Empire in the West in 476, the Christian Church became the most important patron of art in Western Europe. Mosaic played an important part in the decoration of Rome's earliest churches. Sketches left by 16th-century artists show the original mosaics of the Constantinian basilica of St. Peter. The façade was dominated by a 5th-century image of Christ flanked by the Four Evangelists, while the apse featured a mosaic of Christ with St. Peter and St. Paul from the mid-4th century.

Mosaic was also widely used in the interior of the new Renaissance basilica created in the 16th and 17th centuries. In 1727, Pope Benedict XIII (1724–30) founded the Mosaic Studio and a school for mosaic apprenticeships. In 1770, a new form of mosaic manufacture was discovered, using thinner tesserae. All the altarpieces in the chapels of St. Peter's were oil paintings, but oil paint darkens and can disintegrate with age. Using the new technique, artists from the studio replaced all these oil paintings, apart from the fresco of the Trinity in the Chapel of the Blessed Sacrament, with faithful mosaic copies.

Paolo di Buono, the director of the studio, studied archaeology at La Sapienza University before joining the Mosaic Studio. With his team of specialists, he is proud to be the latest in a long line of directors caring for the fabric of St. Peter's. "Mosaic takes a long time to make and a long time to restore," he observes. Although the main work of the Mosaic Studio is to maintain the mosaics of St. Peter's, the studio also carries out commissions. "The pope appreciates our work and he likes to give a mosaic to important people and so we keep a stock of work ready for him. Pope John Paul II gave one of our reproductions from St. Peter's to Fidel Castro when he visited Cuba in 1998."

∧ LOOSE PLASTER
Mosaic pieces are carefully removed and stored. The plaster has dried out over the centuries and must be replaced.

> BELOW THE MEDALLION
Last cleaned in the 18th century, some mosaics are coated in deposits from lamps and candles burning in the basilica.

MOSAIC RESTORER
DIRECTOR OF THE VATICAN MOSAIC STUDIO

< CHECKING THE SURFACE
A mosaic is checked for any loose tiles on its curved surface. These are removed and will be replaced during restoration.

> TESTING FOR STABILITY
Tapping gently with a hammer, an expert can detect by changes in tone any hollows that have formed beneath the mosaic as the plaster has dried out.

∨ MEDALLION OF ST. MARK
Major restoration work is in progress on the circular portraits of the Four Evangelists beneath the central dome, which date from the late 16th century.

< SAFETY CHECK
Glass balls as big as a man's fist represent jewels in this mosaic of a papal tiara. A restorer makes sure they are firmly in place. Any replacements needed are made in ceramic.

> BACK AND FORTH
Paolo and his colleague return to St. Peter's after examining some drawings at the studio. They take great care to keep to the original designs of the mosaics when restoring them.

> **GLASSWORKING**
Using a blow torch, Paolo melts pieces of glass, reducing them once more to a malleable state.

< ˅ **REPRODUCTION STUDIO**
Working under a mixture of natural and electric light, the team fulfills commissions of images such as van Gogh's *Church at Auvers* (below).

˄ **REPRODUCING AN OLD MASTER**
Paolo stops in the reproduction studio for a chat with a colleague about the mosaic copy he is making of a Giotto fresco called *The Flight into Egypt*.

> **ST. JOSEPH'S HALO**
Good eyesight, patience, and skill are required for the painstaking art of mosaic. The Giotto original, which is in Padua, is very famous and the reproduction must be entirely accurate.

˄ **OUR LADY OF GUADALUPE**
The most requested image for reproduction is the 16th-century icon from the Basilica of Our Lady of Guadalupe in Mexico—the world's most popular Marian shrine.

> **THE VIRGIN'S TUNIC**
The board is covered with a photograph of the icon. This is lifted and putty is applied to the board. As the tesserae are set into the putty, the photograph is gradually cut away.

< MAKING A ROD
Paolo draws the glass into a rod. When cooled, this can then be cut very finely, creating miniscule fragments of color.

> MOSAICIST'S TRAY
The pieces of glass from which tesserae are cut start out as long rods. Colors are obtained by adding minerals to the molten glass.

< ʌ PREPARATORY WORK
Paolo makes sure he has the right shades of glass to create the delicate flesh tones of the angel's face and neck. In order to decorate the sky in the background, he shapes glass tesserae with a special hammer.

< ʌ MOSAIC ARCHIVE
The workshop has a vast archive of tesserae, including ones produced in the 16th and 17th centuries, although stocks of these are now badly depleted.

ʌ PRECISION WORK
Paolo carefully positions a tiny tessera with his tweezers. The work is a reproduction of a fresco of an angel playing a lute by Melozzo da Forlì (1438–94) from the Vatican Museums.

> **THE VATICAN MUSEUMS**
Paolo arrives for work each morning just
after 8.00a.m. Already the first tourists have
arrived to explore these fascinating rooms.

ⅴ **VISITING A CHAPEL**
Paolo also works outside the Vatican. Here,
in a chapel in the church of Santa Maria in
Ara Coeli, near the Forum, Paolo checks
the maintenance of frescoes he has restored.

Visitors to the Vatican Museums must wonder how the
enormous treasure trove housed there is kept so well preserved.
Making sure that the works on display do not deteriorate falls to
the Vatican's team of specialist art restorers, among them Paolo
Violini. Paolo has worked at the Vatican Museums since 1988,
and specializes in restoring frescoes. He likens his craft to that
of a detective, using his specialist skills to uncover the past.

Money from entrance tickets to
the Museums proved insufficient to
pay for restoration of the works of
art there. The Vatican reluctantly
considered selling its artworks to
pay for restoration, but some forms
of art, such as the frescoes, could not
be sold. So, in 1983, the Vatican
Museums founded an office for
fundraising: the Patrons of the Arts
of the Vatican Museum. The
Patrons—philanthropists from all
over the world—continue to fund
restoration projects to this day.

Among the many types of work
at the Museums, the restoration of
frescoes is a real speciality. The skill
of making plaster fresco is thousands
of years old and early Christians
employed the technique of frescoes
in their catacombs (underground
burial chambers). However, it was
not until the Renaissance of the
14th–16th centuries that the form
arrived at its perfection. The method
used involved drawing preparatory
sketches on paper, with the drawn
lines then pricked with holes. The
sketches were laid on the damp

plastered wall and patted with a
sponge caked with charcoal dust.
The holes left a charcoal outline
of the design on the wall. Some
painters, like Raphael (1483–1520),
then scored the plaster with a
stylus, leaving a faint outline of
the design. When the fine grained
colors were applied by brush to the
damp plaster, they were soaked
up by the plaster and sealed in the
wall. The challenge for restorers
such as Paolo Violini is to remove
the dirt of centuries and to reveal
the original vivid colors.

Paolo studied art restoration in
Rome at the Institute for Art and
Restoration while also studying
architecture for a time. "I always
enjoyed precision drawing, and I
found that I could combine this
skill with hands-on restoration—
the best of both worlds." Among
Paolo's works are the Stanza della
Segnatura, the Room of Heliodorus,
and, currently, some apartments
commissioned five centuries ago
by Pope Julius II (1503–13)—a great
patron of the arts.

> **INVESTIGATION OF A FRESCO**
Paolo gently taps a stucco frame to hear
what state it is in. If it is hollow, it indicates
that the supporting plaster behind may
have dried out, suggesting problems.

ⅴ **BACK AT THE OFFICE**
Computer programs help Paolo write
up the details of his restoration projects.
When he finishes a project, art historians
will then be able to access a full account
of the details of the restoration.

PAINTING RESTORER

AN EXPERT IN THE RESTORATION OF FRESCOES

‹ EXAMINING THE WORK
Paolo studies photographs of the area where he is working, so he can decide how much more restoration is needed.

› THE PAPAL PATRON
Paolo brushes layers of dust from the burgundy *mozzetta* cape of Pope Julius II. The fresco is in apartments commissioned by the pope in the early 16th century.

˅ KEEPING RECORDS
The day-to-day treatments are recorded on a computer. Paolo enters information about each phase of his work, which will later be published.

˅ BRONZE GRAPPA
Paolo examines a *grappa*, a small bronze sheet in the fresco. These were set into the wall to stop the plaster cracking.

‹ REVEALING THE COLORS
Paolo applies Japanese Paper, dampened with bicarbonate of ammonia. It softens the film of dirt obscuring the color pigments.

› CLEANING THE FRESCO
Once the dirt has softened, Paolo brushes it away with a natural sponge. He then washes the area with ionized water.

⌃ PRESERVED FOR POSTERITY
In order to preserve these works of art for future
generations, Paolo has had to learn many of the skills
of the great masters of the Renaissance. Raphael would
surely be astonished to see his work so lovingly restored.

During the cleaning ... the fresco's material magically resurfaces ... I feel Raphael's soul revive in the freshness of his brushstrokes.

Rodolfo distributes cards for the Felici Studio to the audience. People who are photographed with the pope often wish to obtain a photo of this important day.

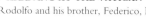

∨ ARRIVING AT THE VATICAN
Rodolfo and his brother, Federico, leave home early on the day of a General Audience and arrive at the Vatican around 8.00a.m. The cameras are ready and loaded.

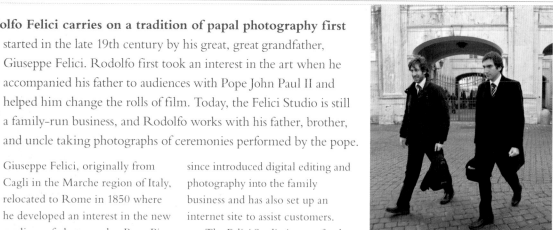

Rodolfo Felici carries on a tradition of papal photography first started in the late 19th century by his great, great grandfather, Giuseppe Felici. Rodolfo first took an interest in the art when he accompanied his father to audiences with Pope John Paul II and helped him change the rolls of film. Today, the Felici Studio is still a family-run business, and Rodolfo works with his father, brother, and uncle taking photographs of ceremonies performed by the pope.

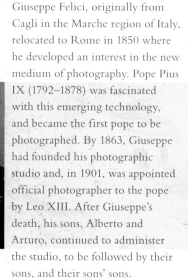

Giuseppe Felici, originally from Cagli in the Marche region of Italy, relocated to Rome in 1850 where he developed an interest in the new medium of photography. Pope Pius IX (1792–1878) was fascinated with this emerging technology, and became the first pope to be photographed. By 1863, Giuseppe had founded his photographic studio and, in 1901, was appointed official photographer to the pope by Leo XIII. After Giuseppe's death, his sons, Alberto and Arturo, continued to administer the studio, to be followed by their sons, and their sons' sons.

Today, Giuseppe's great grandson, Rodolfo Felici, carries on the family tradition, having been involved with photography since he was a boy. One Friday evening, on one of his trips with his father to see Pope John Paul II, the pope's private secretary, Monsignor Stanisław Dziwisz, called over to him: "Go on Rodolfo, take a photograph of us." That was the first photograph he took in the Vatican. Rodolfo has

since introduced digital editing and photography into the family business and has also set up an internet site to assist customers.

The Felici Studio is one of only two studios allowed to photograph papal events in the Vatican. It does not work in conjunction with the Vatican's public relations department, nor are their photographs passed on to the media. The Felici Studio simply provides a service recording events that take place inside the Vatican, often providing copies to those who have come to see or meet the pope.

Rodolfo loves photography, but he is also passionate about the arts and architecture, which he studied at Rome's La Sapienza University. Now an architect, he also retains his role within the family firm.

Today, the Felici Studio still has unique access to the Vatican. The family is trusted and respected by the Prefecture, which arranges for all the pope's public appearances. And for visitors who meet the pope, a photograph from the Felici Studio is still a treasured souvenir.

∧ > THE GENERAL AUDIENCE
Thousands of pilgrims from all over the world pack the Paul VI Audience Hall each Wednesday to hear Pope Benedict XVI deliver a brief discourse. He addresses his audience in several languages.

PAPAL PHOTOGRAPHER
CAPTURING THE VATICAN'S OFFICIAL EVENTS

< GREETING VISITORS
As the audience ends, the pope greets as many people as possible, all chosen by the private secretary and the Prefect of the Papal Household.

< FINAL CHECKS
Waiting on the stage of the Paul VI Audience Hall, Rodolfo makes further checks—that his batteries are fully charged, for example.

⋏ AFRICAN BISHOP
The meeting with the pope only lasts for a minute or two. Rodolfo needs to make sure he does not miss his shot, or the visiting bishop will have no souvenir of the day.

< BACK TO THE OFFICE
As soon as the pope leaves, Rodolfo, with his father and brother, rush back to the studio to deliver the discs from which the day's photographs will be printed.

⌄ **UPLOADING THE PHOTOS**
Rodolfo and Giuseppe upload the images onto a computer and make sure that all is in order. Clients are expected to come into the studio later to select photographs of their audience with the pope.

⌄ ⟩ **RESEARCH IN THE ARCHIVES**
The studio archives house valuable photographs and negatives, some dating as far back as the 1840s. The studio is in the process of restoring some of the photos and then storing all the images digitally.

⟩ **CHECKING QUALITY**
When the pictures have been uploaded, the color and focus of every one is checked individually. Any that are thought to be unsatisfactory are deleted.

⌄ **DEALING WITH CLIENTS**
Rodolfo photographs many types of events. Two newlyweds come in to view pictures of their meeting with the pope on their wedding day.

⟩ **CHOOSING THE PHOTOS**
Two nuns view on-screen digital images of their meeting with the pope. The day has clearly been a very special occasion for them, so it is important to get the right pictures.

⌃ WATERCOLORS BY THE TIBER
Rodolfo has developed a real passion for architecture and often takes the opportunity to paint watercolors. Rome, with its magnificent buildings, is a constant inspiration.

⌃ ⋎ EVENING WORK
An architect, Rodolfo often continues working into the evenings. His eye for detail, honed over years of taking photographs, proves invaluable for this other discipline.

⋖ LEAVING THE STUDIO
After a long day, Rodolfo leaves the office. He decides to spend time relaxing with one of his favorite hobbies, watercolor painting.

> MEDALS AND DECORATIONS
Tiziano begins his day by donning his military uniform, along with the medals he has been awarded since he joined the Swiss Guard in 1994.

∨ > BRASS BUCKLE
As Tiziano gets ready he makes final adjustments to his belt. The monogram on the buckle indicates that the wearer belongs to the Pontifical Guard.

Tiziano Guarneri joined the Vatican's Swiss Guard in 1994.

The first 16 weeks of his period of duty were spent acclimatizing to the world of the Vatican, where he had to learn its geography and the ranks and names of the people working there. The statutory period of service for a Swiss Guard is two years, after which three quarters of them choose to leave. Some, like Tiziano, who is now a Senior Guard, stay on and make a career of protecting the pope.

On January 22, 1506, a troop of Swiss mercenary guards arrived at the Vatican. They had been engaged by Pope Julius II (1503–13), who wanted to ensure his protection and the safety of the Vatican amid the turmoil and upheaval that characterized the Italian peninsula in the 16th century. At that time, Italy comprised a number of duchies, petty kingdoms, and republics. The Papal States were among these various political entities, and only 12 years earlier had been invaded by King Charles VIII of France.

During the Sack of Rome, on May 6, 1527, the troops of Emperor Charles V entered the city, forcing Pope Clement VII to flee the Vatican and take refuge in Castel Sant'Angelo. Of the 189 guards who protected the pope that day, only 42 survived. The others died fighting the invaders at the High Altar of St. Peter's. Subsequently, the popes re-employed a company of guards, and for over half a millennium they have rendered faithful service to the Holy See.

To join the Swiss Guard, which is made up of a company of 110, there are a number of requirements that must be met. The prospective guard must be an unmarried Swiss male Catholic, aged between 19 and 30. He must be at least 5 ft 8 in (174 cm) in height, have a recommendation from his local parish, and also have served in basic military school in Switzerland. Young men join for a multitude of reasons, but the opportunity of spending two years in Rome is attractive and rewarding.

Service in the Swiss Guard includes physical training, learning drills centered around ceremonial halberds, and instruction in combat. Enrolment into the Swiss Guard takes place on May 6 each year, the day in 1527 when their forebears died defending Pope Clement VII. Grasping the papal flag, the young recruits make a pledge to protect the pope: "I promise to the Commanding Captain and my other superiors, respect, fidelity and obedience. This I swear! May God and our Holy Patrons assist me!"

> READY FOR DUTY
Tiziano finshes dressing. On ceremonial occasions, guards wear a silver breastplate and a silver helmet. For everyday duty they wear a red, yellow, and blue uniform.

∨ DONNING THE BERET
While on everyday duty, the guards wear a soft woollen beret, but when they form a Guard of Honor for important guests received by the pope, they must wear a plumed, metal helmet.

> OFF TO WORK
Tiziano gives his young son a kiss as he leaves for duty. Being a Senior Guard means that Tiziano is able to live with his family in an apartment in the Vatican.

SWISS GUARD

PROTECTING THE POPE'S SECURITY

< SIDE ENTRANCE
Wearing a navy, tasselled winter cloak, Tiziano walks to the side entrance of the Apostolic Palace to report for his tour of duty there.

∨ > INSPECTION OF THE GUARDS
Today is Wednesday—the guards will be in attendance on Pope Benedict who will hold a General Audience in St. Peter's Square. The guards line up in the barracks courtyard.

∧ THE GUARDS' BARRACKS
Wearing plumed helmets, the guards march out of the 16th-century barracks on their way to the General Audience.

> WAITING FOR ORDERS
At the entrance to the Apostolic Palace, the guards must await permission from Tiziano before they can enter the building.

∧ MARCHING THROUGH THE PALACE
Inside the Apostolic Palace, Tiziano salutes his colleagues as they march in formation along the main corridor leading up to St. Peter's Basilica.

⋗ THE WING OF MADERNO
The guards march along the Wing of
Maderno, named after the architect who
designed the façade of St. Peter's Basilica,
on their way to the atrium of the basilica.

⋏ FLAG OF THE SWISS GUARD
The flag of the Pontifical Swiss Guard hangs over
the Bronze Door to the Apostolic Palace. The
standard bears the papal insignia and the crest of
Pope Julius II of the Della Rovere family.

⋗ GUARD DUTY
Security is an ongoing concern of the Vatican
authorities. Standing opposite the Bronze Door,
Tiziano checks through lists of people who have
permission to enter the Apostolic Palace.

◁ CALLING AHEAD
Sitting at his desk by the Bronze Door, Tiziano has overall responsibility for all who enter the Apostolic Palace. He phones ahead to tell the guard at the next level that a visitor is arriving.

▷ ON DUTY AT THE BRONZE DOOR
The halberdier stands at the Bronze Door. He uses his halberd to stop visitors at the entrance. When Tiziano gives permission for a visitor to pass, the halberd is raised.

⋏ TAKING LEAVE
When a halberdier comes to the end of his duty, he is replaced by another guard; the outgoing halberdier cermoniously takes his leave of the Bronze Door.

◁ CHANGING THE GUARD
Tiziano presides over the Changing of the Guard. At the end of his duty by the Bronze Door, a halberdier is relieved by another guard, here presenting himself for duty.

⋏ WATCHING EVENTS
From a well-placed window in the Wing of Maderno, Tiziano can follow the progress of those guards who have marched out to attend the General Audience.

ᴧ DISMISSING THE CAPOPOSTO
When one guard is relieved by another,
the *capoposto* (commander) reports
the change to Tiziano, who then tells
the *capoposto* that he too can leave.

When I carry out ceremonial duties I remember our history ... the events of the Sack of Rome ... and the pledge we make.

⟩ KARATE WITH THE MASTER

Since the assassination attempt on Pope John Paul II, in St. Peter's Square on May 13, 1981, the guards have studied self defense and karate with a black belt master.

⌄ MARTIAL ARTS IN THE VATICAN

Surprise is the key element in attack and also in defense. The guards, who are in peak athletic form, undergo martial arts training—one benefit of this is that it teaches them to react rapidly to any threat against the pope.

⋀ ⟩ READY FOR ACTION

Guards train rigorously—in particular to deal with situations that may arise at large public events at the Vatican; if necessary, they will defend the pope with their lives.

⋀ ⟩ IN THE GYM

Each day, after martial arts training, Tiziano goes to exercise in the gym beneath the barracks—he follows a training program laid out by his fitness instructor.

⌄ TAILORING A UNIFORM

To make a Swiss Guard uniform, the tailor needs to cut out and combine 156 pieces of fabric. It takes him around 30 hours of patient cutting and stitching to complete one full dress uniform.

⌃ IRONING

The tailor uses an iron to press the uniforms, which are made from cotton (for summer) and wool (for winter). The uniforms are labeled and hung up ready for collection.

⌄ FATHER AND SON

Tiziano adores his children and, when he is not working, loves to spend time with them. He takes his young son for a walk, leaving through St. Anne's Gate.

⌃ BLUE UNIFORMS

Some of Tiziano's colleagues go to visit the tailor. These guards, who stand duty at St. Anne's Gate, on the east side of the Vatican, wear a simple blue uniform with a navy tasselled cape.

⌄ FAMILY LIFE

All guards who reach the grade of corporal may marry, and all, without exception, live in the Vatican. Tiziano lives with his wife and his two children in an apartment near the barracks.

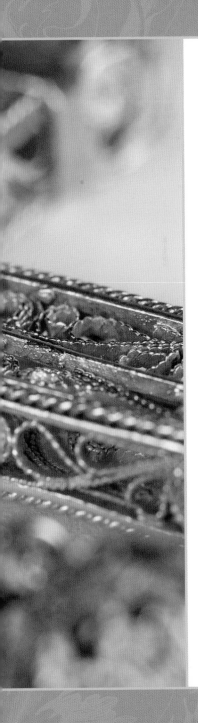

TREASURES

THE PAPAL SACRISTY

Few of the thousands of visitors to the Vatican who gaze each day at Michaelangelo's famous *Last Judgement* in the Sistine Chapel could guess that behind the frescoed wall lies a room filled with priceless treasures. This is the Papal Sacristy, overseen by the Master of Pontifical Liturgical Celebrations, where vestments and liturgical objects once used by the popes are kept. Since at least the 4th century, special vestments and vessels have been reserved exclusively for the Vatican's celebration of the sacraments, and over the centuries, the pontiffs have gathered an incomparable collection of these artifacts. The majority of the objects stored in the sacristy are gifts bestowed by the Church's faithful; some are gifts from royalty and other heads of state. Only the very finest items that human skill could produce have been dedicated for use by the pope in the Divine Service.

The Papal Tiara is one of the most widely recognized symbols of the papacy, historically used to crown a new pope. The tiaras date from as far back as the 8th century and may have developed from a Byzantine form of imperial headdress worn by the rulers of the Eastern Roman Empire.

The earliest style of Papal Tiara was a white headdress, encircled by a simple band over the forehead. By the 10th century, the headband included two crowns and a third was added by the beginning of the 14th century. The three tiers are sometimes referred to as the *triregnum* (Latin for "three crowns") symbolizing the Church's temporal, ecclesiastical, and heavenly authority. Two lappets (embroidered pieces of silk or satin fabric) fringed with tassels hang from the back of the tiara.

The last pope to be crowned was Pope Paul VI in 1963, who subsequently donated his tiara to the people of the United States in recognition of their charity work for the poor and homeless. However, the symbol of the tiara continues to feature on the papal flag and on all official insignia.

GOLD EMBROIDERY

FLEUR-DE-LYS MOTIF

Globe and cross finial

< POPE LEO XIII TIARA
A gift from the Catholics of Bologna in 1903, this tiara is etched with olive branches and medallions of Pope Leo XIII, Pope Pius IX, St. Peter, and an angel.

Filigree gold on silver mesh

False gems representing precious stones

Latin inscription reads "By Divine Right High Priest on Earth"

Silk lappets with gold border and tassels

Coat of arms of Pope Leo XIII

^ POPE PIUS VII TIARA
Made around 1820, this simple gold and silver tiara was a gift from merchants of the French city of Lyons, commemorating Pope Pius VII's visits there in 1804 and 1805.

PAPAL TIARAS
THREE-TIERED JEWELED PAPAL CROWNS

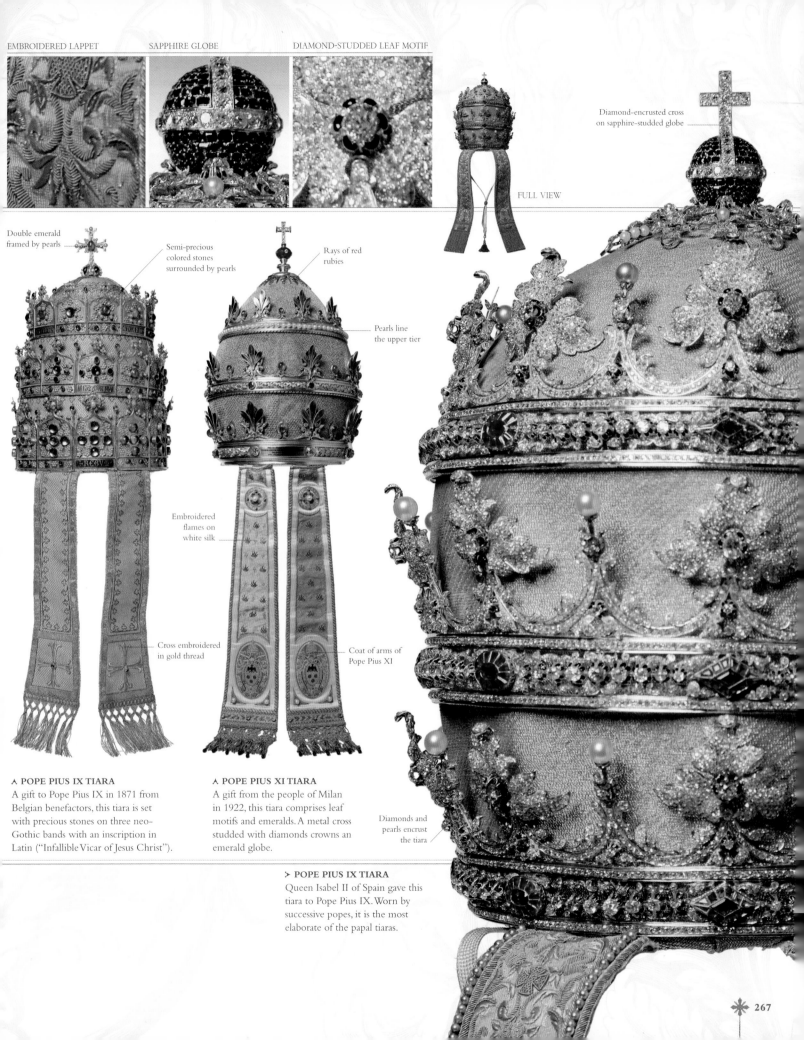

EMBROIDERED LAPPET

SAPPHIRE GLOBE

DIAMOND-STUDDED LEAF MOTIF

Diamond-encrusted cross on sapphire-studded globe

FULL VIEW

Double emerald framed by pearls

Semi-precious colored stones surrounded by pearls

Rays of red rubies

Pearls line the upper tier

Embroidered flames on white silk

Cross embroidered in gold thread

Coat of arms of Pope Pius XI

Diamonds and pearls encrust the tiara

⋏ POPE PIUS IX TIARA
A gift to Pope Pius IX in 1871 from Belgian benefactors, this tiara is set with precious stones on three neo-Gothic bands with an inscription in Latin ("Infallible Vicar of Jesus Christ").

⋏ POPE PIUS XI TIARA
A gift from the people of Milan in 1922, this tiara comprises leaf motifs and emeralds. A metal cross studded with diamonds crowns an emerald globe.

⋗ POPE PIUS IX TIARA
Queen Isabel II of Spain gave this tiara to Pope Pius IX. Worn by successive popes, it is the most elaborate of the papal tiaras.

JESUS THE GOOD SHEPHERD

The word "mitre" comes from the Greek for headband, or turban. It is the distinctive mark of a bishop and is worn only during a liturgy. A tall crown, the mitre is made of two boards covered with a fabric, usually silk. The boards, of equal size, fold together and are bound at the base by a band. From the back hang two lappets (long strips of cloth) made of the same material as the base band, which are often embroidered with the coat of arms of the bishop. The mitre is worn with a cope (a large cape) or a chasuble (sleeveless tunic), which the bishop wears while celebrating the Eucharist, or Mass.

Iconographical evidence indicates that the mitre only came into common use at the end of the first millennium. In the past, mitres were often covered with precious stones or embroidered with elaborate designs. Today, they are simpler; when in the presence of the pope, the cardinals wear an unadorned white damask mitre. In 2005, Pope Benedict XVI replaced the Papal Tiara with the mitre on his coat-of-arms, to underline that the pope is Bishop of Rome.

Embroidered palm tree fronds

Jesus as the Good Shepherd, caring for his flock

Sheep or Jesus's "flock" symbolize the faithful

Gold rosette on lappets

EMBROIDERED ROSETTES

CREST OF POPE PIUS IX

MITRES

CEREMONIAL HEADDRESSES

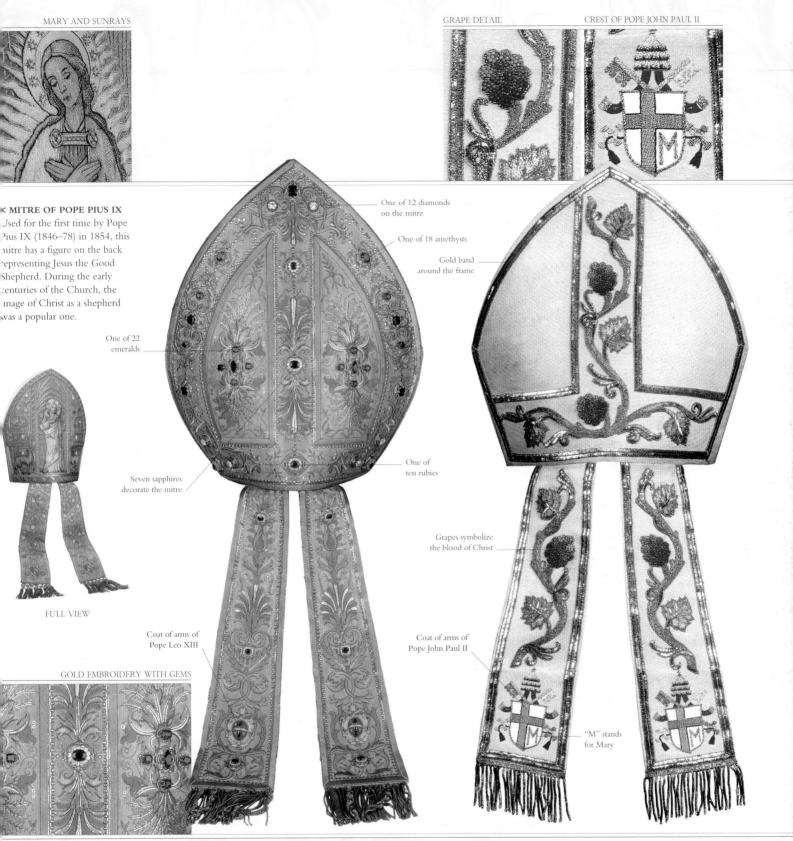

MARY AND SUNRAYS

GRAPE DETAIL

CREST OF POPE JOHN PAUL II

≪ MITRE OF POPE PIUS IX
Used for the first time by Pope
Pius IX (1846–78) in 1854, this
mitre has a figure on the back
representing Jesus the Good
Shepherd. During the early
centuries of the Church, the
image of Christ as a shepherd
was a popular one.

One of 22
emeralds

Seven sapphires
decorate the mitre

FULL VIEW

GOLD EMBROIDERY WITH GEMS

One of 12 diamonds
on the mitre

One of 18 amethysts

Gold band
around the frame

One of
ten rubies

Grapes symbolize
the blood of Christ

Coat of arms of
Pope Leo XIII

Coat of arms of
Pope John Paul II

"M" stands
for Mary

ʌ MITRE OF LEO XIII
Emperor William II of Prussia gave this
elaborately embroidered silk mitre to Pope
Leo XIII in 1888, to mark the Golden Jubilee
of the pontiff's priestly ordination.

ʌ MITRE OF POPE JOHN PAUL I
This mitre was originally used by Pope John Paul I in
1978, during his month-long pontificate. Embroidered
vine branches and grapes decorate the mitre and lappets.
The coat of arms of Pope John Paul II was added later.

⋏ CABINET OF MITRES
This display of 19th- and 20th-century mitres is located within the Papal Sacristy. Although not open to the general public, many objects are kept on permanent display for visiting dignitaries.

COAT OF ARMS

EMBROIDERED MONOGRAM

From the Middle Ages onward, the pope wore special gloves and shoes during the celebration of the Pontifical High Mass, the most solemn form of the Eucharist. The color of the shoes and gloves varied according to the liturgical season and matched the vestments. White was worn for celebrations in honor of Jesus, Mary, and the saints, as well as during Christmas and Easter; purple was used during Lent and Advent; red was worn on Palm Sunday, Good Friday, and the feasts of the martyrs; and green was worn during the ordinary days of the year on which feasts were not observed. Black was worn for funerals and Requiem Mass (Mass offered for the dead). These colors are still worn today by the pope for each of these occasions.

Gloves were employed primarily for outdoor celebrations such as processions and blessings. During the Middle Ages, a special large ring was worn over the finger of the glove, and the faithful kissed the ring as a mark of respect to the bishop. Buskins (silk shoes), often embroidered with gold thread, were also worn during the liturgy. The pope's red *galero* (wide-brimmed hat) was not used during the liturgy but rather in everyday wear, as it still is today.

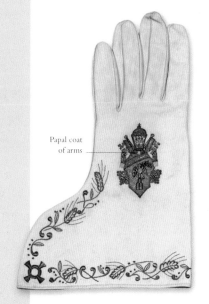

Papal coat of arms ——

—— Monogram

∧ GLOVES OF POPE PIUS XII
The gloves of Pope Pius XII (1939–58) carry the pontiff's crest on the left, and the initials IHS: *Iesu Hominum Salvator* (Jesus Savior of Mankind) on the right.

∨ SHOES OF POPE PIUS VII
The white silk shoes of Pope Pius VII (1800–23) are embroidered with gold thread. Each shoe has a decorative cross with an emerald at its center.

EMERALD

EMBROIDERED SCROLLS

Ribbon laces

Emerald

PAPAL ACCESSORIES

HATS, SHOES, AND GLOVES

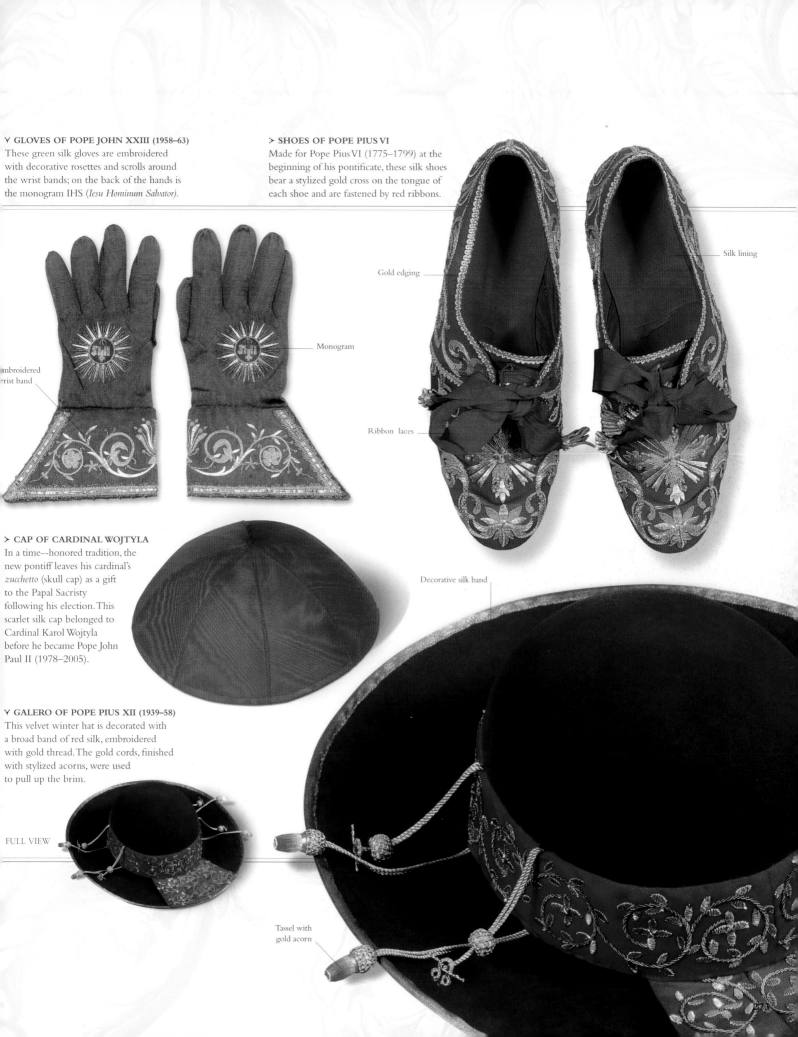

ᵛ GLOVES OF POPE JOHN XXIII (1958–63)
These green silk gloves are embroidered with decorative rosettes and scrolls around the wrist bands; on the back of the hands is the monogram IHS (*Iesu Hominum Salvator*).

> SHOES OF POPE PIUS VI
Made for Pope Pius VI (1775–1799) at the beginning of his pontificate, these silk shoes bear a stylized gold cross on the tongue of each shoe and are fastened by red ribbons.

Silk lining

Gold edging

Monogram

Embroidered wrist band

Ribbon laces

> CAP OF CARDINAL WOJTYLA
In a time--honored tradition, the new pontiff leaves his cardinal's *zucchetto* (skull cap) as a gift to the Papal Sacristy following his election. This scarlet silk cap belonged to Cardinal Karol Wojtyla before he became Pope John Paul II (1978–2005).

Decorative silk band

ᵛ GALERO OF POPE PIUS XII (1939–58)
This velvet winter hat is decorated with a broad band of red silk, embroidered with gold thread. The gold cords, finished with stylized acorns, were used to pull up the brim.

FULL VIEW

Tassel with
gold acorn

Red silk lining

Intricately embroidered
flowers with variegated leaves

Simply meaning "clothing" in Latin, vestments are, in effect, the ritual uniform of the clergy. Since the 4th century, special vestments have been worn in the celebration of the sacraments (Baptism, Penance, Confirmation, the Eucharist, Holy Orders, Matrimony, and the Anointing of the Sick). When the Roman emperor Constantine I proclaimed religious tolerance in 313 and permitted churches to be built, lavish vestments were designed to match the elaborate buildings. From the 8th to the 14th century, vestments became more sumptuous, partly influenced by the Byzantine court where special forms of dress were prescribed for particular occasions.

The most important of the sacraments is the Eucharist, or Mass. The bishop and priest wear the chasuble (long, sleeveless garment) during the Eucharist, and the deacon wears a dalmatic (wide-sleeved tunic). Underneath these garments, a long white ankle-length gown is worn, called the alb. A stole, made of the same material as the chasuble and dalmatic, is worn over the shoulder.

EMBROIDERED FLOWERS

GOLD AND SILVER THREADS

MASS VESTMENTS
CHASUBLES AND DALMATICS

Tulips from Turkey were
introduced into Europe in
the 16th century

Bands on and around
the garment are woven
with gold thread

CENTRAL PANEL EDGING

GOLD EDGING

Exotic, blue-
petalled flower

⊳ SILK DALMATIC
The flowers of this 17th-century
tunic have been embroidered
using silk thread. The design is
symmetrical and is divided into
panels by woven gold bands.

⊲ 17TH-CENTURY CHASUBLE
Dating from the pontificate of
Pope Urban VIII (1623–44), this
sleeveless garment tapers in at the
top to allow the arms maximum
freedom of movement.

Symmetrical
floral design

Serrated petal design
in shades of red

Embroidered
gold edging

FULL VIEW

Papal vestments are stored in the Sacristy,
where they are kept on galley hangers in
specially constructed wardrobes to prevent
the delicate fabric from being damaged.

FLORAL DESIGN

DETAIL OF GOLD SHEETING

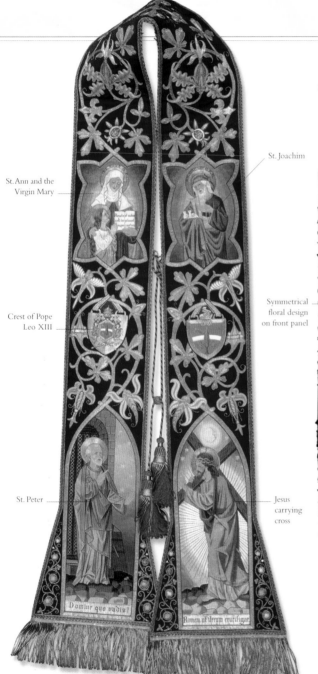

St. Ann and the
Virgin Mary

St. Joachim

Internal straps for
hanging garment

Pieces of sheet
gold sewn on
with fine thread

Crest of Pope
Leo XIII

Symmetrical
floral design
on front panel

St. Peter

Jesus
carrying
cross

Domine quo vadis?

Romam ut iterum crucifigar

Woven gold
edging

∧ **VELVET STOLE**
Images of St. Ann and St. Joachim are
embroidered in the upper panels of this
stole. The lower panels depict St. Peter
meeting Christ carrying the cross.

∧ **19TH-CENTURY CHASUBLE**
This chasuble of red silk, made between
1820 and 1825, is covered with a geometric
floral design created with gold thread and
florets of gold sheeting.

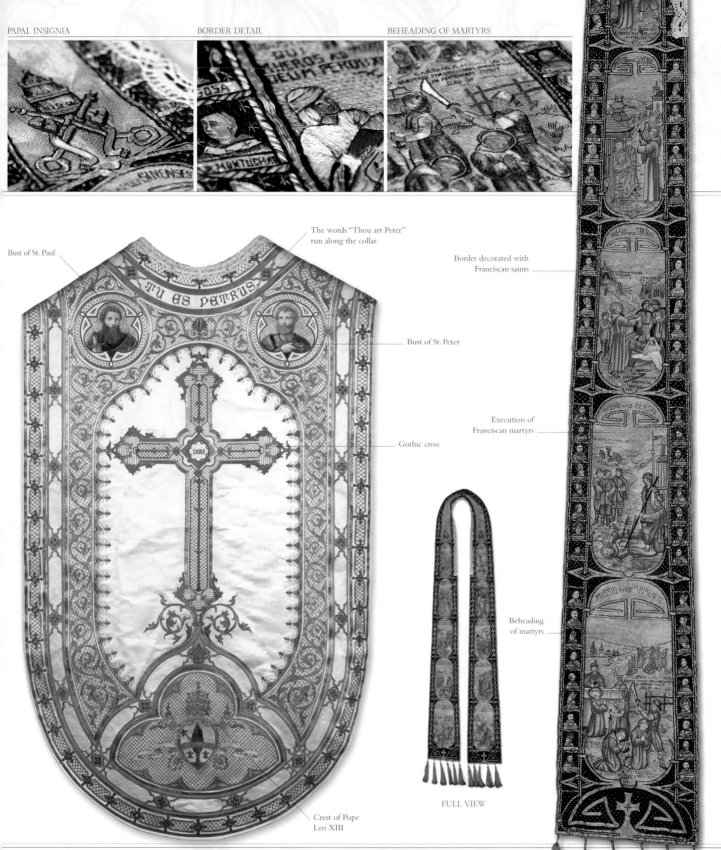

Bust of St. Paul

The words "Thou art Peter" run along the collar

TU ES PETRUS

Bust of St. Peter

Gothic cross

Border decorated with Franciscan saints

Execution of Franciscan martyrs

Beheading of martyrs

Crest of Pope Leo XIII

FULL VIEW

∧ WHITE CHASUBLE

Made of white satin, this chasuble was given to Pope Leo XIII (1878–1903) in 1887 by the people of Milan. In the center is a Gothic cross surmounting the pope's coat of arms.

> EMBROIDERED STOLE

A gift to Pope Pius XI in 1926 by Clarissan Sisters from Mazamet, France, this stole commemorates the 700th anniversary of the death of St. Francis of Assisi.

The cross is the most recognizable symbol of Christianity and comes in a multitude of sizes and differing designs. Catholic priests and worshipers may choose to wear crosses around their necks, but the pectoral cross, worn on a long chain with the cross itself resting below the heart, is usually a sign that the wearer is a senior member of the clergy: a bishop, an archbishop, a cardinal, or a pope. When worn by the pope, the pectoral cross acts as a reminder that the pope's role is to serve Jesus.

Instead of pectoral crosses, priests and laity alike may wear a rosary: a set of beads on a chain that ends with a cross. The beads are held while the wearer says the Rosary, a medieval prayer that recalls events in the life of Jesus. As Catholics recite, they move a bead along during each prayer. The pope recites the Rosary prayer daily during Mass and, at Private Audiences, he presents visitors with a rosary.

Historically, many pectoral crosses and rosaries belonging to the pope were made of precious metals and sumptuously decorated with fine jewels; today, these items tend to be more simple in design.

Ring for chain

Pearl floret

Large pearl

Ring for chain

< PEARL CROSS
This pectoral cross was gifted to Pope Pius XI (1922–39) by the King of Italy in celebration of the 1929 Lateran Treaty.

Ruby

Sapphire

Emerald

Malachite

< PECTORAL CROSS
The Sisters of St. Raphael gave this cross to Pope Paul VI (1963–78) in 1977. The gift marked the canonization of their founder, St. Raphael.

Relic of St. Raphael

< ROSARY OF FATIMA
A gift to Pope John Paul II (1978–2005), this 20th-century rosary of coral beads has a hand-crafted crucifix bearing the pope's coat of arms. On the clasp is an image of the Madonna of Fatima.

ᴧ GOLD AND RUBY CROSS
In commemoration of the beatification of Pope Pius IX in June 2000, this cross was created for Pope John Paul II, and bears his crest on the reverse.

PECTORAL CROSSES
SYMBOLS OF CHRISTIAN DEVOTION

Diamond

Sapphire

Emerald

Gold rope design

< NEO-GOTHIC CROSS
Dating to 1939, this cross
is encrusted with diamonds,
rubies, and emeralds and
is worn suspended from a
gold chain that links through
the top of the cross.

End piece imitating a
Neo-Gothic pointed arch

> CROSS OF POPE PIUS X
Pope Leo XIII (1878–1903) gave
this pectoral cross to Giuseppe
Sarto in 1890 when Sarto was
made a cardinal. The cardinal was
elected Pope Pius X (1903–14)
in 1903 and continued to wear
the aquamarine gem cross.

Aquamarine
gemstone

Cherub with
folded wings

Gold floret

Amethyst

Gold frame

> AMETHYST CROSS
Once belonging to Cardinal Donato
Sbarretti (1856–1939), this simple
cross was left to the Papal Sacristy
in 1939. It was subsequently worn
by Pope Pius XII (1939–58).

FULL VIEW

In addition to vestments, popes wear various pieces of elaborate jewelry. The decorative items are beautifully crafted but some also fulfill a specific function. Clasps, for example, are used to fasten the pope's cope, a long silk cloak worn during the liturgy. Called a "morse" or a "rational," the clasp has two hooks that are used to link it to the center edges of the cope, thus holding it in place. Another useful item is the pin, three of which are used to hold in place the pallium, a long woollen stole that is worn over the shoulders.

Serving a more symbolic function, rings represent the Episcopal office (the office of a bishop), and during ordination ceremonies, each new bishop is presented with a ring, the seal of his office. Rings are also given to bishops when they are elevated to the Sacred College of Cardinals. The design of these particular rings is chosen by the pope himself; under Benedict XVI, the cardinal's ring is a gold band with the crucified Jesus flanked by Mary and St. John.

The rings of the past were more elaborate than those in use today. Once encrusted with sapphires, rubies, diamonds, and other precious stones, today they tend to be simple bands of silver or gold.

DOVE DETAIL

> RING OF POPE PIUS IX
Presented to the pope by Queen Victoria, this 24-carat ring has an aquamarine gem and a papal insignia on the band.

Papal crest

Four garnets

18 pearls surround the central stone

< AMETHYST AND PEARL RING
This gold ring belonged to Cardinal Donato Sbarretti, who died in 1939 and left the ring to Pope Pius XII.

> RING OF POPE PIUS VI
In 1775, Princess Marie Clotilde of France presented this ring to the pope to mark her wedding.

Garnet

Emerald

Inlaid diamonds in the profile of the pontiff

< GOLD CLASP
Dating from 1729, this clasp belonged to Pope Benedict XIII (1724–30). The piece portrays the Holy Spirit as a dove, in a burst of gold rays set with diamonds. Other decorative gems include an aquamarine and six emeralds.

PAPAL JEWELRY
PINS, RINGS, AND CLASPS

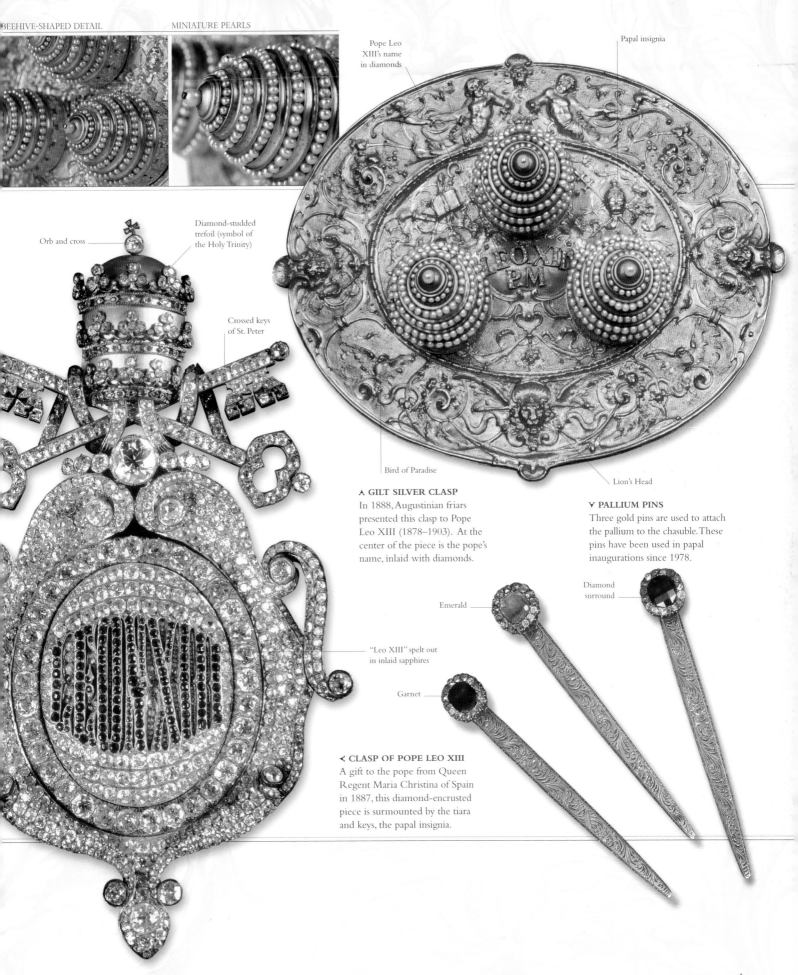

Pope Leo XIII's name in diamonds

Papal insignia

Orb and cross

Diamond-studded trefoil (symbol of the Holy Trinity)

Crossed keys of St. Peter

Bird of Paradise

Lion's Head

"Leo XIII" spelt out in inlaid sapphires

⌃ GILT SILVER CLASP
In 1888, Augustinian friars presented this clasp to Pope Leo XIII (1878–1903). At the center of the piece is the pope's name, inlaid with diamonds.

⌄ PALLIUM PINS
Three gold pins are used to attach the pallium to the chasuble. These pins have been used in papal inaugurations since 1978.

Diamond surround

Emerald

Garnet

⌃ CLASP OF POPE LEO XIII
A gift to the pope from Queen Regent Maria Christina of Spain in 1887, this diamond-encrusted piece is surmounted by the tiara and keys, the papal insignia.

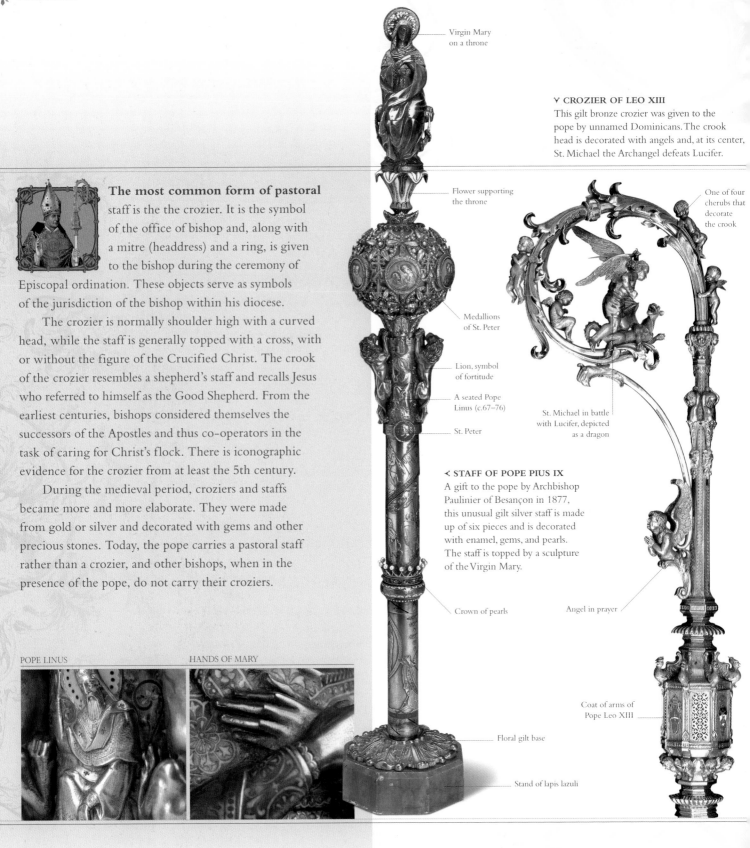

The most common form of pastoral staff is the the crozier. It is the symbol of the office of bishop and, along with a mitre (headdress) and a ring, is given to the bishop during the ceremony of Episcopal ordination. These objects serve as symbols of the jurisdiction of the bishop within his diocese.

The crozier is normally shoulder high with a curved head, while the staff is generally topped with a cross, with or without the figure of the Crucified Christ. The crook of the crozier resembles a shepherd's staff and recalls Jesus who referred to himself as the Good Shepherd. From the earliest centuries, bishops considered themselves the successors of the Apostles and thus co-operators in the task of caring for Christ's flock. There is iconographic evidence for the crozier from at least the 5th century.

During the medieval period, croziers and staffs became more and more elaborate. They were made from gold or silver and decorated with gems and other precious stones. Today, the pope carries a pastoral staff rather than a crozier, and other bishops, when in the presence of the pope, do not carry their croziers.

POPE LINUS

HANDS OF MARY

Virgin Mary on a throne

Flower supporting the throne

Medallions of St. Peter

Lion, symbol of fortitude

A seated Pope Linus (c.67–76)

St. Peter

Crown of pearls

Floral gilt base

Stand of lapis lazuli

ᴠ CROZIER OF LEO XIII
This gilt bronze crozier was given to the pope by unnamed Dominicans. The crook head is decorated with angels and, at its center, St. Michael the Archangel defeats Lucifer.

One of four cherubs that decorate the crook

St. Michael in battle with Lucifer, depicted as a dragon

‹ STAFF OF POPE PIUS IX
A gift to the pope by Archbishop Paulinier of Besançon in 1877, this unusual gilt silver staff is made up of six pieces and is decorated with enamel, gems, and pearls. The staff is topped by a sculpture of the Virgin Mary.

Angel in prayer

Coat of arms of Pope Leo XIII

CROZIERS AND STAFFS
SYMBOLS OF PASTORAL OFFICE

PROFILE OF CHRIST

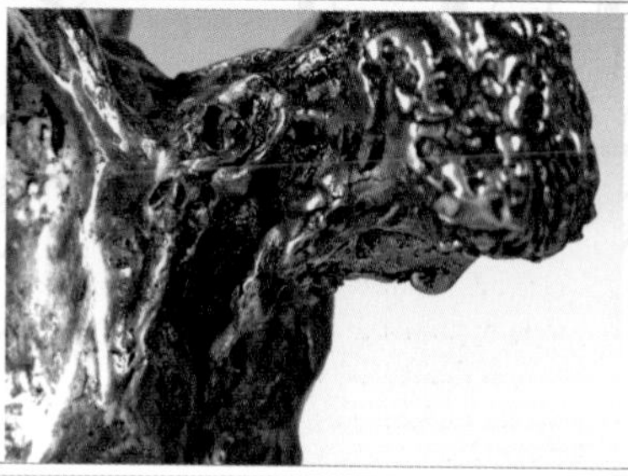

ROPE DETAIL

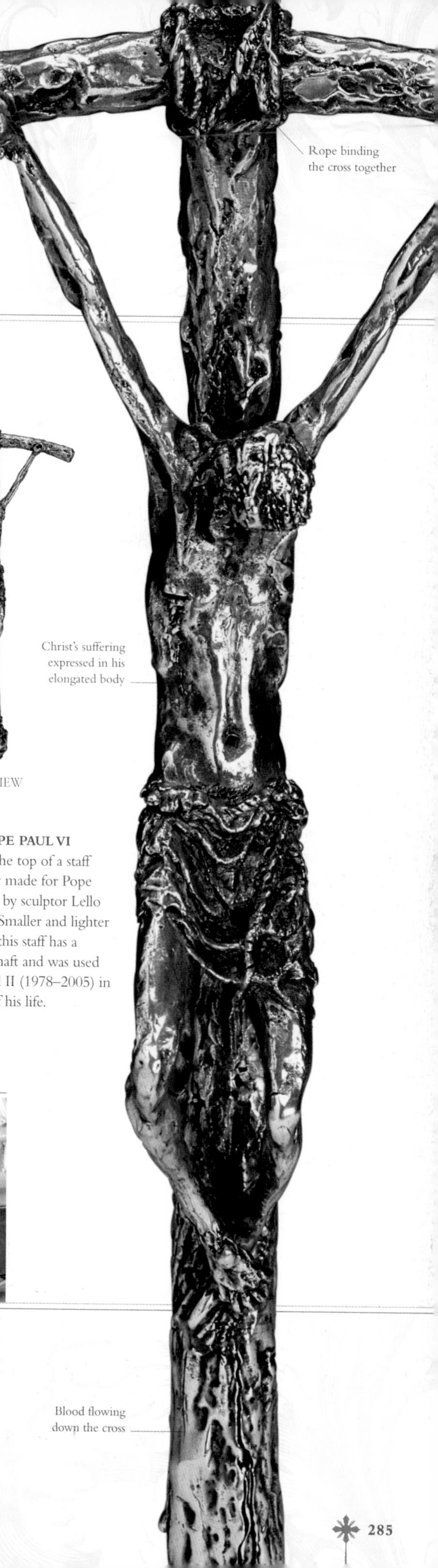

Rope binding
the cross together

Sapphire

Amber

Amethyst

The Virgin Mary on
a flower throne with
the infant Jesus

Christ's suffering
expressed in his
elongated body

FULL VIEW

Carved
ivory stem

MARY WITH INFANT JESUS

> **STAFF OF POPE PAUL VI**
This is a copy of the top of a staff
that was originally made for Pope
Paul VI (1963–78) by sculptor Lello
Scorzelli in 1974. Smaller and lighter
than the original, this staff has a
hollow titanium shaft and was used
by Pope John Paul II (1978–2005) in
the last 15 years of his life.

JESUS, THE GOOD SHEPHERD

SYMBOL OF ST MATTHEW

St. Rupert
of Salzburg

< **MID-19TH-CENTURY CROZIER**
The elaborate crozier of Cardinal Karl-August von Reisach
(1800–69) is made up of four ivory sections along a gilt
shaft. Just below the crook is a panel decorated with fine
miniature statues of St. Charles Borromeo, St. Corbinian of
Bavaria, St. Benno of Bavaria, and St. Rupert of Salzburg.

Blood flowing
down the cross

⟨ PROCESSIONAL CROSS OF PIUS IX
This crucifix is made of silver except for its gilt figure of Christ and the monogram above, which reads INRI, a Latin acronym for "Jesus of Nazareth, King of the Jews". The staff has ornate niches that house 12 Apostle figurines, also in gilt.

Inscription

Four-leaf motif

In the early centuries of the Catholic Church, the cross was seen as a symbol of defeat. In the Roman world, death by crucifixion was reserved for common criminals; the cross reminded Christians of the death of Jesus and man's inhumanity to man. As a result, early Christians used other images and symbols to represent their faith: the anchor represented the faith that could provide stability in the stormy waters of life; the fish was an acronym in Greek for Jesus Christ, savior of humanity; and the lighthouse recalled Christ describing himself as the Light of the World. However, in 312, Emperor Constantine claimed to have seen a vision of the cross on the eve of his victorious battle to win control over Rome. From that point onward, Christians interpreted the cross as a symbol of Jesus's ultimate victory over death. Today, the cross is the primary symbol of those who believe in Jesus as the Son of God.

The Processional Cross leads all liturgical celebrations. It is mounted on a shoulder-high shaft, flanked by two candles, and is preceded by a thurible (*see pp.288–89*), from which rises perfumed incense. Most modern processional crosses belonging to the pope take the form of a crucifix.

Gilt figure of Christ

Garnet

Gilt filigree

Gilt Apostle figure

Silver Christ

⟩ PROCESSIONAL CROSS OF PIUS IX
This cross, presented in 1868, was used for the first time at the opening of the First Vatican Council on 8 December 1869.

Angel holding drinking cup

Silvered staff

APOSTLES IN NICHES

GILT CHRIST DETAIL

PROCESSIONAL CROSSES
LEADERS OF LITURGICAL CEREMONIES

Mary, Mother of God

˅ PROCESSIONAL CROSS OF LEO XIII

This gilt metal triple cross was a gift from Parisian jewelers to Leo XIII in 1887. The three crossbars represent the pope's triple role as Bishop of Rome, Patriarch of the West, and successor of St. Peter. This design of the papal cross was discarded in favor of a simple crucifix by Pope Paul VI (1963–78).

Enamel florets

Four-leaf motif

Alpha and omega symbols flank blue cross design

Salus means "Salvation"

Gilt Christ

˃ MEDIEVAL CROSS

Dating from the late 14th or early 15th century, this cross is made of wood, and covered with beaten strips of metal. The central image of Christ is surrounded by saints and other figures, who also appear on the reverse.

One of 62 garnets

Delicate scroll motif

Doves drinking from fountain

Inscription from donors

Beaten metal

FULL VIEW

Pommel on staff

Cap on staff to affix cross

Incense, an aromatic substance that is obtained from certain resinous trees, is common in the worship of many of the world's religions. Burning the substance releases the aroma, which can be altered by the addition of wood, olive leaves, and other ingredients. Incense was used in Judaism, during worship in the Temple; early Christians may have used it, but it was not until the 4th century, with the construction of churches, that the burning of incense became common practice.

Thuribles, metal containers made of two portions, are used to burn the incense. Charcoal is placed in the lower portion of the thurible, while the lid, the upper half of the container, allows the perfumed smoke to escape through the holes. The thurible is swung from chains attached to the lid to disperse the smoke. During Mass, incense is used in the entrance procession and to incense the altar, the Book of the Gospel, and the bread and wine, as well as the clergy and the faithful. The incense is kept in a specially designed container called an incense boat and is placed into the thurible with a spoon.

Phoenix

Coral cross

ʌ ASH CONTAINER
This silver container is used to hold ashes during Ash Wednesday celebrations. Each handle is decorated with a phoenix, the mythical bird that rose from its own ashes.

Lid

> GILT METAL THURIBLE
This thurible belonged to Pope Pius IX (1846–78). Charcoal is burned in the hollow base, and the lid, divided into sections, is decorated with leaf motifs.

Decorative opening allows smoke to escape

< 19TH CENTURY INCENSE BOAT
Also belonging to Pope Pius IX, this oval, gilt metal boat sits on a circular base and has two lids, each with floral designs. The spoon is used to scoop up incense.

Holder for charcoal

Floral motif on double lid

Incense spoon

Papyrus motif

Finger ring on handle

INCENSE HOLDERS
THURIBLES AND BOATS

OPENING FOR CHAIN

LEAF DESIGN

Finger ring
on handle

Lid of thurible

Incense spoon

∨ SILVER INCENSE BOAT
Catholics in Madrid presented
this incense boat and thurible
(left) to Pope John Paul II in
1995. The boat has a spoon
and two lids that open.

Hinged lid

Smoke holes
in lid allowing
smoke to escape

Upper portion
with holes

Charcoal
container

∧ THURIBLE SET
This silver thurible of
Spanish manufacture forms
a set with an incense boat
(right), which is decorated
with similar floral designs.

Chains used to carry
and work the incense

Finger
ring

≻ SILVER THURIBLE
This 21st-century silver thurible
has a finger ring on the handle to
allow it to be swung easily. Both
the handle and the tall lid are
decorated with stylized leaves.

Handle

Chain used to
swing the thurible

During a visit to the Holy Land in 325–27, Helena, the mother of emperor Constantine, claimed to have found the cross on which Jesus was crucified. She had the cross unearthed from where it was allegedly buried, close to Golgotha—site of the crucifixion—in Jerusalem, and a portion was brought to Rome, where it was installed in her private chapel. It seems that small pieces were removed from the cross, for shortly afterward, St. Cyril of Jerusalem (c.315–87) claimed that "the world is full of the relics of the Cross of Christ".

During the Middle Ages, veneration of the "True Cross" became common. Artists painted, carved, and cast crosses as aids to Christian devotion. This was further expanded by Crusaders returning from the Holy Land bearing religious souvenirs, and it became popular for monks and nuns to keep a cross in their cell, either on a wall or on a desk. This tradition was also observed by the popes; in the 16th century, Pope Alexander VII (1655–67) is said to have kept a skull beside his table cross as a reminder of his mortality.

MONOGRAM DETAIL

CHRIST DETAIL

Monogram indicates "Jesus Christ King of the Jews"

< CROSS OF PIUS VII
Pope Pius kept this cross at his side during his captivity in France in the early 19th century. The cross is set on a silk base.

v CROSS OF JOHN PAUL II
Sculpted by Enrico Manfrini, this bronze table cross was in Pope John Paul's study until his death in 2005. Symbols of the four Evangelists surround Christ.

Eagle represents St. John

Lion represents St. Mark

Base of silver silk cloth with sunray motif

Wooden case

Man represents St. Matthew

TABLE CROSSES
A FOCUS FOR PERSONAL DEVOTION

Sapphire above the
head of Christ

Inset pearl

Sunburst of
diamonds

Pearl set in
leaf motif

Sapphire surrounded
by diamonds and pearls

Ox represents
St. Luke

Angel seated on
mount of cross

Inset emeralds
on scroll design

Inscription in Greek
commemorating the
donation of the cross

Glass
pendant

Angel head
surrounded
by six wings

Date of
presentation

Shell motif
on base

▷ TABLE CROSS
OF JOHN PAUL II
This silver cross, inlaid with
enamel and gemstones and hung
with four glass pendants, was a
gift to Pope John Paul II from
Patriarch Demetrius I in 1987.

◁ TABLE CROSS OF LEO XIII
A gift from Emperor Franz Josef
of Austria in 1887, this gold cross
stands on an elaborate mount, and
is adorned with pearls, sapphires,
diamonds, and emeralds.

Candles have always had special significance in Catholic churches. During the Middle Ages, beeswax candles were used to illuminate church interiors, and were placed on the altar in specially made candleholders. Six candles were placed on the altar for Mass and when the pope joined the celebrations, a seventh candle was added.

During the Renaissance (14th to 16th centuries), candlesticks were finely wrought from silver and gold. It became the practice when greeting a prelate (high-ranking church dignitary) at the door of the church to accompany him with a candle. On the night of Holy Saturday (the day before Easter), Catholics light the Paschal Candle. For the 50 days of Easter this candle burns at Mass, and many churches have elaborate stands for this purpose. The Paschal Candle is also lit during the celebration of all the other sacraments to underline their link with the resurrection of Jesus. In popular devotion, people light candles before images of the saints and the Virgin Mary, to honor the memory of those who have died.

Candles are also used with altar sets, consisting of a crucifix and a number of matching candlesticks, which are placed on a church altar as a reminder of Christ's sacrifice.

Leaf motif

Harp design

< SILVER CANDLEHOLDER
This 18th-century four-leafed candleholder is edged with a cord motif. The candle is held in place by the silver wire in the center.

Enam[el] flor[al]

Floral inlay of green enamel

Detail in blue enamel

< FRENCH CANDLEHOLDER
Belonging to Pope Pius IX (1846–78), this colorful holder dates to 1867. The scroll beneath the handle balances the arm.

Text from the scriptures

Crest of Leo XIII

St Ambrose

St. John

Enamel inlay

< NEO-GOTHIC CANDLEHOLDER
A gift from the people of Milan to Pope Leo XIII (1878–1903), this 1887 gilt silver holder carries the busts of St. Peter, St. Ambrose, and St. John.

CREST OF LEO XIII

BUST OF ST JOHN

CANDLEHOLDERS
CANDLESTICKS AND ALTAR SETS

FULL VIEW

Figure of Christ

Symmetrical design depicting sunrays

Cup to collect melted wax

Stem

Shell motif

The martyr, St. Stephen

Decorative floret

Stem

Central panel with figure of Christ

Pedestal

Central panel decorated with figures of saints

A SILVER ALTAR SET

Dating from the end of the 18th century, this elegant altar set is made up of six candlesticks and a matching crucifix. Each piece stands on a wide, three-footed base and rises on a slender stem.

< A ALTAR SET OF LEO XIII

This Neo-Gothic altar set, dating to 1887, consists of a gilt metal cross and six candlesticks. Each piece stands on a triangular pedestal, decorated with saints.

Lamb of the Apocalypse

Arch studded with
turquoise-inlaid stars

Scene from the
birth of Jesus

Peace is one of the central themes of the Jewish and Christian faiths. Throughout the Bible hopes for peace are constantly repeated. The first words of the Risen Christ to his apostles were "Peace be with you", and this is also the greeting the bishop uses when celebrating the Eucharist.

During the service, there is a short rite—"The Sign of Peace"—before the congregation receives Holy Communion. The priest greets the faithful with the words "the peace of the Lord be with you." It was customary at this point for the clergy to offer a gesture of peace to each other, normally by an embrace or a kiss. For elderly or infirm clergy, who were unable to rise from their place to participate in the greeting, a devotional tablet was introduced. The earliest of these date to the 13th century. It was called the *tabella pacis* ("board of peace"), or more colloquially, the Pax, from the Latin for "peace". The priest or bishop presiding over the service kissed the devotional tablet and this was then carried to other clergy.

Over time, the Pax became a liturgical item and was used at all High Masses with a number of clergy attending. Today, however, it is no longer a part of the Mass; instead, it is customary to shake hands as a sign of peace.

Prophet Isaiah

INLAID TURQUOISE   INLAID GARNET

ISAIA

REDEMISTI NOS DEO
IN SANGUINE TUO

PAXES
DEVOTIONAL TABLETS

Translated, the Latin reads: "You
redeemed us, O God, in your bloo[d]

Chalice and Host

Cherubs guarding
the Host

Archangel Raphael

The Risen
Jesus appears
to the Apostles

Neo-Gothic cross

Two miniature
archangels flank an
image of Christ

...ne depicting
...Deposition,
...s being
...en down
...m the cross

...ing David

Arms of Pope
Leo XIII

...pacem meam do vobis.

‹ PAX OF PIUS IX

Dating from 1872, this silver Pax
depicts the deposition of Christ
from the cross. The Pax is set in a
Renaissance-style cornice studded
with turquoises and garnets.

ʌ PAX OF LEO XIII

Ecclesiastical lawyers gave this
gilt silver Pax to Pope Leo XIII
(1878–1903) in 1887. The Pax
marked the Golden Jubilee of the
pope's ordination to the priesthood.

DETAIL OF THE DEPOSITION

DETAIL OF KING DAVID

Latin inscription
translates as "My
peace, I give you"

ʌ PAX OF LEO XIII

Dating from 1887, this Neo-Gothic Pax depicts
the moment when Christ is presented to the
crowds by Pontius Pilate. At the base of the Pax
is Pope Leo XIII's coat of arms.

< MONSTRANCE OF LEO XIII
This monstrance was gifted to the pope in 1888. Putti (winged infants) encircle the Host, bearing instruments associated with the Passion of Christ—the suffering of Jesus on the cross.

Putti carry a chalice, ladder, hammer, pincers, and a spear—objects relating to the Passion

∨ 19TH-CENTURY "SOLAR" MONSTRANCE
This typical sunburst monstrance includes two doves, symbolic of the Holy Spirit, atop vine tendrils symbolic of Christ as the Vine. A cross surmounts the monstrance

During Mass, Catholics have the opportunity to eat the Host (a wafer of unleavened bread) in a ritual called Holy Communion, or Eucharist. Though its appearance remains the same, this bread is believed to be changed by God's grace into the body of Christ. Those unable to come to the altar are traditionally brought the Host, and it became practice in some monasteries to preserve the Eucharist Host for those too sick to attend church. By the 13th century, it had also become popular in France and Italy to pray before the Eucharistic bread. For both these purposes, beautiful receptacles, called monstrances, were designed to store and display the consecrated Host.

The monstrance displays the Host behind glass in the center of an elaborate "sunburst" shape. After a period of display, usually an hour, the Host is removed from the monstrance, placed in a pyx (a special container), and stored in a tabernacle—a small cupboard of precious metal set behind the altar—until it is consumed.

Putto head

Space for Host in center of sunburst

Putto playing a horn

Dove, symbol of Holy Spirit

Vine tendrils, symbol of Christ

Enamel of saint

DECORATIONS OF PUTTI (WINGED INFANTS)

MONSTRANCES
VESSELS FOR DISPLAYING THE HOST

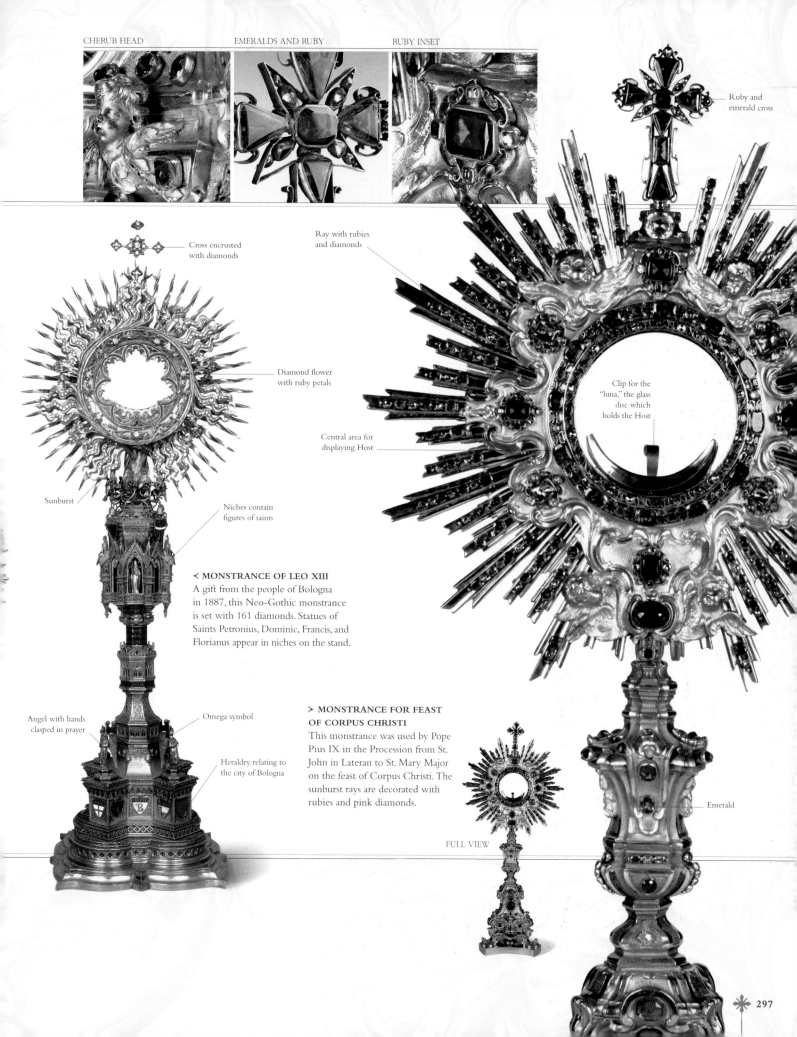

CHERUB HEAD

EMERALDS AND RUBY

RUBY INSET

Ruby and
emerald cross

Cross encrusted
with diamonds

Ray with rubies
and diamonds

Diamond flower
with ruby petals

Clip for the
"luna," the glass
disc which
holds the Host

Central area for
displaying Host

Sunburst

Niches contain
figures of saints

< MONSTRANCE OF LEO XIII

A gift from the people of Bologna
in 1887, this Neo-Gothic monstrance
is set with 161 diamonds. Statues of
Saints Petronius, Dominic, Francis, and
Florianus appear in niches on the stand.

Angel with hands
clasped in prayer

Omega symbol

Heraldry relating to
the city of Bologna

> MONSTRANCE FOR FEAST
OF CORPUS CHRISTI

This monstrance was used by Pope
Pius IX in the Procession from St.
John in Lateran to St. Mary Major
on the feast of Corpus Christi. The
sunburst rays are decorated with
rubies and pink diamonds.

Emerald

FULL VIEW

297

The **Mass recalls the Last Supper of** Jesus at the feast of Passover, when Jesus changed the substance of bread and wine into his body and his blood. Although the unleavened bread used in the sacred rite remains bread in appearance, Catholics believe that Jesus is truly present in the bread, transforming it entirely. It has been the tradition of the Church to treat the portion of bread, called the Host—from the Latin *hostia*, meaning "victim" or "sacrificial animal"—with the utmost reverence and devotion, for it is believed to be the very body of the Risen Jesus. As a result, Catholics have always provided the most precious containers in which to store the Host.

During the Mass the Host is distributed from a vessel called a ciborium, from a Medieval Latin word for "drinking cup." The Host might also be given from a paten (small plate), a pyx, (circular, lidded container), or even, occasionally, a chalice. The ciborium has a lid to protect the Host during transport. After the Mass, the Host may be taken to any sick people unable to attend the ceremony; traditionally, pyxes are used for this purpose.

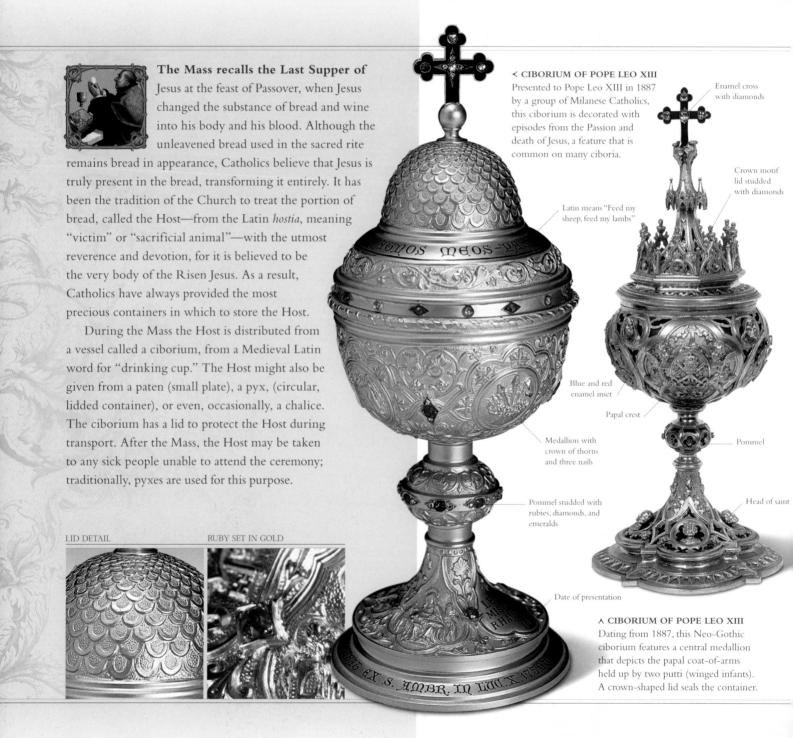

LID DETAIL

RUBY SET IN GOLD

< CIBORIUM OF POPE LEO XIII
Presented to Pope Leo XIII in 1887 by a group of Milanese Catholics, this ciborium is decorated with episodes from the Passion and death of Jesus, a feature that is common on many ciboria.

Enamel cross with diamonds

Crown motif lid studded with diamonds

Latin means "Feed my sheep, feed my lambs"

Blue and red enamel inset

Papal crest

Pommel

Head of saint

Medallion with crown of thorns and three nails

Pommel studded with rubies, diamonds, and emeralds

Date of presentation

^ CIBORIUM OF POPE LEO XIII
Dating from 1887, this Neo-Gothic ciborium features a central medallion that depicts the papal coat-of-arms held up by two putti (winged infants). A crown-shaped lid seals the container.

CIBORIA

SERVING AND STORAGE VESSELS

Cross adorned
with sapphires

A saint holding
a book and quill

Filigree
pommel

Sapphire

Papal coat of
arms on enamel
background

Cross with ruby
and diamonds

Sphere of red and
black marble

Ruby set in
floral design

Roundel
with date of
presentation

Cameo of Christ wearing
crown of thorns

Handle with
acanthus leaves

White diamond

> CIBORIUM OF PIUS IX
Given to Pope Pius IX prior to
1877 by Count Gabriele de Caix di
Saint Aymour, this was part of a set
that included a matching chalice
and wine and water cruets.

Filigree cross inlaid
with miniature pearls

Enamel medallion

Six medallions alternate
between cherub and
cross motifs

∧ CIBORIUM OF POPE LEO XIII
This elaborate Neo-Gothic ciborium was
a gift from Spanish Catholics in 1887.
The cup has four roundels and four
panels, each set in miniature pearls.
The lid and cross are set with sapphires.

∧ LATE 19TH-CENTURY CIBORIUM
This gilt ciborium was left to Pope Leo
XIII by Cardinal Simonetti around 1892.
The ciborium is decorated with
diamonds, rubies, and sapphires. At the
center of the cup is a cameo of Christ.

FULL VIEW

⌄ CHALICE OF LEO XIII
Presented to the pope in 1893, this chalice
from Portugal marked his 50 years as a
bishop. The pommel is decorated with
scenes from the Passion of Christ.

Gilt silver cup

The word "chalice" comes from the
Latin *calix*, meaning "drinking cup." The
chalice has a long and meaningful history
within the Catholic Church. At the Last
Supper, Jesus commanded his apostles to
drink wine from a cup "in memory of me." Catholic doctrine
teaches that during the Mass the wine, at the moment of
consecration, although remaining wine in appearance, in actual
fact becomes the true blood of Jesus, and thus allows worshipers
to make a spiritual communion with the risen Jesus. For that
reason, followers have always sought to make chalices as beautiful
as possible, crafting them from the finest materials available, such
as gold or silver and precious stones. In this way, faith transforms
these simple vessels into stunning works of art.

Most chalices comprise a cup, stem, and base. The middle of
the stem has a globe, or "pommel," making the chalice easier to
grip. Chalices are also accompanied by a small flat dish called a
"paten," from the Latin *patena*, meaning "plate." The paten is
made in similar style and from similar materials as the chalice, and
holds the Host during the Mass. The chalice is placed on a linen
cloth, and a linen band is used to clean the rim in between each
offering. While the Host may be preserved after the Eucharistic
celebration, the wine is always consumed during the Mass.

Floral motif

Sheaf of wheat

Inscription
"Take and
drink" from
the words
of the Mass

Evangelists
Matthew, Mark,
Luke, and John

Crown of thorns
on pommel

Dedication to
Pope Leo XIII
from the women
of Portugal

Sapphires set
in diamonds

Winged griffins
on base

⌃ CHALICE OF LEO XIII
This French chalice was given
to the pope in 1887. It is set
with enamel and sapphires with
statues of the Four Evangelists
adorning the stem. The base
features four papal emblems set
with diamonds and pearls.

PAPAL INSIGNIA   STATUES OF EVANGELISTS

Latin dedication

Papal insignia of
diamonds and pearls

CHALICES
SACRED VESSELS OF THE EUCHARIST

ST. MATTHEW   CHERUB SET WITH PEARLS   ST. JOSEPH AND JESUS

Scriptural quotation

Crucifix

Christ shown enthroned

Pommel

Paten

One of three red gems

The Eye of God, symbolizing God's all-seeing nature

St. Joseph and Jesus

Croatian coat of arms

Cherub

FULL VIEW

Angel head

Shell of St James

24 garnets

Pearl clusters of grapes and wheat sheaves evoke the Eucharist

St. John

∧ CHALICE OF PIUS XI

Presented in 1925 to Pius XI by Croatian Catholics, the cup depicts Christ enthroned and attended by angels. The base shows Slavic saints interspaced between noble crests. Three large gems decorate the pommel.

∧ CHALICE OF PIUS IX

This gilt chalice, presented in 1867 to Pius IX, is clad in blue enamel and delicate filigree, and bears a crucifix on the cup. The base is decorated with statues of the Old Testament figures of Melchisedech, Abraham, and Abel.

⟩ CHALICE OF PIUS IX

This Neo-Gothic Spanish chalice was given to Pope Pius IX in 1877. The cup bears inlays of four saints and the pommel is decorated with shells and angels. The base depicts the Four Evangelists.

During the ritual of Holy Communion or Eucharist, which forms part of the Mass, a pair of small containers called cruets are brought to the altar. Usually presented on a tray, one cruet contains water and the other wine. During the Eucharist, the wine and water are combined in a chalice to commemorate Jesus's Last Supper.

Cruets are usually made from glass, though they may also be made of metal or other material, and are topped with a lid and a lip for pouring. The cruets are differentiated from each other through decoration; the wine cruet may be marked with a grape symbol, while the water cruet might display shell or fountain motifs. Sometimes the ringing of a bell is incorporated into the Mass to signal the most significant events occuring at the altar (*see p.304–05*), and some cruet sets include a bell for this purpose. During Pontifical High Mass, celebrated by a bishop or the pope, a drinking straw called a fistula, from the Latin for "tube", was used by the bishop to partake from the chalice. This was both for reasons of hygiene and to prevent any of the wine from spilling. Use of the fistula originated in the Byzantine Empire, and though it is no longer used in the Catholic Mass, it remains part of the Orthodox Church tradition.

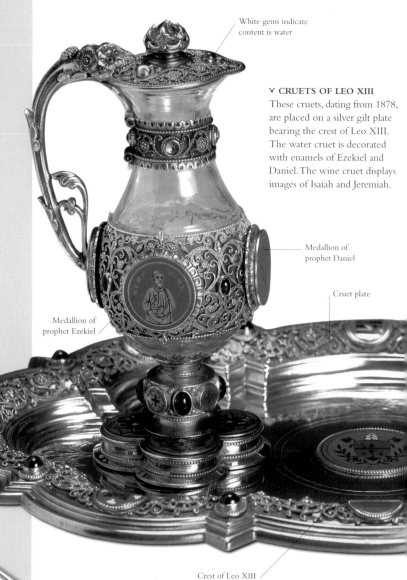

White gems indicate content is water

∨ CRUETS OF LEO XIII
These cruets, dating from 1878, are placed on a silver gilt plate bearing the crest of Leo XIII. The water cruet is decorated with enamels of Ezekiel and Daniel. The wine cruet displays images of Isaiah and Jeremiah.

Medallion of prophet Daniel

Cruet plate

Medallion of prophet Ezekiel

Crest of Leo XIII

Stopper on mouthpiece

Lip piece   Shaft

∧ SILVER GILT FISTULA
Until the reforms of the Second Vatican Council in the 1960s, the pontiff drank from the chalice during Pontifical High Mass using this gilt silver straw. The fistula is composed of three tubes, of which the central is the longest.

CRUETS
CONTAINERS FOR WATER AND WINE

⌄ CRUETS OF PIUS IX

These silver gilt ampoules and bell on an oval plate date from around 1854. The wine cruet shows the Wedding Feast at Cana, while the water cruet shows Moses striking the rock. The bell is decorated with leaves and shells.

Shell indicates contents of water

Grape cluster indicates contents of wine

Cherub head

Red gems denote wine cruet

Hand bell

Red ribbon indicating wine cruet

Red ribbon indicating wine cruet

Moses strikes water from the rock with his staff

Christ at Wedding of Cana

Medallion of prophet Jeremiah

Enamel floral design

Angel holding staff

Hand bell topped by an angel

Cherub

Saint's head

Crest of Leo XIII

⋏ CRUETS AND BELL

These gilt wine and water cruets date from the late 19th century, and are reminiscent of Classical Roman decorative jars. The cruets are presented on an oval plate, and accompanied by a hand bell (*center*) surmounted by an angel.

Bells have been used for a variety of purposes, both religious and secular, for thousands of years. By at least the 6th century, they featured in the Christian liturgy and by the 8th century, it was common to cast large bronze bells to be hung in bell towers that were attached to the sides of churches.

For those worshipers who did not understand Latin, the bell proved a useful tool during the liturgy. Latin had once united people throughout the Roman Empire, and despite the later development of vernacular languages throughout Europe, the liturgy continued to be celebrated exclusively in Latin until the early 1970s. Bells were rung at various stages to let the congregation know exactly what was happening at the altar. They indicated when to kneel and when to stand; when the priest pronounced the words of consecration ("this is my body, this is my blood"); and when the priest elevated the Host (bread venerated as the body of the Risen Jesus) and the chalice containing wine (venerated as the blood of Jesus) for all to see and honor. In small churches, a single bell was usually considered to be sufficient, while larger churches often had a set of chimes with a magnified sound.

DETAIL OF FLORAL DESIGN

Floral design

Double loop handle

Acanthus leaf design

ʌ GILT METAL BELL
The surface of this early 20th-century bell is decorated with flowers and acanthus leaves, a popular motif derived from antiquity. The bell is divided into three sections and rung from an unusual curved handle.

The distinctive design of this bell displays typical Eastern workmanship

< SILVER BELL
This elaborate bell originated in Istanbul, Turkey. Used in Orthodox liturgies, it was given to Pope John Paul II (1978–2005) by leaders of the Greek Orthodox Church.

BELLS
CHIMES TO SIGNAL THE LITURGY

Statue of Mary

Upper band

Central band

Handle

> **19TH-CENTURY BELL**
Dating from the first half of the
19th century, this French gilt
silver bell has gems on its handle
and is surmounted by a statue
of Mary. The surface of the bell
is decorated with scenes from
the lives of Mary and Jesus
inside four porcelain ovals.

Pommel

Leaf design

Incised handle

Lower band

Garnet

The bells are of
different weights
to vary their tone

St Ann
with Mary

One of four
wolf heads

Mary with
infant Jesus

ᴧ **SET OF FOUR BELLS**
Dating from either the late 19th or early
20th century, this bell set hangs from a
stylized trellis of leaves and fruits. The
handle is decorated with leaves.

For many religions, and especially for Christianity, water is a symbol of life. The Bible makes reference to water on many occasions: God created the waters at the beginning of the world; Jesus was baptized by his cousin, John the Precursor or Baptist, at the River Jordan; and, at the marriage feast of Cana, in the town of the same name, Jesus turned water into wine.

Water is considered holy and it is used during one of the Church's most important rituals, baptism, the sacrament by which people enter the Church and become Christians. In the early centuries, baptisms were only carried out on Holy Saturday but today the sacrament is celebrated regularly, in parishes throughout the world. During the baptism ceremony, special containers, in the form of shells and other shapes, are used for pouring water over the baptized in order to "cleanse" them in preparation for entering the Church. Water is also used during the liturgy when a holy water sprinkler (aspergillium) is dipped into a container of holy water (aspersory) and used to sprinkle the church congregation. Holy Water fonts are also kept by many Catholics and can often be seen by the front door of their home.

DETAIL OF CHERUBS

Y GILT METAL SHELL CONTAINER
This shell-shaped holy water vessel of Cardinal Giovanni Simeoni has been used for baptisms by Pope John Paul II (1978–2005) and Pope Benedict XVI.

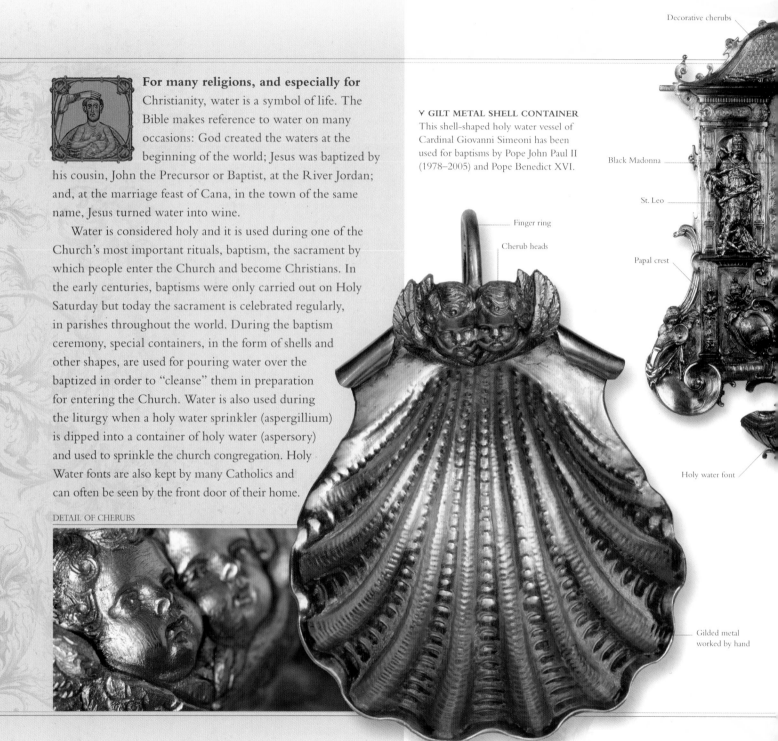

Decorative cherubs

Black Madonna

St. Leo

Papal crest

Finger ring

Cherub heads

Holy water font

Gilded metal worked by hand

WATER VESSELS
HOLY WATER CONTAINERS AND FONTS

‹ HOLY WATER FONT

This font was a gift from the Polish College in Rome to Pope Leo XIII (1878–1903) in 1887. At its center is a relief of the Black Madonna of Czestochowa, flanked by two saints, Leo and Canisius.

St. Canisius

Polish crest

Cherub head

Handle with animal heads

˅ ASPERSORY OF POPE PIUS IX

Dating to 1858, this elaborate gilt metal aspersory is decorated with saints and the seated figure of Christ. The sprinkler has an ornate trellis design on its handle.

FULL VIEW

Decorative rim

‹ SILVER ASPERSORY

This water carrier of Cardinal Raffaele Fornari (1787–1854) sits on a circular base and is decorated with the crest of Pope Pius IX (1846–78).

Coat of arms of Pope Pius IX

St. John the Evangelist

Handle

Silver aspergillium

Holy water sprinkler

307

∨ FRAMED MASS TEXTS OF LEO XIII
Until the reforms to the liturgy following the
Second Vatican Council it was common to place
framed texts of the Latin Mass on the altar. The
texts below were presented to Leo XIII in 1888.

The prayers that are offered during the
Mass date back to the oral tradition of the early
Church. Over the centuries, these prayers were
formulated and written down. As early as the
late 6th century, the official prayers of the Mass
were collected in a book known as a sacramentary. The
word "missal" refers to a book containing these prayers—plus all that
is officially read or sung in connection with the Mass—and is
derived from the Latin word for mass: *missa*.

The early missals were written on vellum—a type of
parchment made from animal hide—and bound in leather
covers. Some were covered with jewels. With the invention of
the printing press in the mid-15th century, it became possible
to produce missals cheaply and in large quantities; however,
the bindings remained notably elegant and finely crafted.

Until the liturgical reforms of the Second Vatican Council
in 1962–65, Mass and the other sacraments were celebrated in
Latin. Following the reforms, Pope Paul VI (1963–78) published
new missals and prayer books in the vernacular, or local
language, for the first time. Today, people have the choice of
attending Mass in Latin or in their own language, and missals
are now published in scores of different languages and dialects.

The Sacred
Heart of Mary

Christ holds a book
bearing Alpha and
Omega symbols

The Sacr
Heart of
Christ

Illustration of
the Baptism of
Jesus by St John

Text on the blessing of water
and washing of hands

Text of the Gospel
according to St. Joh

Lamb of God

Text recited during Mass

DECORATED CAPITAL

LAMB OF GOD DETAIL

MISSALS

PRAYER BOOKS FOR CELEBRATING MASS

Emperor Constantine's vision of the cross

Coat of arms of Pope Leo XIII

Priest administering sacraments

Arrival of Columbus in the New World

MISSAL OF LEO XIII
This missal was printed in Germany in 1882 and given to Pope Leo XIII. Four enamels at each end of the cross depict the Four Evangelists with their accompanying symbols (clockwise)— John (eagle); Luke (ox); Matthew (represented as a man); and Mark (lion).

MISSAL STAND OF LEO XIII
A gift from Spanish Catholics in 1888, the rectangular Neo-Gothic stand comprises a filigree base decorated with stone and enamels. The moveable stand can be raised and lowered.

Man represents St. Matthew

Lamb and cross symbol

FULL VIEW

> MISSAL OF JOHN PAUL II
This missal was given to John Paul II by Hungarian priests to commemorate the pontiff's visit to Poland and Hungary in 1991. It is printed in Italian, and the cover is detachable.

Sacred Heart of Jesus encircled with 11 rubies in gold (one missing)

Red velvet on red leather

Priest with cross of Christ on gilt medallion

Moveable stand

Ox represents St. Luke

Enamel of lamb

Sacred Heart of Jesus

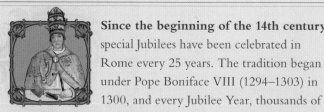

RAISED FLORET   CREST OF POPE LEO XIII

Since the beginning of the 14th century, special Jubilees have been celebrated in Rome every 25 years. The tradition began under Pope Boniface VIII (1294–1303) in 1300, and every Jubilee Year, thousands of pilgrims continue to flock to Rome to pray at the tombs of St. Peter and St. Paul. The pope formally initiates the Jubilee Year on Christmas Eve, when he ceremonially opens a door in St. Peter's Basilica that has been sealed for a quarter of a century. Millions of pilgrims pass through this Holy Door during the 12-month period of the Jubilee Year; other Holy Doors are also opened in St. John Lateran, St. Mary Major, and St. Paul-Outside-the-Walls. The Holy Door is highly symbolic; Jesus referred to himself as "the Door" and urged people to pass through him to God the Father. Pilgrims who enter the basilica through the Holy Door and pray are granted remission of their sins.

At the end of each Jubilee Year, the pope ceremonially closes the door for the next 25 years. The essential ritual has changed little over the centuries, but the ceremonial hammer for knocking on the closed door and the trowel for laying bricks to reseal the door at the end of the year were not used by Pope John Paul II on the eve of 2000, the last Jubilee Year.

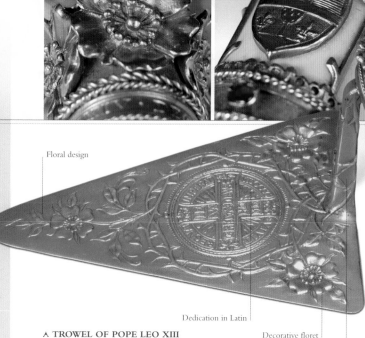

Floral design

Dedication in Latin

Decorative floret

Stem encircled with branches

ʌ TROWEL OF POPE LEO XIII
Used by the pope to close the Holy Door in 1900, the trowel was ceremonially dipped in cement and a layer applied to the sill of the door.

Bronze dove

Christ surrounded by emblems of the Evangelists

ʌ HOLY YEAR CONTAINER
This box is embedded in the Holy Door when it is bricked up at the end of each Jubilee Year. It contains the Papal Bull proclaiming the given Holy Year, medallions of the pope, and the keys to the Holy Door.

‹ HOLY DOOR, ST. PETER'S
The bronze Holy Door to St. Peter's Basilica will remain walled up until the next Jubilee Year (2025), when it will be opened by the pope. In the wall is a hole where a box (*right*) containing the Papal Bull of the Jubilee Year is placed. Above the door is a mosaic, placed there by Pope Clement X in 1675.

CEREMONIAL TOOLS

HAMMERS AND TROWELS

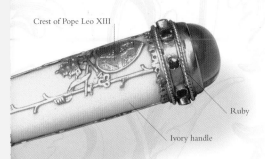

Crest of Pope Leo XIII

Ruby

Ivory handle

Flat-edged blade

Medallion of
an Evangelist

Nail

Latin inscription on
handle commemorating
the Holy Year of 1975

∧ BRONZE HAMMER
This hammer is a copy of the silver
original used to open the Holy
Door on Christmas Eve 1974, the
start of the 1975 Jubilee Year.

The coat of arms of
Pope Paul VI (1963–78)

➤ CEREMONIAL BRICK
At the end of the Jubilee Year of 1975, ceremonial
bricks were used in the closing up of each of the
Holy Doors in the four major basilicas.

∨ TROWEL OF POPE PAUL VI
This bronze trowel is a copy of
the silver original kept in St.
Peter's Basilica. It was used by
the pope to close the Holy
Door at the end of the 1975
Jubilee Year.

Latin inscription on
handle commemorating
the Holy Year of 1975

Depiction of pligrims
en route to Rome

∧ CLOSING THE HOLY DOOR
On January 6, 2001, Pope John Paul II
(1978–2005) symbolically closed the
Holy Door in St. Peter's Basilica, thus
ending the 2000 Jubilee Year.

CHRONOLOGY OF POPES

124 STEPHEN VIII *929–31*

125 JOHN XI *931–35*

126 LEO VII *936–39*

127 STEPHEN IX *939–42*

128 MARINUS II *942–46*

129 AGAPETUS II *946–55*

130 JOHN XII *955–63*

131 LEO VIII *963–64*

132 BENEDICT V *964*

133 JOHN XIII *965–72*

134 BENEDICT VI *973–74*

135 BENEDICT VII *974–83*

136 JOHN XIV *983–84*

137 JOHN XV *985–96*

138 GREGORY V *996–99*

139 SYLVESTER II *999–1003*

140 JOHN XVII *1003*

141 JOHN XVIII *1003–09*

142 SERGIUS IV *1009–12*

143 BENEDICT VIII *1012–24*

144 JOHN XIX *1024–32*

145 BENEDICT IX *1032–45*

146 SYLVESTER III *1045*

147 BENEDICT IX *1045*

148 GREGORY VI *1045–46*

149 CLEMENT II *1046–47*

150 BENEDICT IX *1047–48*

151 DAMASUS II *1048*

152 ST. LEO IX *1049–54*

153 VICTOR II *1055–57*

154 STEPHEN X *1057–58*

155 NICHOLAS II *1058–61*

156 ALEXANDER II *1061–73*

157 ST. GREGORY VII *1073–85*

158 BLESSED VICTOR III *1086–87*

159 BLESSED URBAN II *1088–99*

160 PASCHAL II *1099–1118*

161 GELASIUS II *1118–19*

162 CALLISTUS II *1119–24*

163 HONORIUS II *1124–30*

164 INNOCENT II *1130–43*

165 CELESTINE II *1143–44*

166 LUCIUS II *1144–45*

167 BLESSED EUGENE III *1145–53*

168 ANASTASIUS IV *1153–54*

169 HADRIAN IV *1154–59*

170 ALEXANDER III *1159–81*

171 LUCIUS III *1181–85*

172 URBAN III *1185–87*

173 GREGORY VIII *1187*

174 CLEMENT III *1187–91*

175 CELESTINE III *1191–98*

176 INNOCENT III *1198–1216*

177 HONORIUS III *1216–27*

178 GREGORY IX *1227–41*

179 CELESTINE IV *1241*

180 INNOCENT IV *1243–54*

181 ALEXANDER IV *1254–61*

182 URBAN IV *1261–64*

183 CLEMENT IV *1265–68*

184 BLESSED GREGORY X *1271–76*

185 BLESSED INNOCENT V *1276*

186 HADRIAN V *1276*

187 JOHN XXI *1276–77*

188 NICHOLAS III *1277–80*

189 MARTIN IV *1281–85*

190 HONORIUS IV *1285–87*

191 NICHOLAS IV *1288–92*

192 ST. CELESTINE V *1294*

193 BONIFACE VIII *1294–1303*

194 BLESSED BENEDICT XI *1303–04*

195 CLEMENT V *1305–14*

196 JOHN XXII *1316–34*

197 BENEDICT XII *1334–42*

198 CLEMENT VI *1342–52*

199 INNOCENT VI *1352–62*

200 BLESSED URBAN V *1362–70*

201 GREGORY XI *1370–78*

202 URBAN VI *1378–89*

203 BONIFACE IX *1389–1404*

204 INNOCENT VII *1404–06*

205 GREGORY XII *1406–15*

206 MARTIN V *1417–31*

207 EUGENE IV *1431–47*

208 NICHOLAS V *1447–55*

209 CALLISTUS III *1455–58*

210 PIUS II *1458–64*

211 PAUL II *1464–71*

212 SIXTUS IV *1471–84*

213 INNOCENT VIII *1484–92*

214 ALEXANDER VI *1492–1503*

215 PIUS III *1503*

216 JULIUS II *1503–13*

217 LEO X *1513–21*

218 HADRIAN VI *1522–23*

219 CLEMENT VII *1523––34*

220 PAUL III *1534–49*

221 JULIUS III *1550–55*

222 MARCELLUS II *1555*

223 PAUL IV *1555–59*

224 PIUS IV *1559–65*

225 ST. PIUS V *1566–72*

226 GREGORY XIII *1572–85*

227 SIXTUS V *1585–90*

228 URBAN VII *1590*

229 GREGORY XIV *1590–91*

230 INNOCENT IX *1591*

231 CLEMENT VIII *1592–1605*

232 LEO XI *1605*

233 PAUL V *1605–21*

234 GREGORY XV *1621–23*

235 URBAN VIII *1623–44*

236 INNOCENT X *1644–55*

237 ALEXANDER VII *1655–67*

238 CLEMENT IX *1667–69*

239 CLEMENT X *1670–76*

240 BLESSED INNOCENT XI *1676–89*

241 ALEXANDER VIII *1689–91*

242 INNOCENT XII *1691–1700*

243 CLEMENT XI *1700–21*

244 INNOCENT XIII *1721–24*

245 BENEDICT XIII *1724–30*

246 CLEMENT XII *1730–40*

247 BENEDICT XIV *1740–58*

248 CLEMENT XIII *1758–69*

249 CLEMENT XIV *1769–74*

250 PIUS VI *1775–99*

251 PIUS VII *1800–23*

252 LEO XII *1823–29*

253 PIUS VIII *1829–30*

254 GREGORY XVI *1831–46*

255 BLESSED PIUS IX *1846–78*

256 LEO XIII *1878–1903*

257 ST. PIUS X *1903–14*

258 BENEDICT XV *1914–22*

259 PIUS XI *1922–39*

260 PIUS XII *1939–58*

261 BLESSED JOHN XXIII *1958–63*

262 PAUL VI *1963–78*

263 JOHN PAUL I *1978*

264 JOHN PAUL II *1978–2005*

265 BENEDICT XVI *2005–2013*

266 FRANCIS *2013–*

GLOSSARY

 ACOLYTE Originally one of the lower orders of clergy, the acolyte assists the priest in the liturgical celebrations—especially the Eucharistic liturgy—holding candles in the procession and during the reading of the Gospel.

ALTAR A raised table built in the sanctuary of the church at which the Mass is celebrated.

ANGELUS A brief prayer that came into usage in around the 12th century. It recalls the visit of the archangel to Mary, announcing that God had chosen her to be the mother of Jesus.

ANTIPOPE A rival who opposes the legitimately elected pope, and who is elected in opposition to the chosen pontiff.

APOSTOLIC PALACE The official residence of the pope at the Vatican.

APSE Situated at the end of the church above the altar, the apse is a domed or semicircular recess. It was a common feature of ancient Roman basilicas, which were the prototypes of the early Christian churches.

ARCHBISHOP A bishop of the highest rank.

BASILICA The Roman law courts were called *basilicas*, derived from the Greek word for king. The Roman emperor Constantine I (r.306–337) chose the basilica as the ideal architectural model for Christian churches.

BISHOP From the Greek word meaning "administrator", bishops are the successors of the twelve Apostles—the companions of Jesus.

BYZANTINE EMPIRE The Eastern part of the Roman Empire, which survived for a thousand years after the fall of the Western Roman Empire until it was conquered by the Ottoman Turks in 1453.

CANONIZATION The public declaration by the pope that—after careful investigation by the Holy See—a person may be venerated by the Universal Church as a saint.

CARDINAL Senior members of the clergy, cardinals are the exclusive electors of the pope and also act as his closest advisors.

CATACOMB Underground burial place consisting of tunnels and tombs, where primitive Christian art first developed.

CONCLAVE The process and ceremonies surrounding the election of a pope by the College of Cardinals.

CORINTHIAN A Classical architectural decoration based on stylized acanthus leaves.

COUNTER-REFORMATION The reform movement of the 16th and early 17th centuries that called for religious renewal, discipline, and learning, bringing about a Catholic revival. Also known as the Catholic Reformation.

CRUSADE A military campaign with a religious objective. The first crusade—an attempt to recapture Jerusalem from Muslim hands—was called in 1095 by Pope Urban II (1088–99).

DEACON An ordained minister ranking below a priest. The word deacon originally derived from the Greek work for servant. In the Bible, the apostles appointed seven deacons to care for the widows, orphans, and poor.

DIOCESE The district which is administered by a bishop. The Holy See is the pope's diocese.

DOCTRINE The official body of teaching that is taught by the Church.

DOGMA The teaching of the Church that has been defined by the authority of the pope.

DORIC A Greek-inspired style of architecture, noted for its fluted columns and simple capitals.

EASTERN ROMAN EMPIRE *see* Byzantine Empire.

ENCYCLICAL A document, or letter, composed by the pope for the whole Church that addresses important issues of doctrine, morals, and discipline.

EUCHARIST The ritual re-enactment of the Last Supper and of the death of Jesus, commemorated by the consecration of the Host (bread) and wine. Also called the Holy Sacrifice of the Mass.

EXCOMMUNICATION A formal pronouncement that confirms that an individual is not in communion or agreement with the Church. People who are excommunicated may not receive the Sacraments.

FRESCO The Italian for "fresh," a fresco is painted on the wet plaster of a wall so that when it dries, the painting is set in the plaster.

GENERAL AUDIENCE A weekly event where the pope addresses a large gathering of people. General Audiences are held on Wednesday mornings at the Vatican.

GREEK CROSS A cross with all four arms of equal length.

HABSBURG DYNASTY A major European royal and imperial family. From 1438 to 1806 all Holy Roman Emperors but one belonged to the Habsburg house.

HERETIC A person who holds beliefs contrary to the teachings of the Church.

HOHENSTAUFEN DYNASTY German dynasty that ruled the Holy Roman Empire from 1138 to 1208 and from 1212 to 1254.

HOLY COMMUNION The act of receiving the Host of bread and the cup of wine, which the Catholic Church teaches is the body and blood of Christ.

HOLY LEAGUE Either of two leagues (the first in 1571 and the second in 1683) that the papacy formed with European powers to protect Italy from the threat of Ottoman Turkey.

HOLY ROMAN EMPIRE An alliance of territories in middle Europe under one emperor, several of whom were crowned by the pope. It was dissolved by Napoleon in 1806.

HOLY SEE Also known as the Apostolic See, the term refers to the Roman pontiff, the Roman Curia and the government of Church.

INTERCESSION The act of offering a petitionary prayer to God on behalf of others. Catholics ask the assistance of saints to accompany their prayers to God.

LATERAN PALACE Between the 4th and the 14th century, the residence of the popes was beside St. John Lateran, the Cathedral of Rome. Even though papal residency transferred to the Vatican, the Lateran Palace today serves as the official office of the Vicar of Rome.

LATERAN TREATY The pact signed in 1929 between the Holy See and the Italian

...overnment. The papacy recognized the state [o]f Italy and, in return, Italy recognized papal [so]vereignty over the Vatican City, granting full [in]dependence to the pope.

[L]ATIN CROSS   A cross shape where the [ba]se stem is longer than the other three arms. It [w]as the traditional plan for churches during the [m]edieval period, with the longer arm of the [cr]oss forming the nave of the church.

[L]ITURGY   The public act of worship, [pr]esided over by a member of the clergy.

[L]OGGIA   A gallery or room, sometimes [pi]llared, that is open on one side. It may be part of a building, or it may be separate.

MARTYR   A Christian who dies for his or her faith, rather than renouncing his or her beliefs in the face of persecution.

MASS   The word "mass" comes from the dismissal of the people at the end of the Eucharistic Liturgy: *ite missa est* ("go, it is sent"). The Mass is the more popular name for the Eucharistic Service.

NUNCIO   The Apostolic, or papal, nuncio is an ambassador appointed by the pope to be his representative in a country, and to present the views of the Holy See to the government of that country.

NUN   A woman who takes lifelong religious vows of poverty, chastity, and obedience to God. Most nuns, or sisters, live in convents.

ORDINATION   The rite of appointment of a deacon, priest, or bishop to the Holy Orders. Ordination is one of the Seven Sacraments of the Catholic Church.

PAPAL BULL   An official letter or document written by the pope. The name comes from the *bulla*, a wax or metal seal traditionally affixed to the document.

PAPAL STATES   Also known as the Patrimony of St. Peter, the Papal States were territories over which the pope was civil as well as spiritual ruler from 756 to 1870. The states—comprising regions in modern-day central and northern Italy—were absorbed by the Kingdom of Italy in 1870.

PASCHAL   From the Hebrew word *Pesach*, meaning Passover, the word Paschal refers to the redemptive death and resurrection of Jesus. It is most commonly known as Easter.

PIAZZA   A large, open public space, normally in front of an important building. Most of the great Roman basilicas had such a space in front of the main entrance.

PONTIFICAL GUARD   A police force created in the 19th century to protect the pope and Vatican City. In 1970, the various categories of the Pontifical Guard were disbanded by Pope Paul VI, leaving only the Swiss Guard intact, who now handle the role of papal security at the Vatican.

PONTIFF   Derived from the Latin word *pontifex* (priest), the pontiffs were the high priests of the Roman Empire. The term is now used principally to refer to the pope.

PREFECT   In the Roman Empire, prefects were those with positions of authority in the civil administration. The title is used today by the heads of the most important congregations or Curial offices within the Vatican.

PREFECTURE OF THE PAPAL HOUSEHOLD   The administration which oversees the pope's appointments. All public and private audiences are arranged through this office, which is presided over by the prefect, a high-ranking prelate.

PRELATE   A title of honor given to high-ranking members of the clergy, in particular to bishops.

PRESBYTER   From the Greek word meaning "elder", the presbyter was traditionally appointed by the bishop to assist him in the care of a diocese. In modern usage, it is synonymous with priest.

PRIEST   In many religions, the priest leads people in public or congregational prayer. In Catholicism, the priest is also the principal celebrant at the Eucharist and of the Sacrament of Penance and Reconciliation.

PROTESTANT REFORMATION   A movement of religious reform and renewal in the 16th century led by Martin Luther and John Calvin. It became the basis for the founding of Protestantism, where supporters split from the Catholic Church and rejected the authority of the pope.

PUTTO   A representation of a naked, pudgy boy, often with wings, found especially in Renaissance and Baroque art. Plural "*putti*."

QUIRINAL PALACE   Built on the Quirinal Hill by Pope Gregory XIII in 1573 as a summer residence, many conclaves took place here. Reluctantly surrendered by Pope Pius IX in 1871, it is today the official residence of the President of Italy.

ROMAN CURIA   The central government of the Catholic Church is administered by the Roman Curia. It consists of a number of offices, under the Secretariat of State. The sole purpose of the Curia is to serve the pope and assist him in his ministry.

ROSARY   A contemplative prayer in honor of Mary, the Mother of Jesus. The devotion was spread by the preaching of St. Dominic (1170–1221) and his followers in the 13th century.

SACRAMENTS   In Catholicism, the seven sacred ceremonies or rites: Baptism, Penance, Confirmation, the Eucharist, Holy Orders, Matrimony, and the Anointing of the Sick.

SACRISTY   The area where the clergy dress in preparation for the celebration of the Sacraments. The Sacristy is also the storage place for liturgical vessels and vestments.

SANCTUARY   The area where the liturgy is performed, and which is occupied by the clergy and their assistants.

SCHISM   Since the early centuries of Christianity, it has been common for members of the Church to break away, forming new groups in opposition to the Holy See. Many of these schisms are started by a genuine desire for reform. Known as the Great Schism, in 1054, the Church divided into two branches: the Western (Latin) and Eastern (Greek), which later became the Roman Catholic Church and the Eastern Orthodox Church respectively.

SEMINARY   Literally meaning "seed bed", a seminary is a college where students for the priesthood prepare for ordination through theological and philosophical studies.

STUCCO   A method of decoration, especially of walls, used in churches. It is a durable, slow-setting plaster made of gypsum, lime, and sand.

TRAVERTINE   A type of stone which is found in abundance around Rome. Travertine was extensively quarried for the buildings of Ancient Rome. Much of the stone was used again during the Middle Ages and Renaissance period to build churches.

WESTERN ROMAN EMPIRE   The Western part of the great Roman Empire, which was divided into two in 395 AD, after the Empire became increasingly difficult to govern. The Western Empire, with its capital at Milan, fell in 476, although the eastern part – the Byzantine Empire – survived a further thousand years.

INDEX

Page numbers
in *italics* refer to
illustrations